The real power game

A guide to European industrial relations

Jack Peel

McGRAW-HILL Book Company (UK) Limited

London · New York · St Louis · San Francisco · Auckland · Bogotá · Guatemala · Hamburg · Johannesburg · Lisbon · Madrid · Mexico · Montreal · New Delhi · Panama · Paris · San Juan · São Paulo · Singapore · Sydney · Tokyo · Toronto

Published by
McGraw Hill Book Company (UK) Limited
Maidenhead · Berkshire · England

British Library Cataloguing in Publication Data

Peel, Jack
    The real power game.
    1. Industrial relations — Europe
    I. Title
    331'.094   HD8376.5   79-41028

ISBN 0–07–084534–4

To Dorothy, Vicky, and Robin without whose tolerance this book would not have been written, and to Brian Towers for his invaluable assistance and Mike Wade for sparking off the whole idea

Contents

Foreword

It was at the Paris Summit Meeting nearly seven years ago, in October 1972, that the Community declared that:

> Economic expansion is not an end in itself. Its firm aim should be to enable disparities in living conditions to be reduced. It must take place with the participation of all social partners. It should result in an improvement of the quality of life as well as in standards of living.

This declaration represented a renewed resolve by the Community to make social policy a new reality for the 100 million workers and their families who live in the Community. And at the heart of a successful social policy lies an effective industrial relations strategy. Indeed, as Jack Peel argues in this book, our ability to achieve sustained growth to maintain political cohesion and to face up to new problems, whether created by energy shortages or rapid technological change, depends crucially on our ability as a Community to develop a real dialogue between the social partners. Jack Peel has a unique range of experience and practical knowledge. He has served on the shop floor, as a trades union general secretary, as a member of the National Coal Board, and for six years as the Director of Industrial Relations in the European Commission. And from that has emerged a book which is not another academic treatise but a practical guide written with authority about the options before us in this essential area of Community life. Its blend of common sense and commitment deserves to be read widely, both on the shop floor and in the board room.

Roy Jenkins

1. Introduction: European industrial relations—no neat formula

An old Chinese epigram sagely observes that 'harmony soon loses its attractiveness if it does not have a background of discord'. By this criterion, at least, industrial relations will be an absorbing topic during the 'eighties. The social barometer shows rough weather ahead for industrial relations practitioners. Fresh bargaining criteria, new participative management styles, more international trade union activity, schemes for job enrichment, disclosure of information and a complex network of protective legislation at national and European level are trends already in train. Unemployment figures are creeping up relentlessly as European governments falteringly try to find short-term solutions to the problem which could easily degenerate into social and political catastrophe. With this daunting scenario we may simply pray for a social Edison, or like Shakespeare's Hamlet, '. . . rather bear those ills we have, Than fly to others that we know not of . . .'. Industrial relations, always important, now assume a crucial relevance to our future.

There is an urgent need for a constructive, readable book on European industrial relations. Existing publications tend to be highly technical, academic or legalistic in scope. This book is aimed at managers, trade unionists, and politicians at all levels, and hopefully at the general reader. It probes the human attitudes and reasons behind the controversies in all the main areas of industrial relations. It is designed to inform, provoke, and encourage industrial relations practitioners. The book has five sections, the first describing the main European institutions and how they work and can be influenced. The second section discusses the strengths and weaknesses of the trade union and employers' organizations at European level, the role of multinational companies and the possibility of Euro–bargaining. Section 3 presents some of the controversial industrial relations issues, including job enrichment, disclosure of information, industrial democracy, and incomes policy. Section 4 looks at the future effect on industrial relations of the European Parliament after direct elections and the enlargement of the European Community. The final section traces the effect of European labour legislation on Britain and to provoke thought—and action—reconstructs British industrial relations—Euro/style.

Industrial relations problems began to look unusually serious when the energy crisis ruptured the full employment boom and compounded the business decline in 1974–75, which produced record unemployment figures. For the first time for nearly fifty years political leaders are using the term 'depression' to describe the jobless situation. Although the crest of economic growth came to a peak in 1974 it did not diminish the deep–seated and almost universal expectations of rising living standards. Indeed, to the new generation of workers and their children, these expectations have now become entitlements and many European countries have an enlarged burden, often crippling, of social costs to support the non–working population.

In short, society with its mass media, new educational systems, welfare services, and boring jobs has been changing faster than the workplace. Changing attitudes towards work, combined with this revolution in social values, have aroused new interest in improving the quality of working life, the production process, the hierarchical structure, the working environment, prospects for advancement and participation in decision–making. There is no panacea for this industrial arthritis which can be rubbed on to society like a social liniment. If this existed, its inventor would deserve and receive a rainbow of eulogies. The aim should be to change the adversary style of industrial relations for something more cooperative and productive. It means giving workers more influence and responsibility.

Good industrial relations are not measured solely by the tangible though negative yardstick of working days lost in strikes, official or unofficial. They are based on more intangible though positive factors, such as a willingness to cooperate, especially in the introduction of new techniques, and a readiness to assist in solving modern commercial and production problems. Industrial relations are about the human links between people in a working unit or in the working community. Their needs and problems, the way they inform, consult, instruct, and negotiate are the patterns of behaviour which decide whether an industry flourishes or declines.

Solutions to problems arising out of this framework must also be sought in a European and world context, as industry now operates in these wider dimensions. Such activity is not a mere academic jaunt. Jobs may depend on industrial leaders being aware of these wider implications and drawing the right conclusions from them. It matters very much that a Japanese steelworker produces $5\frac{1}{2}$ tons for every ton produced by a British steelworker. It matters even more to find out how and why this happens. In the same way, a Belgian car production worker and a Luxembourg lathe operator receive substantially higher hourly rates than their British counterparts. They are also entitled to four weeks' annual holiday with double pay. Is this low investment, overmanning, and political ineptitude in Britain, or higher production and a wider bargaining spectrum on the Continent?

In a fiercely competitive world, these questions are relevant. Industrial success is linked to economic strength and political power. It is significant that the richer countries like Germany, Sweden, Denmark, Austria, and Switzerland have progressive, harmonious industrial relations systems; though this correlation seems to rest on the predominance of industrial trade union structures, and more professionalism and economic realism in management and trade unions. The simple fact is that a business, like a family, a trade union or a country, must in the long run live within its income or take the consequences. But just as expenditure must be matched by income, so the rights of workers must be linked to corresponding responsibilities. If we are to survive 'the consumption of the purse' which afflicted Shakespeare's Falstaff, our prosperity must be earned. If we give priority to improving the lot of the old, the young, and the underprivileged, it means others must get less, unless we produce more wealth.

Britain, victorious in the Second World War, has suffered almost permanent economic troubles, while Germany and Japan have not only restored their shattered economies, but virtually achieved 'economic miracles'. It is easy to refer to American aid or hard work to explain this puzzle, but the fact is that Britain received vast amounts of money and most Britons have worked hard too. There are many possible answers—the strain of the war, economically speaking, and an extremely high level of postwar overseas military expenditure—but the two that matter are that we have consistently awarded ourselves a higher standard of living than we could afford, and that Britain's industrial relations have been infinitely worse than on the Continent. The emulation of Continental life–styles without the corresponding productivity base has kept Britain trailing in the prosperity league.

Here, then, is the relevance of industrial relations to current affairs. We are in the midst of a conflict between high social expectations, relatively low economic growth rates, and political parties playing the auction game for votes. In short, a world that was politically and socially passive is now becoming truly activist, thus producing a rising tide of political and social demands not always related to given national resources. This is one of the important factors contributing to inflation and unemployment. Most people accept that mass unemployment is a disgrace to a civilized society. It is fashionable and easy to call for shorter hours, longer holidays, and earlier retirement as a way of dealing with the problem. Then comes the crunch question—if incomes and work opportunities are to be shared more equitably without lowering industrial efficiency, what steps will be necessary to bring about the fundamental changes in human attitudes without which such sharing would be meaningless?

This is the minefield through which industrial relations experts must pick their way with meticulous care. There is a comradely ring about the phrase 'work–sharing'—indeed the European trade unions are sincere though a

3

little desperate in its advocacy. It implies, on the face of it, a degree of sacrifice on the part of those who are working, for those who are unemployed. In some cases it may mean just this. At best the concept is a palliative; but if the working week is shortened in order to share the available work among more people and the same level of wages is maintained, then, unless productivity is raised substantially, the industry in question will rapidly become less competitive as its labour costs rise. Its unemployment problem would soon become worse.

In more indirect ways, the giving of longer holidays and earlier retirement could have the same effect. Trade unions in the community argue that past experience of reducing hours shows that, after the adjustment, production and productivity gradually rise. Whether this would happen in the cautious, uncertain atmosphere of a recession seems doubtful. The European employers' organizations have serious doubts about the economic viability of work–sharing measures, however well–intentioned they may be. They argue that, unless such measures were applied uniformly throughout the European Community, competition would be distorted. From the standpoint of the European Commission, there are further complications in connection with the Community's global trading arrangements where the same competitive comparisons apply.

On the other hand, the costs, risks, and limits of work–sharing measures should be balanced against the equally serious problems inherent in the present recession, which will not be conquered easily. It is pointless to radiate false optimism or to become engulfed in gloom. The average annual rate of economic growth in the European Community between 1974 and 1977 was less than two per cent, whereas it had been over four per cent in the period 1970–73. Along with this reduced growth, the working population in the community is likely to increase by 1 million per year for the next seven or eight years, due to the high birth rates of the 'sixties. The number of elderly persons retiring has also dropped considerably, due to the low birth rates in the early years of this century.

A period of reduced growth and high unemployment does not mean, however, that we should no longer seek improvements in social policy in Europe; it does mean that such improvements will require greater solidarity between the two sides of industry and the governments. The key role of industrial relations experts will be to ensure that both sides of industry bring their contributions to bear on the difficulties facing society. In a democracy there will always be things which divide people, but the concept of conflict about sharing the proceeds of industry should not be inconsistent with cooperation to produce a worthwhile amount to share. Much of the present *malaise* in Western society can be traced to the erratic and negative attitudes we show towards industry and those who work in it.

4

This is a serious ethical dilemma. A society which cannot affirm the basic values of the activities by which it lives can hardly be expected to take a positive view of its own future. In a purely material sense, work is essential for our survival. We cannot have goods, services, hospitals, houses, schools, and better pensions, for example, unless people have first made them or created the wealth to pay for them. But ideally, too, work should also give people the spiritual benefit of satisfying activity. No doubt the poet Shelley had this in mind when he said, 'joy's soul lies in the doing'. Prolonged indolence makes a man lose confidence in himself and sometimes he becomes a prey to envy and hate. A bored or cynical nation is hard to govern, but a nation occupied and enthused by work is already a happy one, whatever its problems.

Given the existence of a European Community, there is a logical case for an industrial relations system which fits the whole Community. There are four chief reasons why this can only evolve extremely slowly. First, each country's industrial relations system is devised to meet the needs of its industrial situation, though the cynic would say it was designed to achieve the opposite result. It would be nice to be able to transfer an imaginative, harmonious industrial relations plan to another country with a more disturbed industrial scene. The fact is that you cannot transplant in this way unless by some magic you also transplant the historical soil and the cultural fertilizer.

Secondly, a kaleidoscope of social change is currently swirling over European countries and influencing training standards and industrial behaviour. We are witnessing an explosion in proposed worldwide legislation on corporate information disclosure. A survey recently taken in 10 countries covers 32 closely typed pages. Such collective agitation may well lead to eventual tranquillity in the industrial relations field, but it makes the task of constructing a set of common, acceptable rules extremely difficult at the present time. The third obstacle to the neat formula is unemployment, now running as we have seen at unprecedented levels across Europe and producing acute anxieties in the member states of the Community. The combination of fairly generous benefits to large numbers of people for not working, and high taxation to help to pay this bill, is already putting strains on the social fabric of many countries.

A full range of palliatives is understandably being tried in various countries, but coordinating these is difficult. In Belgium compulsory schooling to the age of 16 years is being debated. Men may retire from work at 60 and women at 55, provided unemployed workers under 30 years of age are employed in their place. France is offering large financial bonuses to immigrant workers who are willing to return home. The French government is also waiving social security payments by employers—normally about 30

5

per cent of total wages—if they employ young people. Britain is using some of these measures but is also hamstrung by the overtime problem. Incredibly, in approximately half of all sectors of British industry the full–time equivalent (40–hour week) of the overtime worked exceeds the registered unemployed figures.

The fourth problem blocking the desired European relations system is fundamental—it is the conflict between nationalism and industrialism. During the nineteenth century more than 80 modern democratic nation states were being formed. There are now more than 160. The ending of Western colonial experience has been accompanied by the universalization of the nation state as a basic unit of political organization. For industry, materials and markets are needed and sought all over the world, but nationalism tends to divide the world into smaller compartments and segregate the human race into smaller groups. The demand for protectionism to alleviate unemployment gives a further twist to this nationalistic thinking. These are the daunting obstacles to the achievement of a European dimension in industrial relations. There are, of course, technical difficulties such as wage relativities and differentials, the use of wage and price restraints, and many structural disparities between trade union and employer organizations and their attitudes to the law, which further complicate the issue.

The dilemma is that in spite of these well–known difficulties there is still an urgent need to give a European flavour to the industrial relations scene. The implications of the Treaty of Rome are the free flow of labour, capital, goods, and services across the boundaries of the member states of the community. With these barriers removed and company law harmonized between European countries to facilitate more trade, industrial relations systems must adjust to this wider spectrum. The general strategy of the European Commission in the field of industrial relations has two aspects—the legislative and the participative, both designed to achieve a higher degree of social responsibility, especially in the multinational companies. On the legislative side more than thirty draft directives have been sent by the Commission to the Council. So far only a few of these have been agreed, including a directive removing gross disparities between national laws on mass redundancy procedures and a directive protecting workers' rights when transfers of ownership take place. The other measures are still being studied in the light of their political sensitivity.

The purpose of this new and developing code of labour law is to give companies the autonomy and economic elbow–room they need to operate successfully, but within a new social framework giving greater weight to the human aspects of business. It is clear that large firms are an integral part of the drive to increase the wealth of the Community and to ensure its fairer distribution, but more power means more responsibility. The participative side of the industrial relations work in the Commission is extensive and varied in scope and includes more than seventy consultative bodies of different kinds, tripartite and bipartite. These will be described in detail later in the book and their significance to industry fully explained.

The economic problems in the European Community make this work urgent, but financial stringency induces opposition to social reforms, especially those ambitiously conceived. Here the role of the European Commission is often misunderstood. Its job is not to harmonize the whole field of social welfare benefits and working conditions throughout the Community; though there might be some justification in the Treaty of Rome for taking an opposing view, since different social welfare provisions theoretically distort the competition between member states. In practice, this is not an important factor. To improve the social basis of the Community, it is more important to ensure that at a Community level minimum standards are set which should apply to all advanced industrial countries. On the basis of these standards individual countries can take their own legislative measures. Richer countries will obviously set higher standards, but the Commission sees its job as setting the level below which a member of the European Community should not fall.

It is a matter of cooperation and learning from each other, with a view to improving and harmonizing social policies, but not standardizing such policies. An industrial relations policy for the European Community is, therefore, an integral part of social policy and must take account of all these complexities. There are practical problems, too, arising out of the differences in structure and operational styles of the various trade union organizations. The Continental rule is industrial trade unionism, legally binding agreements, better fringe benefits and most important of all, higher productivity. Continental unions see British unions with a basic reverence, as the pioneers, tinged with dismay and amazement at the masochism sometimes practised. The British trade union pattern seems to be a happy chaos: tremendous camaraderie, strong influence on governments and ingeniously devised collective bargaining systems. British unions generally regard their Continental brethren with a mixture of suspicion, disbelief, and envy.

They are also sensitive about outside interference, as shown by the following exchange in the letters–to–the–editor column of a British newspaper.

Sir,

Outside my window, I have just watched five workmen spend the entire morning watching another dig a hole in the road.

Yours faithfully,

Julian Chumley–Phipps.

7

Sir,
And what exactly was Mr. Chumley–Phipps doing all morning?
Yours faithfully,
Alf Digger.

On the Continent there are two, sometimes three, national trade union centres in each country. These are based on religious or political links. As they cover the same industrial ground, there is some duplication; but because the affiliated unions are industrially based, this does not pose undue problems. Works councils have evolved into powerful bodies with legal rights and do much to compensate for the fragmented nature of Continental trade unionism. Like the TUC, the German Trade Union Federation (DGB) is the main national trade union centre. Second in European size to the TUC, the DGB owns the fourth–largest bank and the second–largest insurance company in Germany. It also owns the biggest building society and construction firm in the world, and runs a travel firm. Top managers in Europe tend to be graduates in subjects related to their work. The ratio of such trained people is as high as 90 per cent in France, Belgium and Germany. The comparable figure for Britain is 40 per cent. British industry has always felt that business experience is the best training ground for top managers—a dangerously naïve view in the ruthless sophistication of modern industry.

The industrial relations scene on the Continent tends to be less volatile than in Britain. This is partly due to the legal framework previously mentioned, but is also related to the persistence of dissident elements in a number of key British industries. It seems sad that the good sense of the majority of British trade union leaders is overshadowed by the militant extremism of a few. It is equally sad that the hard work of most managers is often lost in the disreputable arguments involving a handful of speculators, who capture the public eye and thrive on their temporary notoriety. Industrial relations are about organized civility. Militants and moderates have a role to play provided it is within a framework of rules and does not ride rough–shod over human dignity.

Management and unions in Britain often seem obsessed with money. Obviously, if a firm is making losses it will not stay in business very long, so profits are a necessary pre–condition. But for industrialists to say that their sole function is to make profits is ridiculous. Food is a similar pre–condition of life, but few would argue that eating is a man's exclusive function. This leads to profit being regarded as a dirty word, which is the other extreme. Trade unions have the same problems. They must obviously do their best to see that their members are well paid and fairly treated; but many other issues are dealt with, from shop–floor level to the union executive committee.

8

Too often the public image of unions is of bodies which seldom think in terms other than of money—and disruption and hardship to the public if they don't get it.

In Britain, trade unionism is still on the cheap, and the movement suffers accordingly both in its public relations and in the crucial area of education. There are roughly 300 000 British shop stewards, 100 000 branch officials and 5000 full–time officers. The TUC estimates that the annual turnover of these part–time and full–time officials is about 20 per cent, or 80 000 officials. Yet in 1976 the TUC reported that only 30 000 officials received training of any kind. Denmark trains 30 000 trade unionists a year, with one tenth of Britain's population. West Germany trains 170 000 trade unionists each year in 21 colleges, compared to the 6 used by the TUC. This is not the fault of the TUC, whose dedicated staff work wonders with limited resources. There is now a substantial government grant given each year to the TUC to help with this work. There is no substitute for professionalism in this field, even for the TUC.

So there is no neat formula for a European industrial relations system. This does not mean that chaos exists. Three main systems of industrial relations can be discerned in the European Community. First, we have the German system of co–determination, based on works councils, designed to foster cooperation and confine conflict and collective bargaining to levels outside the factory. Works councils are composed of worker representatives only, and in particular have the right of decision or co–determination on social as well as technical and economic matters. The closed shop is illegal and unions are industrially based.

The second system is in Britain, where the shop steward is the chief medium of worker representation. Voluntary, elected works councils are rare, and where they exist are usually considered superfluous or too compliant. Accordingly, they have been reduced to discussing trivia. Factory relationships in Britain, therefore, are conducted through institutions set up to resolve conflict rather than promote cooperation, and through worker representation nominally aiming to challenge management rather than to work with it. Voluntarism pervades industrial relations in Britain, except for the historical quirk of the closed shop, which covers more than four million workers and has now become a political shrine. More than 480 trade unions operate alongside 500 or more employers' organizations and myriad *ad hoc* negotiating bodies.

The third industrial relations pattern is based on joint consultative works councils. These operate, for example, in France, Belgium, and the Netherlands. These councils are established by law, or by national agreement between trade unions and employers' organizations. Their specific purpose is to promote cooperation between management and workers and

9

they are the main vehicle of worker representation at local level. The councils are advisory, and require management to give information to workers on progress, performance, and plans. They also give management the opportunity to consult workers on matters concerning change, efficiency, welfare, safety, and productivity. But councils are not allowed to indulge in collective bargaining on pay and conditions. These activities are conducted outside the plant, at industry or national level. Here again, factory relationships have an organizational form which excludes conflict and leaves the initiative and prerogative to manage in the hands of management.

These three patterns of industrial relations will be gradually mixed by the sheer pressure of events, though the process may well produce apoplexy among trade union officials and employers. First, the harmonization of company laws and loosened trade barriers will push collective bargaining inexorably into European framework, starting with fringe benefits, as these are less controversial than wages. A foretaste of this trend was given in 1976, when British miners' leaders, serving on joint committees in the European Commission with their Community counterparts, became acutely aware that the retirement provisions enjoyed by miners in Belgium, France, and Germany were infinitely better than those received by British miners. Improvements were rapidly secured, largely on the basis of these comparisons.

Secondly, solutions to the unemployment problem must be sought on a Community–wide basis. Even the palliative measures must be applied in a coordinated European context if a slide into protectionism is to be avoided. Extensive work–sharing seems inevitable, if only to give baffled politicians and bemused economists time to think of more durable and credible remedies. The critical aspect of work–sharing is how the various schemes will be financed. Finally, all Europeans are learning the lesson that countries, like families, businesses, or trade unions, must live within their means or take the consequences. Simple economic realism, linked with outspoken leadership at all levels of society, is the way forward. Trade unions and employers' organizations need more money, to mount special educational programmes to equip workers and managers with the knowledge they will need to cope with the frightening new responsibilities which events are thrusting on them.

Good industrial relations used to be advocated purely on the grounds of efficiency. Now they are necessary for our survival. The stirring opening words from *A tale of two cities,* written over a hundred years ago by Charles Dickens, have a prophetic and disturbing relevance in Europe today: 'It was the best of times, it was the worst of times, it was the age of wisdom, it was the age of foolishness, it was the epoch of belief, it was the epoch of incredulity, it was the season of Light, it was the season of Darkness, it was the spring of hope, it was the winter of despair.' Industrial relations trends will surely decide whether we cross the threshold to a new prosperity, or slide over the brink into economic disaster.

Part 1
Industrial relations institutions: supranational and international

2. How the European Community works

To many people the European Community seems more like a bag of marbles, jostling noisily together, than a melting pot in which a new Europe is being forged. Walter Hallstein, the first President of the European Commission said: 'The European Community is like one of the Dutch old masters—parts are painted in great detail and other bits are left blurred.' Working in the European Commission too, is said to resemble being swallowed by a whale. It is big though not particularly vicious and it is certainly warm–blooded. At first it is dark inside and there are lots of shrieks and rumblings as civil servants from nine member states are slowly and painfully digested. Occasionally the whale spouts and well–chewed policies emerge on various topics in six languages.

Yet with all its faults and absurdities, real and apparent, the Commission has an unusual concentration of international brains and talents. Despite the inevitable frustrations, you can really feel the dedication, as most Eurocrats are emotionally deeply involved in the Community idea, and see it both in political and personal terms as an escape from the trammels of nationalism. Unlike the other polyglot bureaucracies, such as the OECD, UNESCO, NATO and the FAO, where national governments have a direct influence, the European Commission has been designed as a supranational engine, to turn national interests into international ideas. It is one of the few places in the world where people are no longer expected to represent just their own country. In the words of Jean Monnet: 'Europe has never existed. It is not the addition of national sovereignties in a conclave which creates an entity. One must genuinely create Europe.'

The European Economic Community was set up by the Treaty of Rome in 1957, the six signatories being France, West Germany, Italy, Holland, Belgium, and Luxembourg. Four countries signed the Treaty of Accession in 1972 agreeing, subject to ratification procedures during that year, to join the Community on 1 January 1973—United Kingdom (UK), Ireland, Denmark, and Norway. The first three joined, but Norway opted out. So in historical terms the Community is still in its infancy and according to some cynics it has not been very impressive. Its growth and development have admittedly been uneven and crisis–ridden in recent years, but it is maturing and solidifying. It is now a functioning international force which outstrips the Soviet Union in economic progress and challenges even the United States in economic power.

It was bad luck that the recession and the energy crisis coincided with enlargement, but it is clear that the Community's existence has helped to restrain protectionist forces. The Community is a convoy of nine nations moving at the speed of the slowest member. They have united their national markets in a single trading, farming, and industrial system which embraces a large part of Western Europe. It is often called a 'common market', because its member states are surrounded by a protective wall of customs duties within which there is a free movement of goods. Firms are able to buy and sell in all other member states almost as freely as they buy and sell across county and regional boundaries in their own countries. The name 'Community' indicates the wider aspects of the grouping. The method of decision–taking, for instance, has created a new political relationship between the nine member states.

Ministers of all the national governments are required to hold regular meetings in Brussels to exercise what are called 'community powers' for reaching decisions on EEC policy. The British minister, for example, can veto any proposal which the government feels is damaging to British vital interests. The ministers of other countries can act in the same way if they consider their vital interests are threatened. But once a Community law is agreed in Brussels, it is automatically binding on Britain and on all other member countries. There are four main institutions in the European Community—the Commission, the Council of Ministers, the European Parliament and the Court of Justice. The Commission and the Council provide the main day–to–day impetus in the Community's decision–making process. The Commission makes policy proposals after consulting a wide range of experts and interested parties. The Council takes the final decisions after consulting the European Parliament and the Economic and Social Committee. The Court of Justice is the ultimate court of appeal.

The Commission consists of 13 members, who are appointed by agreement between the governments of the member states for a renewable four–year term of office. The Commission's role is to serve the Community in general; its members are completely independent of the governments which appointed them. More specifically, its task is fourfold:
1. To initiate Community action by making proposals to the Council of Ministers.
2. To supervise the implementation of Council decisions.
3. To use its autonomous powers of decision.
4. To act as the guardian of the Treaties.

The Commission is collectively responsible to the European Parliament, which can force it to resign by means of a motion of censure.

The Council of Ministers is composed of representatives of member

states—normally the ministers with functional responsibility for matters under discussion—the Minister for Foreign Affairs being the person most frequently involved. The Presidency of the Council rotates among the member states in alphabetical order, each country holding it in turn for six months. The functions of the Council as set out in the Treaty are:
1. To ensure that the objectives in the Treaty are attained.
2. To ensure coordination of the general economic policies of member states.
3. To have power to take decisions.

In practice, the Council's decisions on important matters tend to be taken on a unanimous vote though in principle, under the Treaties, some decisions can be taken by a qualified majority. Votes are weighted in such a way that the interests of the smaller member states are protected. France, Germany, Italy, and the UK each have 10 votes, Belgium and the Netherlands 5, Denmark and Ireland 3, and Luxembourg 2. Of these 58 votes, 41 are required for a majority. Efforts have been made recently to make more use of majority voting, as the council is aware of the dangers to the effectiveness of decision taking through over–insistence on the unanimity principle. In a Community of Twelve this point will have even greater force. The European Council is the name now given to the meetings of Heads of States or governments which take place three times a year, usually once in each of the states holding the Presidency and once in Brussels. Such meetings provide an opportunity for the Heads of State or governments to discuss matters of European interest and to ensure greater progress and cohesion in Community activity. In many ways the European Council is the successor of the Summit Conferences held between 1961 and 1974. In contrast to them, however, the European Council can take decisions, like the Council of Ministers, within the Treaty framework.

The European Parliament (or Assembly) is charged with the task of exercising the advisory and supervisory powers given to it by the Treaty. It must discuss the annual general report of the Commission and it has the power to remove the Commission *en bloc* on a two–thirds majority vote. Normally, however, its decisions are taken on a simple majority vote. The Parliament also has certain powers in relation to the Budget. Political groupings in the Parliament cut across national party lines. There are at present six groups within the Assembly—Socialists, Christian Democrats, Liberals and associates, Conservatives, Progressive Democrats, and Communists and associates. Each group endeavours to take up a common political position on all matters dealt with in Parliament. Direct elections to the Parliament have given the Assembly a new political authority. At the

17

same time, it has reinforced the democratic legitimacy of the whole European institutional apparatus.

The Court of Justice, which sits in Luxembourg, consists of nine judges, assisted by four advocates–general. They are appointed by the governments of the member states acting in agreement for a six–year term of office. The Court's task is twofold: to ensure the application and interpretation of Community law. In its first task it has jurisdiction in disputes between institutions and member states, and between individuals and institutions. In the second, it gives preliminary rulings on questions of interpretation which are referred to it by national courts during the course of legal proceedings at national level. The Court's judgements have executive force in each member state. In this respect the Court of Justice is unique among international tribunals.

A large number of other institutions are associated with the Council and the Commission, some of them provided for in the Treaty, others by legislation to meet political and administrative needs.

The Economic and Social Committee, an advisory body, is composed of representatives of the different categories of economic and social activity. In practice, three groups can be distinguished among its 144 members: employers, employees, and a group representing various other interests (such as consumers, for example). The task of the Committee is to give advice to the Council and the Commission. In certain matters this is obligatory under the Treaties. In other cases the Commission and the Council consult the Committee if they think it desirable. The Committee can also give advice to the Commission on its own initiative. Being a full Community institution under the Treaty, the Committee has its own secretariat, unlike other consultative committees which are serviced by the Commission or the Council as appropriate.

The European Investment Bank (EIB) is another important Community body provided for in the Treaty. It consists of the nine member states, all of whom have subscribed to the Bank's capital, which stands at approximately £1500 m. The objective of the EIB is to contribute to the balanced development of the European Community. It tries to do this by giving long–term loans and guarantees to finance investments which favour the development of less advanced regions and areas undergoing industrial reconversion. It also helps to finance projects which serve the interests of several member states or of the Community as a whole. The Bank's activities also embrace those countries associated with the EEC, including the African, Caribbean, and Pacific countries covered by the Lome Convention (1975). A basic

Figure 1   How policy is made

1. Commission staff consults experts, committees, and interest groups.
2. Staff completes first study documents.
3. Commission examines first study and sets general guidelines
4. Commissioner concerned may consult relevant committee of European Parliament; Committee may ask that European Parliament be consulted officially.
5. Commission staff prepares draft proposal.
6. Commission settles final text, orally or by written procedure.
7. Commission sends formal proposal to Council and, usually, European Parliament.
8. Council asks Committee of Permanent Representatives to advise on whether to consult European Parliament and Economic and Social Committee; on some subjects, consultation of European Parliament is obligatory, and as a rule is consulted on all important matters.
9. As appropriate, Council sends proposal to these bodies.
10. Economic and Social Committee discusses proposal and sends opinion to Commission and Council. Meanwhile—
11. Appropriate committee of European Parliament prepares draft report on proposal.
12. European Parliament debates draft report, with Commissioners present, votes on it (including any amendment replying to original proposal), and sends opinion to Commission and Council.
13. Commission reports to European Parliament on action in response to its advice.
14. Appropriate Council working party reports on proposal, and on Parliament's advice, to Committee of Permanent Representatives.
15. Committee of Permanent Representatives debates proposal, dividing it into 'A' points where agreement already informally reached and 'B' points where further discussion needed in Council.
16. Council discusses points at issue: in light of discussion, Commission may modify proposal.
17. If no agreement reached, points at issue may go back to Committee of Permanent Representatives and/or Council working party.
18. At request of European Parliament, Council gives reasons if disregarding its advice.
19. When agreement reached, proposal adopted and published in the Community's *Official Journal.* The results may be:

☐ *Regulations,*   or Community laws, legally binding on member countries, and applied directly, like national laws;

☐ *Directives,*   equally binding on member States as regards the aim to be achieved, but leaving national authorities to decide how to carry them out;

☐ *Decisions,*   binding in every respect on those to whom they are addressed, whether member States or firms or private individuals; or

   ☐ *Recommendations and Opinions,*   which have no binding force.

The Commission, as well as the Council can issue regulations, directives, decisions, recommendations and opinions on certain subjects such as the day–to–day application of farm policy.

policy of the Bank is that two thirds of its loans within the Community should be devoted to regional development.

More than 70 committees and groups are also associated with the Commission and the Council. Many of these are technical and specialized. Those with relevance to industry are set out in Chapter 4, pages 36–39. The joint committees which have great significance for industrial relations, are described in Chapter 10 pages 99–100. A step–by–step description of how policy is made is given in Figure 1. A list of Commission departments, or

Figure 2   The Directorate-General of the Commission at September 1978 (Source: European Commission)

The Commission is divided into 23 Directorates-General and other services each of which is subdivided into a number of Directorates with responsibility for a specific area of Commission policy.

DG I External Relations
Director-General: Sir Roy Denman

DG II Economic and Financial Affairs
Director-General: Ugo Mosca

DG III Internal Market and Industrial Affairs
Director-General: Fernand Braun

DG IV Competition
Director-General: Willy Schlieder

DG V Employment and Social Affairs
Director-General: Jean Degimbe

*DG VI Agriculture*Director-General: Carlo Facini
Director-General: Claude Villain

DG VII Transport
Director-General: Raymond Le Goy

DG VIII Development
Director-General: Klaus Meyer

DG IX Personnel and Administration
Director-General: Pierre Baichère

DG X Spokesman's Group and Information
Director-General: Enzo Perlot

DG XII Research, Science and Education
Director-General: Günter Schuster

DG XIII Scientific and Technical Information
Director-General: Raymond Appleyard

DG XIV Fisheries
Director-General: Eamon Gallagher

DG XV Financial and Fiscal Institutions
Director-General: O Bus Henriksen

DG XVI Regional Policy
Director General: Pierre Mathijsen

DG XVII Energy
Director-General: Leonard Williams

DG XVIII Credit and Investments
Director-General: Antonio Nicoletti

DG XIX Budgets
Director-General: Daniel Strasser

DG XX Financial Control
Director-General: Carlo Facini

Legal Service
Director-General: Claus D. Ehlermann

Statistical Office
Director-General: Aage Dornonville de la Couz

Administration of the Customs Union
Director: Klaus Pingel

Environmental and Consumer Protection Service
Director: Michel Carpentier

Directorates-General, as they are called, including 'staff' services such as the secretariat–general, legal service, translation services and statistical service, is given in Figure 2. This may all seem incredibly complicated, but it is merely the framework within which activities take place. It will, however, help the reader to understand how things happen in the Commission, or why they often happen slowly. A later chapter will indicate the pressure points which can be used by industrial relations specialists who wish to secure information or influence policy.

Two other pieces of general information are needed to round off this broad picture of the working procedures. The first concerns the commissioners, each of whom has responsibility for different functional areas (see Figure 3). Each Commissioner also has his personal staff, headed by a *Chef de Cabinet,* comprising a small group of experts, recruited either within the Commission or from outside, to advise the commissioner on the many proposals coming before the Commission for decision. The Cabinet also helps the commissioner to develop proposals within his own area of responsibility, working in close collaboration with the relevant Directorate–General. A key task of the Cabinet is to assist, at the political level, in gaining the support of Cabinets of other commissioners for the proposals being prepared by the responsible member of the Commission. It is often a question of striking a balance between an assessment of what is politically feasible, bearing in mind national viewpoints, on the one hand and the Community desiderata on the other. The importance of contacts, political and administrative, within the Commission, and in relevant national capitals, is crucial.

Second, when looking at the decision–making procedures in the EEC, a distinction should be made between:
1. those actions which lead to legislation (treaties, regulations, directives, or rules) whether made by the Council or Commission, and
2. administration by the Commission of existing Community legislation (for example, management of the agricultural, regional, and social funds, or the policing of competition rules).

The legislative process, including the approval of the Community Budget, forms part of the strategic policy–making role of the Community; while the management of funds and legislation is largely an executive function, although it too has strategic implications, in so far as it leads to changes from time to time in the policy followed by the Community institutions in response to developing situations.

This daunting battery of institutions and committees is bound to be baffling to the average person, but it is important to keep in mind that the Community is the first attempt ever made to unite independent European countries by voluntary assent. It is also grappling with arguably the most

21

Figure 3 Special responsibilities of the members of the Commission (Source: European Commission)

President	Roy Jenkins	Secretariat-General Legal Service Information Spokesman's Group Security Office
Vice-Presidents	François-Xavier Ortoli	Economic and Financial Affairs Credit and Investments Statistical Office
	Wilhelm Haferkamp	External Relations
	Finn Olav Gundelach	Agriculture and Fisheries
	Lorenzo Natali	Enlargement Protection of the Environment Nuclear Safety Contacts with Member Governments and public opinion on preparation for direct elections to the European Parliament
	Henk Vredeling	Employment and Social Affairs Tripartite Conference
Members of the Commission	Claude Cheysson	Development
	Guido Brunner	Energy Research, Science and Education Euratom Scientific and Technical Information Common Research Centre
	Raymond Vouel	Competition
	Antonio Giolitti	Coordination of Community Funds Regional Policy
	Richard Burke	Taxation Consumer Affairs Transport Relations with the European Parliament
	Étienne Davignon	Internal Market Industrial Affairs
	Christopher Tugendhat	Budgets and Financial Control Financial Institutions Personnel and Administration

difficult economic and political problems encountered during this century. Given the existence of these problems it is unthinkable that we should return to a system of nationalistic rivalries. Indeed, prominent politicians in different member states have stated that had the European Community existed during the early part of this century, both world wars would have been avoided. Just the same, the many obstacles to progress and the various dilemmas being faced by the Community must be mentioned, to enable a balanced view to be taken.

Our problem is to develop a social policy appropriate to the scale of the current economic crisis. In British terms, social policy covers anything handled by the Departments of Employment, Health and Social Security, Housing and Environment. It is a wide field and yet the Treaty of Rome is not too specific on social policy. The underlying philosophy of the Treaty is *laissez-faire*. The belief is that the removal of obstacles to the free movement of labour, capital, goods, and services, will bring the optimum growth rate, the optimum allocation of resources and, as a corollary, the optimum social system. But the social crudity of the *laissez-faire* theory is soon apparent at any level, nationally or internationally. This is why the Summit Meeting in 1972 planned a Social Action Programme comprising three dozen measures, most of which have been implemented.

Further social measures are currently in train, including a directive on the protection of workers in the event of the employer's bankruptcy, measures to oblige management to inform and consult staff, and wider trade union rights for migrant workers. The continuing economic crisis makes these measures urgent, but financial stringency tends to induce opposition to social reforms, especially those ambitiously conceived. Another problem is finding the necessary consensus within the Council of Ministers without diluting the social proposals into a meaningless formula. As we have already seen, Commission approval is necessary to start any measure's progress through the pipeline. At the end comes the Council's approval, provided a consensus view can be reached. It is then the responsibility of the nine member states to ensure that they have legislation which conforms to the new measure. In most cases they will have a fixed time, usually one or two years, in which to do this.

There is no 'standard time' taken by these laws to traverse the pipeline. Nor is there a guarantee that they will emerge into operation at the end, even if they reach the table of the Council of Ministers. The Fifth Directive on Company Law, for example, which embodies the controversial provisions for worker directors on company boards, began its current journey in 1972 and is still in legislative orbit. Sometimes a directive may go straight through at a fairly fast speed. One of the fastest in recent years in the field of social affairs was the Directive on Acquired Rights, which was approved within three and a half years of the Commission deciding to do something in this area. The carefully designed procedures, involving checks, balances, references to all interested parties, and occasionally the use of the veto,

23

sometimes seem to the harassed civil servants in the Commission to be an overdose of democracy and a sure prescription for eternity. Most Eurocrats seem to have limitless reserves of stoicism!

Moreover, the Commission's role in the social field is often misunderstood. Its job is not to harmonize the whole gamut of social welfare benefits and working conditions throughout the Community, though in fact wide differences in these provisions can distort the competition between the member states. To improve the social facilities in the Community, it is more important that the Commission aims to set minimum standards, which should apply to all advanced industrial countries. On the basis of these standards member states can then develop their own legislative measures— the richer countries will obviously set higher standards. In short, the Commission believes in improving and harmonizing the social policies of member states, but not in standardizing them.

The high level of unemployment in the Community also has obvious implications: a drift towards a protectionism amongst some member states, and a growing cynicism amongst young people who cannot find work. The political uncertainty in member countries transmits itself to the Council of Ministers, thus making it difficult for the Commission to launch new initiatives without attracting a frosty response from the Council. The size of the economic differences between the weaker and stronger members of the Community is another frustrating aspect, as the Community is in many ways a transitional institution. If it were a federal state, then the economic weaknesses of certain areas in it would be compensated by a redistribution of resources from the centre.

The approaching enlargement of the Community introduces further political sensitivities. The fact that Greece, Spain, and Portugal are poorer countries means that the social and regional policies of the Community, as well as the Common Agricultural Policy (CAP), will have to be changed substantially to meet these new pressures. All these negative factors reflect the problems of member states who are unable to find solutions themselves. Therein lies the paradox. For the Commission to make a solid impact on the major difficulties facing the Community, it would need to be given more power and authority, especially in fields such as manpower planning, investment, taxation, and incomes policies. Understandably, there is no question of these levers of power being given to the Commission; many argue that the European Community is historically too young for the Commission to be given such significant authority.

On the other hand the Commission is often criticized for its inability to produce solutions from a magic box. The Commission's staff, the Eurocrats, all of whom are dedicated Europeans, are trying to push the Community forward against the drag of narrow nationalisms. They are criticized for not doing what they are not allowed to do anyway! Nothing can be quite as frustrating as that. In the teeth of all these difficulties, however, the Community is making steady though unspectacular progress. The customs union now exists. Social and regional policies are steadily gaining momentum. More than eighty directives have been approved to remove the technical barriers to trade and a start has been made on the formidable task of harmonizing company laws and fiscal policy. Social standards and a code of labour laws are being gradually extended. There is a growing realization, especially amongst the trade unions in the Community, that the economic forces on which prosperity and welfare depend, escape the control of individual governments acting alone. Interdependence is not only a theory but essential for our survival.

The key to an understanding of the baffling complexities of the European Community is to remember that it was formed on the basis of a compromise between European federalists and a miscellaneous group which came to be known as the European functionalists. Each wanted to unite Europe, but differed on how they felt it should be done. The federalists saw the root of the problem in Europe in the twenty or thirty fragmented, self–interested nation states, separated by trade barriers and acting unilaterally to change the balance of power until nothing but a power vacuum was left. The federalists believed these ideas had led to economic collapse and two world wars, not to mention mass unemployment.

The functionalists were more cautious. They advocated a gradual advance towards unity. They wanted national states to keep their independence, but to pool enough sovereignty to allow institutions to exercise general powers over sectors of their economies or industries. Some functionalists only wanted to form organizations for international cooperation, whilst others wanted a phased programme to full federalism. Against this turbulent background, the Community's hesitant and sporadic progress is encouraging. But how it works will determine whether we can master the great problems of our time, or be constantly at the mercy of international forces which will threaten the security, stability, and welfare of us all.

3. Birth pangs of a Euro–law

There are several ways in which a Euro–law can be conceived and the period of confinement is often long and difficult. In every case, however, the Commission is the watchful and competent midwife, though there are more late deliveries than premature births! The Council of Ministers can simply instruct the Commission to prepare draft legislation on a particular subject; or it can call for a general action programme in a specific field, which in turn can lead to proposals requiring the eventual decision of the Council. The Social Action Programme, for example, was one of the general measures called for at the Paris Summit in 1972 and resulted in approximately forty measures being produced during the ensuing three years. Some of these measures were Euro–laws. Three directives were adopted to improve the situation of women in industry. One provides for equal pay for equal work; another gives women equal access to employment, vocational training, promotion, and comparable working conditions; the third gives women equal social security treatment. Other directives stemming from the Social Action Programme include those on collective redundancies and workers' acquired rights.

Another method is for the Commission itself to initiate work on new legislation, after studying problems in certain regions or industrial sectors. The Commission is responsible for carrying out the provisions of the Treaty of Rome and the decisions of the Council of Ministers. It also has powers of initiative, which means that under the Treaty it has the authority to propose ways in which the general aims of the Community can be achieved.

The Treaty of Rome is in many respects only a framework treaty. For example, it states that there is to be a common agricultural policy, but without defining in detail what the common policy should be. In such a case the Commission must consult all the relevant interests and then make proposals to the Council. But the Commission can make proposals even when there is no specific Treaty requirement. For instance, the Treaty refers several times to the need to assist backward areas of the Community. The Commission has accordingly initiated several proposals in the field of regional development policy.

The third way is for the Commission's services to start things moving by preparing a report outlining proposals for the consideration of the responsible commissioner. This approach might be used following persistent pressures by employers and trade unions, in their frequent contacts with the

Commission's services in the various committees which meet to discuss a wide range of topics.

Whichever of these trigger mechanisms is used, a meticulously careful pattern of consultation takes place—between the relevant services of the Commission, and with the national experts and various interest groups. On all major matters, the opinions and advice of the European Parliament and the Economic and Social Committee are sought before the Council is finally called upon to take a decision on whether a new Euro–law should be born. A step–by–step description of how such policy is made is shown in Figure 1 on page 19, and this demonstrates that the Commission does not work in a void, trying to impose its ideas on member countries without taking their interests into account.

It has close contact with the representatives of economic life in the nine countries. This is why members of the Commission are essentially politicians rather than civil servants. Their task in formulating legal proposals is not just to take account of the Community interest, but to consider what is likely to be politically acceptable to the member governments and parliaments. The previous experience which they have had as ministers, senior civil servants, or government advisers in their own countries, ensures their awareness of the pressures to which national governments are subject. Before a Commission proposal is submitted to the Council there is full consultation with national experts and interest groups. In Brussels, for instance, there are more than 300 organizations representing trade union, manufacturing, agricultural, professional, consumer, and other interests. So when Euro–law proposals go to the Council for a decision, the Commission has a good idea of their acceptability. This sometimes slows down progress to a snail's pace, but there is little point in pressing legal proposals which seriously embarrass particular member states, on the grounds that the European Court of Justice will force them into line. As Ben Jonson said: 'Many punishments discredit a prince as many funerals a physician.' The dilemma of the Commission is to reconcile the inevitable dilution of its proposals which results from this democratic accountability, with the need to make progress in improving the conditions of life and work for citizens of the European Community.

Another more sophisticated complication is that most member states are governed by civil law rather than common law (Denmark has a legal system which is quite distinct from the others). The essential difference between the civil law and common law systems is that the civil law consists mainly of statutes or codes, in which laws and the principles on which they are based are fully set forth, so the judges' rulings are deductive rather than inductive. Judges in civil law countries are specially trained and are aloof from the bar. Their decisions and courtroom work are more anonymous and written than

27

the personalized, oral labours of judges and lawyers in common law countries such as the UK and Ireland. Under the common law, every case makes its own law and precedents are most important. Statutes may be quite detailed, but their specific applied meaning is often omitted from the legislation. The judge, therefore, becomes a 'legislator', when he interprets the meaning of the statute or case (inductive reasoning). Judges in common law countries are trained as lawyers before they become judges. EEC jurists often go far outside the wording of a given piece of legislation in order to determine its meaning and the intention of the legislators. This again highlights the differences between the civil law and common law systems. Strangely enough, although France is a civil law nation (*Code Napoléon*), and in spite of French influence on Community law, common law concepts (the case–law system) still seem to be the basis for much of the judicial deliberation of the Court of Justice.

This does not occur by the usual system of precedents, which is prohibited in civil law systems, but rather by 'interpretation' of the law. Normally, civil law courts and judges do not have the power to 'interpret' law and precedents do not count for much. Yet the European Community courts often exert a legislative function. This tendency is most apparent in the administrative courts dealing with claims involving EEC agencies, where the scope for relying on precedents is greatest. The Community's Court of Justice has three advocates–general. Their function is to act impartially to evaluate the law and the facts of each case appearing before the court, and to present their opinions to the court in the interests of justice. Their findings are not binding but their influence is great. These general considerations create a mood of great caution and sensitivity where lawmaking is concerned in the European Community. 'The end of the law,' said John Locke, 'is not to abolish or restrain, but to preserve or enlarge freedom.' This idealistic conception of the law does not find an automatic acceptance in the Community's institutions. First, there is the difficulty of finding a consensus view through elaborate consultations. Secondly, there are the differing legal backgrounds of member states, each shrouded in varying degrees of sanctity. Thirdly, there is the drive for more accountability and the view that law–making powers should be gradually transferred to the newly elected European Parliament.

The reasons why the Community is so pre–eminently an organization operating by law are not difficult to discern. They come from the nature and purpose of the Community. It is the lawmaking character of the Community which marks it off sharply from the OECD or EFTA. It was precisely because the OECD (then the OEEC) proved inadequate to serve the purposes they deemed essential, that the founders of the Community decided to proceed on a different basis. The OECD proved inadequate because its

28

method—operation not by law but by seeking a general alignment of policies, and an approximation of conduct of its member states through consultation and consensus but without the compulsion of the law—could not, except for short spells, keep those members sufficiently in line to ensure the achievement of key economic objectives. With EFTA, law was not absent from its method of working, but it was relatively inconspicuous, because EFTA's objectives were comparatively uncomplicated and un-ambitious. A free trade area must be based on treaty and customs law but these need not be identical. Separate national laws are enough provided they can achieve, as they can, an identical objective. In the European Community it is easy to see why Community law must take precedence over national law.

The purpose of the Community is to advance the common interests of the member states by applying common, or at least harmonized policies, which are expressed through legislation. It would entirely frustrate this purpose if national governments were free to retain, or to enact, national legislation inconsistent with Community law. This clearly means that national law must, in the last resort, be brought into line with intended Community law before the latter, by an act of the Community in which all member states participate, comes into effect. National legislatures, too, must refrain from enacting law inconsistent with Community law. Given the existence of a European Community, these constitutional implications are entirely logical. There is no point in joining an important and prestigious club and then saying that you intend to defy all the rules and regulations. Nevertheless, these constitutional effects were hard for many people to swallow in the UK, for instance, where opposition to the European Community was, and still is in some cases, deep–rooted to the point of fanaticism. Incidentally, all treaties to which the UK is party bind the UK in international law not to act inconsistently with them. But they do not have effect as law within the UK until made applicable by Parliament.

A number of treaties have obliged the UK to repeal or modify existing national laws to enable them to take effect. The unique aspect of the UK's membership of the European Community is that it obliges the UK not merely to clear the way for the direct effect and direct applicability of its existing treaties and laws, but to undertake to do likewise for any which (with the UK's participation) it might enter into or enact in the future. It is this fundamental nature of the changes which troubles those opposed to the European Community, especially in the political field. The precedence of Community law, has, in fact, the effect of introducing a somewhat novel feature into the UK constitution. So long as the UK remains in the Community, the Treaties and Community law remain entrenched. They cannot be modified or repealed by the ordinary action of the UK

Parliament. To that extent, they differ from other laws and are what amounts to a written part of the British constitution. So a Euro–law is an elaborate exercise in political diplomacy and consultation. It is often shorn of its bite and positiveness in return for the comprehensiveness of its provisions, which have to be acceptable to all member states.

The complex background factors surrounding the preparation of Euro–laws have been briefly explained in order that the problems and opportunities might be more fully understood. To complete the survey, an outline now follows of the introductory arguments presented by the Commission's services in support of a proposal for a Directive on Insolvency Procedures. It was 'The Proposal for a Directive on the approximation of laws of the member states concerning the Protection of Employees in the event of the Insolvency of their Employers'. The Council of Ministers decided to approve this law in June 1979. The same basic presentation was used for the Commission, the European Parliament and the Economic and Social Committee. It does not include the suggested articles and technical aspects of the directive, only the key arguments.

Directive on insolvency procedures

INTRODUCTION

The provisions of bankruptcy law in force in member states do not afford employees adequate protection with regard to claims arising from their employment relationship. The proposed directive therefore requires the member states to set up suitable institutions to settle the outstanding claims of employees, arising from their employment relationship and originating prior to suspension of payments by the employer, irrespective of the available assets and of the progress of the bankruptcy proceedings. The organizing, financing, and operation of these institutions are, however, matters which fall within the competence of the member states, subject to compliance with a number of rules laid down in the proposed directive.

ECONOMIC AND SOCIAL CONSIDERATIONS

A feature of the difficult economic situation in the Community is the increasing number of company bankruptcies, especially of those where there are no available assets. Since there are no Community statistics on the subject, reference must be made to national figures. The statistics available for Germany show that, during 1976, in approximately 70 per cent of bankruptcies there were insufficient assets to enable insolvency proceedings to be opened. The annual losses suffered by employees as a result of bankruptcies, before the bankruptcy deficiency laws of 17 July 1974 came into force, fluctuated between DM20 million and DM50 million. In the UK it has been established that the annual sum of such losses is £4 million. The situation in other member states is presumably comparable.

In these circumstances the following conclusions must be drawn:

1. The preferential ranking accorded by the bankruptcy law of the member states to claims arising from employment relationships does not adequately protect employees, since experience has shown that the available assets are frequently insufficient to meet such claims.
2. Employees are totally unprotected where their employer's insolvency does not result in bankruptcy proceedings, because it is considered pointless to initiate or open such proceedings on account of the total absence of available assets.
3. The employees have no alternative available, such as the provision of a security or the reservation of title to property, that can protect them from the consequences of their employer's insolvency. It is therefore necessary to ensure that, in the event of their employer's insolvency, employees are remunerated for services rendered. The guarantee must be provided by special institutions, independent of the employer's financial position and of the procedures in the event of insolvency that apply in such cases. For these reasons the majority of member states have introduced into their law guarantees designed to protect employees against losses arising from their employer's insolvency.

OBJECTIVE OF THE PROPOSAL FOR A DIRECTIVE

The principle on which the proposal for a directive is based is to require member states to set up suitable institutions to settle the outstanding claims of employees arising as a result of their employment relationship, and originating prior to suspension of payments by the employer. The organization, financing, and operation of these institutions are, however, matters which fall within the competence of the member states, subject to compliance with a number of rules laid down in the proposal for a directive. This approach will enable those member states which have already set up suitable institutions to maintain, to a large extent, their existing arrangements—and the other member states to opt for such solutions as are most appropriate to their own situation. The proposal for a directive specifies, *inter alia:*

1. the criteria which define suspension of payments;
2. the nature of employees' claims arising from an employment relationship;
3. that member states may set limits, in certain cases, to the payment obligations incumbent on the institutions.

31

The proposal for a directive lays down minimum rules which do not restrict in any way the right of member states to apply rules that are more favourable to employees.

LEGAL BASIS

The proposed directive is based on Article 100 of the Treaty.

Article 100

> The Council shall, acting unanimously on a proposal from the Commission, issue directives for the approximation of such provisions laid down by law, regulation or administrative action in member states as directly affect the establishment or functioning of the Common Market. The Assembly and the Economic and Social Committee shall be consulted in the case of directives whose implementation would, in one or more member states, involve the amendment of legislation.

Increasing economic interdependence imposes the requirement that employees' claims arising from the employment relationship against insolvent employers should receive equal protection in all member states. Major differences between the systems for the protection of employees' claims against insolvent employers, and the fact that there is no adequate protection in some member states, increase social imbalances within the Community and thus directly affect the functioning of the common market. It is therefore necessary to promote the approximation of laws in this field while maintaining the improvement described in Article 117 of the Treaty.

Article 117

> Member States agree upon the need to promote improved working conditions and an improved standard of living for workers, so as to make possible their harmonization while the improvement is being maintained. They believe that such a development will ensue not only from the functioning of the Common Market, which will favour the harmonization of social systems, but also from the procedures provided for in this Treaty and from the approximation of provisions laid down by law, regulation, or administrative action.

RELATIONSHIP TO OTHER COMMISSION WORK

The proposed directive does not conflict with the Convention on bankruptcy, winding–up arrangements, compositions and similar proceedings currently being prepared by DGIII. The draft convention provides, in respect of contracts of employment that the effects of the bankruptcy on the contract of employment, are determined in accordance with the law applicable to the contract of employment, where this is the law of the contracting state. As regards the preferential rights of employees, the draft convention lays down that all employees of the undertaking which has become bankrupt may invoke their right of preference, in all member states in which assets are located, in accordance with the law applicable in the member states concerned. Accordingly, employers are treated equally as far as possible, but the exercise to the full of a right of preference which gives favourable ranking to a claim is, of course, possible only where the available assets are adequate.

ASSESSMENT

The object of the proposed directive is to align, in the member states other than Italy and Ireland, the development of guarantees, already existing under their law, which are designed to protect employees against losses arising as a result of their employer's insolvency. It may be concluded that most member states will warmly welcome this initiative and also that the support of the majority of the members of the Economic and Social Committee and of the European Parliament can be relied on.

CONCLUSION

It is proposed that the Commission approve the proposal for a directive, its explanatory memorandum, and their submission to the Council.

Enshrined in the submission just outlined are all the points previously discussed: carefully phrased language; indications that meetings with national experts have taken place; the hint of a consensus already hammered out in informal talks with the interest groups; and suggestions that the Economic and Social Committee and the European Parliament are likely to give the measure a fair wind. Above all, there is a strong thread of social responsibility knitting all the sections together, making it difficult for reasonable people to disagree. These, indeed, are the birth pangs of a Euro–law.

4. How to influence the Commission

When asked what impressed him most when viewing the earth from the moon, one astronaut said recently: 'I could put up my thumb and blot out the whole earth.' Such dimensional tricks are reserved for spacemen, though one sometimes feels that the more rabid critics of the European Commission would revel in its disappearance if lifting a thumb would suffice. This chapter tries to explain how individuals and pressure groups can help themselves and the Commission by lifting a finger, so to speak, and talking to the right people at the right time. There are at least six different ways of influencing the Commission in a positive direction and these will be outlined, along with the important Committees and Commission departments which give platforms for the presentation of views and opinions. Although there are more than three hundred interest groups with representation in Brussels, there is a surprising reluctance to exploit all the available channels of persuasion. This is partly due to the fact that many people interpret 'influence' in a negative sense, as embracing complaints about bureaucracy or as a means of extracting the maximum of Community funds for their use.

But public ignorance of the Commission and its working methods is sometimes matched by Commission officials' ignorance about conditions or situations in countries or regions for which they are preparing legislation. The Commission's services are badly overstretched—there are fewer people in the services *in toto* than in many individual ministries in the British civil service, for instance. Consequently Commission officials do not always have time to absorb all the nuances of the social, economic, and legal systems of the member states. This sometimes gets the Commission a bad name. Moreover, the failure on the part of interest groups and political parties to understand the lengthy process by which draft directives become Euro–law, means that they often over–react to the initial proposals, and then find themselves in entrenched positions from which they have difficulty in extricating themselves without serious loss of face. Nor do the mass media help in this connection; they tend to present all Community issues in clashing, conflictual terms involving different national interests, instead of patient efforts designed to establish a European Community from which in the end all may benefit. This means that a Community is being created which seems psychologically incapable of realizing its full potential, due to ignorance, naïvety, and misunderstandings. The way to improve this situation is to mobilize the talents, brains, and criticisms of key people in the

Community, through the many avenues of communications and influence, as fully and effectively as possible.

The six ways of influencing the Commission are like railway lines, carrying traffic in both directions. They are as follows:

Direct approaches to Commission officials

These can be made by individuals or groups, subject to the normal courtesies of arranging appointments in advance on a reasonable time basis. Senior Commission officials, such as Directors–General, Directors and Heads of Division, and sometimes Commissioners, are perfectly willing to listen and talk to those willing to come to Brussels. A telephone call and a letter indicating the relevance of the subject (and the visitor) is usually all that is required. This openness on the part of the Commission is partly due to the fact that Eurocrats, unlike national civil servants, do not have to worry about parliamentary privilege.

A further aspect of these direct contacts is that it helps to balance the complex and sometimes difficult relationship between the Commission and member governments. Since governments have the ultimate power of decision, progress can only be made if the governments and Commission work together and reconcile differences. But the Commission has obligations to see that the provisions of the Treaty of Rome are met and this can sometimes result in a temporary deadlock. Direct contacts are therefore mutually beneficial, bearing in mind language difficulties and the fact that Commission officials recognize their knowledge limitations of countries other than their own. Due to this openness of the Commission, it is often easier to influence the drafting of a Commission directive than the drafting of a piece of national legislation, where these relationships are more tightly controlled by considerations of protocol and secrecy. Details of the various Commission services are given in Figure 2, page 20.

Using the committee network

In addition to the Community institutions more than 70 consultative bodies assist the Community with its work. These bodies are chiefly of an advisory nature and a number of them have a special relevance for industrial relations. They include the following:

THE ECONOMIC AND SOCIAL COMMITTEE

A 144–member body representing employers' organizations, trade unions, and other interests (including consumers) in equal numbers. The

35

Commission and the Council of Ministers must consult the Economic and Social Committee on all major proposals and it may also give advice on its own initiative.

THE CONSULTATIVE COMMITTEE

An 81–member body, plus one observer, which fulfils a similar role for coal, steel, iron ore, and scrap.

THE MONETARY COMMITTEE

A 20–member body, two of whom are appointed by each member government, usually from the civil service or the central bank, and two by the Commission. It advises the Commission and the Council on the member states' and the Community's monetary and financial position and on the general payments situation of the member states.

THE ECONOMIC POLICY COMMITTEE

National and Commission representatives whose task is to help coordinate member states' economic policies.

THE COMMITTEE OF CENTRAL BANK GOVERNORS

This meets to discuss credit, money–market, and exchange matters with a member of the Commission attending.

THE COMMITTEE OF THE EUROPEAN SOCIAL FUND

Representatives of governments, trade unions, and employers' organizations, presided over by a member of the Commission. It assists the Commission with the administration of the Fund.

THE STANDING COMMITTEE ON EMPLOYMENT

Representatives of workers, employers and, in some cases, of member states, under the chairmanship of the representative of the member state currently presiding over the Council.

THE ADMINISTRATIVE COMMISSION FOR THE SOCIAL SECURITY OF MIGRANT WORKERS

National officials and Commission representatives, whose task is to help protect the welfare of Community citizens working in a member country other than their own.

THE TRANSPORT COMMITTEE

Experts designated by the member states to advise the Commission on transport problems.

THE SCIENTIFIC AND TECHNICAL COMMITTEE

This comprises 27 experts appointed by the Council to advise the Commission on the peaceful uses of nuclear energy.

THE NUCLEAR RESEARCH CONSULTATIVE COMMITTEE

This comprises government representatives, under the chairmanship of the Commission, which also provides the secretariat.

THE SCIENTIFIC AND TECHNICAL RESEARCH COMMITTEE (CREST)

National officials responsible for scientific research under the chairmanship of the Commission.

THE MANAGEMENT COMMITTEES

One for each of the 17 main groups of farm products. These consist of representatives of the national administrations, under the chairmanship of a Commission representative. If a management committee votes against a Commission proposal, the Commission can still take a contrary decision, which remains in force unless the Council decides against it within one month.

THE ARTICLE 113 COMMITTEE

Representatives of member states, under the chairmanship of the representative of the member state currently presiding over the Council, whose task is to assist the Commission in trade negotiations with non–member countries.

THE ADVISORY COMMITTEE ON VOCATIONAL TRAINING

Representatives of governments, trade unions, and employers' organizations, presided over by a member of the Commission.

ADVISORY COMMITTEE FOR THE FREEDOM OF MOVEMENT OF WORKERS

Representatives of governments, trade unions, and employers presided over by a member of the Commission.

MINES SAFETY AND HEALTH COMMISSION

Representatives of governments, trade unions, and employers, presided over by a member of the Commission.

STEEL SAFETY AND HEALTH COMMISSION

Representatives of governments, trade unions, and employers, presided over by a member of the Commission.

The various committees mentioned so far are either composed of experts or have a tripartite composition which permits a balanced industrial representation. The 'bipartite', or joint committees, are discussed in detail in Chapter 9 and give further, more specific opportunities for influencing Commission policies. These committees, which are exclusively employer and worker orientated, cover at the moment coal, steel, agriculture, road transport, inland waterways, sea fishing, rail transport, and footwear. Sectors where contacts are being made with a view to eventually forming a joint committee include civil aviation, shipbuilding, sea transport, public services, teaching, sugar, food, breweries, banks, insurance, distribution, construction, commercial travellers, and textiles. Of course, representatives of trade unions and employers are already playing a valuable role in the work of many of these committees; but the point is, whether interest groups fully understand the wide scope and strategic importance of this network enough to use it for more than just the presentation of grievances or enquiries about available funds. Some sectors have several committees working on their behalf, which poses the need for a considered, coordinated strategy on the part of the interest group concerned. Transport and agriculture are examples of this situation.

Approaches via the ETUC and UNICE to the President of the Commission

The top trade union and employers' organizations in the European Community have what amounts to a 'hot line' to the President via the Social Partners' Bureau—a small office attached to the President's Cabinet through which top–level meetings or contacts are made, often at short notice. If trade unions or employers' organizations have a serious problem which they feel warrants the attention of the President, and they can convince the ETUC or UNICE (Union des Industries de la Communauté Europèene) of the importance of the issue, such an approach might be made at a high level. Obviously, this route must be used with discretion or it will defeat itself by becoming trivialized.

Approaches via national organizations of trade unions and employers

Where a national organization like the TUC or CBI, for example, feels very strongly about a particular issue but does not have the time nor the inclination to press it through the ETUC or UNICE, then a direct approach to the President, through the Social Partners' Bureau, or to the appropriate Commissioner may get things moving quickly.

Approaches to national governments

On major issues, the most effective way of exerting influence is for interest groups in particular countries, like the TUC and CBI in the UK, to pressurize their own government, with the aim of persuading the government to instruct its minister who attends the Council of Ministers meeting in Brussels to reflect the concern of the interest group. This might lead to changing, delaying, or even stopping important measures or decisions.

Approaches to the European Parliament

Now that direct elections have taken place and the newly elected MPs are anxious to show their mettle to their Euro–constituents, pressures can be put on MPs either by individuals or by groups to take up particular issues. Often these will relate to legislation being considered by the institutions, including the European Parliament; which means that MPs who have been briefed about a particular problem and are convinced of the validity of the remedies called for, may ask pointed questions, both in the Parliament and perhaps with greater effect in the specialist Parliamentary Committees which are considering the subject.

So those are the six ways of influencing the Commission (and perhaps making friends in the process). It will be observed that the approaches fall into three categories. The first level could be said to be the Commission itself (approaches 1 and 2); the second level those institutions outside the Commission (approaches 3 and 4); and third, the Ministerial level (approaches 5 and 6). The ability of the many European federations to express a concerted view on behalf of their component members varies greatly from one organization to another, as do their influence on the Community institutions and their value as sources of information and influence.

In general, organizations representing special branches especially affected by Community powers have been more effective in all these respects than the 'peak organizations' (UNICE and the ETUC), even though the Commission gives special recognition to these leading federations, because of their size and authority. This might simply reflect the fact that the

39

development of Community policy and administration has been uneven. The European Farmers' Organization (COPA) is generally regarded as one of the most effective pressure groups and one of the most closely involved in Community decision–taking. In the same way, representative bodies in coal and steel have a longer and better record of representation at European level than those in other parts of industry, but this no doubt relates to their earlier close involvement in the ECSC (European Coal and Steel Community). Two hard facts need to be faced by the European interest groups, however. Firstly, the decisions which matter most to them are still taken mainly at the level of member states. Secondly, the power transferred from member states to the Community level still rests primarily with the representatives of the member states' governments in the Council of Ministers.

Sir Herbert Beerbohm Tree is reputed to have said to a man whom he saw staggering in the street under the weight of a grandfather clock: 'My dear chap, why not carry a watch?' The complex consultative systems attached to the Commission are a heavy though necessary piece of Community furniture: they prove the open and democratic nature of the Community, where time is not as critical as honest argument and wise administration. There is one worrying aspect of the many pressures put on the Commission by interest groups, especially those linked with crisis industries. The European Commission is sometimes accused of seeking to prevent national governments from giving state aid to ailing industries. In principle this is not so, but the Commission is the guardian of the Treaty of Rome and must ensure that any such aid does not contravene Community rules on fair competition. Under the threat of increasing unemployment, many governments are yielding to pressure to give financial aid to struggling industries. State aids to industry are consequently on the increase and it is the responsibility of the Commission to ensure that these aids do not upset basic trading conditions within the common market. Guarding the free play of market forces does not necessarily mean banning state aids to industry—many are in fact in the Community's general interest. They have to be judged case by case and should be permitted when they are likely to correct market conditions which:

1. hinder progress towards certain economic or social objectives;
2. only allow those objectives to be achieved with unacceptable social conditions;
3. intensify competition to the point where it becomes self–destroying.

The Commission's view is that aid should be authorized when it is necessary (and the need has been clearly demonstrated) to correct severe regional imbalances; to help accelerate industrial growth or change; to permit certain industries to be run down without too much social distress; or to neutralize, at least temporarily, distortions of competition due to outside factors. The Commission's approach is to allow aid for struggling industries, to ensure an orderly run down of their activity without serious repercussions for employment in general, and to ensure that national aid does not simply transfer the ills of one country to a Community partner. The Commission allows aid which permits a crisis–stricken industry to adapt to new market conditions.

In concrete terms, this means that the Commission applies three guiding principles:
1. the aim of the aid should not be to preserve the *status quo*—aid for production cannot be permitted unless it is part of a reorganization programme;
2. rescue measures are permitted when they provide a breathing space for long term solutions to be implemented. They should be limited to those industries with the most acute social problems;
3. investment assistance should not expand capacity, since overcapacity is prevalent in all crisis sectors.

The Commission has also given its views on other types of aid to crisis sectors. Employment aids, for example, can be intended either to create jobs or to maintain existing jobs. In the latter case they should only be allocated to troubled sectors if they are a part of a reorganization programme, otherwise they will simply transfer the social and industrial problems to other Community countries. With regional aid, too, in sectors with large surplus capacity (like shipbuilding and man–made fibres) the Community has requested that no aid be given—even regional aid—which would be likely to increase overcapacity further.

5. Other European institutions—ILO— OECD—GATT—Council of Europe

It was Disraeli who said that 'the test of political institutions is the condition of the countries whose future they regulate.' By this criteria, all four of the bodies with which this chapter is concerned are justified and have great significance for industrial relations. The ILO, the OECD, and the Council of Europe deal with conventions, recommendations, or moral commitments in the field of industrial relations, while the GATT helps to set the standards and patterns of international trade. The looser structure of these bodies tends to make them in some ways less effective than the European Community, but their work often sets the pace, for example, in the field of multinationals, job enrichment, vocational training, and the role of women in industry. It is important for industrial relations practitioners to understand the differences and similarities between these four bodies and the European Community.

The International Labour Organization

The ILO, with its headquarters and permanent secretariat in Geneva, is of course a world organization with 139 member countries, but it is well-rooted in European history. It is sometimes criticized for trying to be a super–state, while others dismiss it as an elaborate and ineffective talking-shop. In fact it exerts a considerable influence on the European industrial relations scene, by building up a code of international law and practice: the labour standards are set by the International Labour Conference, which takes place annually, in the form of conventions and recommendations. Each convention is a legal instrument regulating some aspect of labour administration, social welfare, or human rights; it is conceived as a model for national legislation, but a convention is only binding on those member states which have ratified it.

When a member state ratifies a convention, it undertakes that its legislation and national practice will be brought into line with the standards laid down in the convention concerned. A recommendation, however, is not binding in the same sense as a convention. In either case, however, there is the indefinable but powerful moral authority which a worldwide organization possesses and which is bound in the long run to influence the actions of the national units of which it is composed. Since 1919 the ILO has adopted 151 conventions and 159 recommendations; these deal with topics as diverse as night work, sickness insurance schemes, guarding of machinery, paid educational leave, and protection against radiation. Until a convention is ratified it is rather like a recommendation—without being binding, its clauses serve as a guide for action.

When all the clauses have been progressively put into effect, the convention can be ratified. The total number of ratifications of ILO conventions has now passed the 4600 mark, more than 3000 of them having been registered since the end of the Second World War. Apart from these conventions and recommendations, which are known as 'international instruments', there are resolutions, conclusions, or model codes, which can be adapted either by the Conference, the ILO governing body or by technical meetings. For instance, in 1977 the ILO governing body adopted 'The Tripartite Declaration of Principles Concerning Multinational Enterprises and Social Policy'. The 58 paragraphs in the declaration, which took five years to complete, cover most aspects of employment, vocational training, conditions of work and life, and industrial relations in multinational enterprises.

Galsworthy may have been right when he said that idealism increases in direct proportion to one's distance from the problem, but there is nothing phoney about the sincerity and idealism which pervades the ILO. It is the first international institution in history in which workers, employers, and governments have worked together on a worldwide scale to deal with problems related to working life. It became clear during the First World War that the coming peace would have to take account of the rising aspirations of the workers. Various factors brought the ILO into being in 1919 at the Paris Peace Conference, together with the League of Nations, but the need to base peace firmly on a foundation of social justice was undoubtedly the most important influence. In the words of its constitution: 'conditions of labour exist involving such injustice, hardship and privation to large numbers of people as to produce unrest so great that the peace and harmony of the world are imperilled.'

In 1946, the ILO became the first specialized agency associated with the UN. During its early years the ILO encountered difficulties concerning the powers with which it was to be endowed. A choice had to be made between two apparently irreconcilable alternatives. The agreements on labour standards which the new body was to adopt could take the form either of mere resolutions or mandatory national instruments. To escape this dilemma an imaginative compromise was worked out by the ILO: international labour legislation was to be discussed and adopted by a conference composed of government, employer and worker representatives. Decisions which had secured a two–thirds majority in this forum were to be communicated to member countries with a view to legislative action within twelve or eighteen months.

This tripartite structure, and the safeguard of a two-thirds majority voting rule, are distinctive features of the ILO. Moreover, the compromise satisfied trade union leaders, who would not have been content with pious resolutions on industrial problems. Nor did it arouse the opposition of those who might have balked at delegating authority to an international body comprising non–government as well as government representatives. The automatic link was therefore established between the international tripartite body which defined standards, and the national legislations, which had a chance to discuss and either accept or reject the proposal. This unique tripartite structure means that each member country sends two government delegates, one employers' delegate and one workers' delegate to the ILO's annual International Labour Conference. The employers' and workers' delegates speak and vote independently. They may, and often do, disagree with their governments and with each other; but it is this tripartite system which has given the ILO much of its strength and that has helped it to survive wars and depressions.

The International Labour Conference is the supreme deliberative body of the ILO. It normally meets once a year at the Palace of Nations in Geneva, but some earlier sessions have been held in Montreal, Philadelphia, Paris and San Francisco. The Conference sessions are usually attended by more than 1000 delegates, technical advisers, and observers. Many of the government delegates are cabinet ministers responsible for labour affairs in their own countries. The International Labour Conference:
1. adopts international labour standards in the form of conventions and recommendations;
2. adopts the ILO Budget and also the scale of percentage assessments which determine the contributions of member states;
3. elects every three years the members of the Governing Body of the International Labour Office;
4. provides a world forum for the discussion of social and labour problems of concern to governments, employers and workers in all member countries.

The theme of the general discussion is set each year by the Director–General in his report to the Conference and is usually one of pressing international importance.

Apart from this general activity, there are three specific areas of ILO work which have great relevance to industrial relations. The first is the International Institute for Labour Studies, which was established by the ILO in 1960 as a centre for advanced studies in the social and labour field. It has two broad aims—education for leadership in the industrial relations field and research for developing useful social and labour policy ideas. This provides the opportunity for discussions amongst influential policy–makers on current issues, in an atmosphere removed from problems and negotiations. The research conferences of the Institute bring together social thinkers and social practitioners from various parts of the world. They are drawn from management, trade unions, government service, universities and the professions. The second area of relevant activity is the International Centre for Advanced Technical and Vocational Training, which was established in Turin, Italy, by the ILO in 1965. This Centre gives advanced technical and vocational training, primarily for the benefit of developing countries in Asia, Africa, Latin America, and the Near and Middle East, for persons who are considered suitable for more advanced training than they could obtain in their own countries or regions.

Finally, the ILO committees play a crucial part in ensuring the transmission of the ILO's lofty idealism into practical measures. Two key committees are the Committee of Experts on the Application of Conventions and Recommendations, and the Committee of Social Security Experts, both comprising independent persons of international standing. Since 1945 eight Industrial Committees have been formed to consider labour and social questions in particular industries. These committees, which have the normal ILO tripartite representation, cover:

1. Building, civil engineering and public works
2. Chemical industries
3. Coal mines
4. Iron and steel
5. Metal trades
6. Petroleum
7. Textiles
8. Inland transport

The ILO also frequently convenes *ad hoc* meetings to study special problems in other industries. The state of industrial relations in a particular country generally provides a good indication of its approach to social problems. If industrial relations are bad, they poison the social climate and impede economic progress. Good industrial relations, on the other hand, can contribute materially to better living standards. The ILO considers relations between employers and workers are 'good' when they are based on the full recognition of freedom of association in both theory and practice, and when they enable elected representatives of employers and workers to tackle problems of common concern in a spirit of mutual respect and through democratic discussion.

To further this aim, the ILO has adopted Conventions on Freedom of Association and the right to bargain and organize collectively. It has also

45

adopted recommendations dealing with collective agreements, voluntary conciliation, arbitration, and cooperation between public authorities and employers' and workers' organizations. In the words of one of its former Director–Generals, David Morse: 'The ILO's main responsibility is to ensure that the goals of social improvement remain uppermost within the total process of change.' It was perhaps an awareness of this basic goal which led to the first serious challenge to the validity of the ILO's tripartite principle in November 1977. At that time the US withdrew from the ILO on the grounds that it was becoming too 'politicized', and allowing political campaigns to be mounted against the US and Western nations in general. The US, which contributed one quarter of the ILO's Budget, now running at more than eighty million dollars a year, argued that the ILO had allowed the Communist Third World Axis to dominate its affairs and to raise international political issues which were beyond the competence and mandate of the ILO.

The US felt that the tripartite principles of the ILO were being distorted for political motives. It was felt that Soviet employers, for example, if not Soviet trade unions, were in effect agents of the state. Similarly, many Third World countries had trade unions which were an arm of government. Thus the effect of the tripartite rule was to give a massive, whipped voting advantage to the anti–western nations; whereas the tripartite delegations from the Western countries were often genuinely divided and this showed in their split votes. The US gave two years' notice of its intention to quit unless changes were made. This period expired and the withdrawal took place in November 1977. Even so, in withdrawing, President Carter acted against the advice of all nine member states of the European Community, the International Confederation of Free Trade Unions and his own State Department. The gut feeling was that the place to hammer out the argument was within and not outside the embattled organization. Shock therapy may well have been the intention of the US in withdrawing from the ILO; but many believe that the problems of US re–entry into the ILO may be more complex and difficult than those surrounding its departure. Since 1977 the financial effect of the US withdrawal has been to reduce the ILO Staff of 1700 by more than 200. This has imposed limits on the services and administration and some research work and a number of technical studies have been postponed or abandoned. On the other hand, most of the ILO's employment programme, which provides some of the input into work on multinationals, is financed by the United Nations Development Programme (UNDP) and is unaffected by the US withdrawal. Finally, an encouraging and generous gesture was made by the US Department of Labour in 1978, by offering a grant of 250 000 dollars to accelerate the international exchange of information on occupational hazards.

The Organization for Economic Cooperation and Development

The OECD is a direct descendant of the Marshall Plan in the shape of the OEEC (Organization for European Economic Cooperation) set up in 1948, which became the OECD in 1961 with the entry of Canada and the United States. This club of 25 nations is an all–purpose economic agency, perhaps best known for its work in producing economic strategies for its member states on the basis of highly sophisticated analyses and detailed economic studies. It also carries out research work in a wide variety of fields. It has a staff of 2000, of which one–quarter are experts (economists, scientists, statisticians, and sociologists, etc.) The cynics say it is simply a watchdog which does nothing but bark, though occasionally loud enough to wake up the whole neighbourhood.

The convention, signed in Paris in 1960, provided that the OECD should:
1. achieve the highest sustainable economic growth and employment and a rising standard of living in member countries, while maintaining financial stability, and thus contribute to the development of the world economy;
2. contribute to sound economic expansion in member as well as non–member countries in the process of economic development;
3. contribute to the expansion of world trade on a multilateral, non–discriminating basis in accordance with international obligations.

Some 25 per cent of the OECD's 50 million dollar budget comes from the US. The rest is contributed by the other members in proportion to their Gross National Products. Members are the main Western European nations, Canada, USA, Japan, Turkey, Australia, New Zealand, and Yugoslavia. Each member state has the right of veto and understandably tries to advance its own interests and maintain its autonomy. Nevertheless, the club has provided the framework for the industrialized world to work out the policies of cooperation and development it so badly needs.

The key organizations in the OECD are: the Council, which comprises representatives of the member countries; the Executive Committee, which meets in special session; and the General Secretariat which coordinates the activities of the various working committees and carries out the Council's directives. The Secretary–General needs above all to be a diplomat, as the OECD lives on compromises and the concessions it can persuade governments to grant. Its economic studies are carefully worked out in close consultation with the governments concerned. Its role is to develop a consensus based on persuasion, as it is not possible for the OECD to impose a policy line or formulate an overall economic policy with any assurance that it will be applied. From an industrial relations viewpoint, the OECD has done much valuable work in the fields of social policy, job enrichment, multinational companies, and the mobility and productivity of workers.

47

The wider aspects of its activities, which again are highly relevant to the shop–floor worker, are shown in its advocacy of the principle that where the environment is being polluted the polluter should pay, and in its exposure of the futility of protectionist tendencies.

Its role, in fact, is to strengthen relationships between governments and where necessary to mediate. It also enables feedback to the countries whose economies appear most threatened by particular industrial activities, or whose actions appear to threaten the world economic balance. Like all large organizations it carries the risk of becoming top–heavy with officialdom and internal power games. On the other hand, the OECD is performing a vital function in extending multinational economic cooperation between nations and between international organizations. Its work removes or lessens many of the tensions which complicate industrial relations activities in its member states.

The Council of Europe

The Council of Europe's system of institutionalized cooperation, created in 1949, was the first to appear on the European scene, in Strasbourg, after 50 governments had signed the UN Charter in San Francisco in 1945 in the aftermath of the Second World War. Its assembly was the first international parliamentary assembly in Europe. In the flush of idealism which followed the war, Winston Churchill had made a speech in Zurich urging the reorganization within a world context of the European family, and, as a first practical step, the setting up of a Council of Europe. Many had urged the creation of a common government and parliament, but governments at that time were not prepared to go so far. Originally comprising 10 founder countries, it now has 18 member states representing the joint interests of 320 million citizens.

The aims of the Council are to work for greater European unity, to improve the conditions of life and to develop human values in Europe. It upholds the principles of parliamentary democracy, the rule of law, and human rights. The Council does its work by using flexible methods of cooperation between parliamentarians and experts, who work together to harmonize member countries' policies and to adopt common standards and practices. The parliamentary assembly thrashes out in public issues of European importance, and puts its recommendations for joint action by governments to the Committee of Ministers, which in turn decides on the action to be taken and directs the Council's work. The plenary sessions of the Assembly are prepared by parliamentary committees and other committees of government experts, who carry out the work for the ministers and also put proposals for joint action to them. A staff of 700 international civil servants serves the various organs of the Council.

A circle of 12 gold stars on a blue background was adopted as an emblem in December 1955 by the Committee of Ministers on an Assembly recommendation—and with cultural flair Beethoven's Ninth Symphony was chosen in 1972 as an anthem for Europe. The budget ran to about 112 million French francs in 1975 and is shared by the 18 member states. This is equal to the budget of a small European town of about 20 000 inhabitants. Although without legislative powers, the Assembly acts as the 'motor' of the Council, initiating European actions in key areas by sending recommendations to the Committee of Ministers. As the widest parliamentary forum in Western Europe, the Assembly also acts as the 'conscience' of the area by voicing its opinions on important current issues. These are embodied in assembly resolutions. There are also 'written declarations', which commit only the signatories. The Assembly can check on the fate of its recommendations by written questions, at any time.

The Assembly holds a public one–week meeting three times a year in Strasbourg, and an annual session of parliamentarians and ministers takes place once a year to discuss a political question of current importance. The work of the Council is wide–ranging, covering important subjects like human rights, education, environmental pollution, crime prevention, and regional planning. With the 'European Social Charter', the Council laid the basis for social justice and progress in member states. This Social Charter is currently in force in 10 European countries and guarantees fundamental social and economic rights, including work (under fair conditions), collective bargaining and trade union rights, equal pay for men and women, training, and family rights, etc. There is international supervision of how countries are applying the Charter.

The procedure for member states is to aim to reach the standards of the Charter so that they can then ratify it. Control is exercised through biennial national reports which are submitted to an independent expert committee and a government committee (which includes observers from the European Federation of Employers and Trade Unions). The Council's parliamentary assembly and the Committee of Ministers also share in the controlling function. Moreover, national reports are sent to national trade unions for comment. Being anxious to avoid the formation of a new sub–proletariat, the Council has concentrated on the social problem of foreign workers, which it is well placed to tackle, since member countries are both providers and receivers of foreign labour, and the Council is open to cooperation with non–member states. The problems of women workers and young workers also receive continuous attention. The Council has in recent years made a series of recommendations to governments, designed to improve the social

49

and living conditions of special groups in society—unmarried mothers, the aged, the homeless, and the disabled. The Council is also working on the problem of preparing for retirement.

The General Agreement on Tariffs and Trade

The industrial relations scene in Europe is affected regularly, and sometimes traumatically, by the workings of the international trading system, which is mainly the result of the six rounds of multilateral trade negotiations which have been completed since the end of the Second World War. Each of these negotiations has been carried out under the auspices of the GATT, which was formed in 1948. It has no statutory authority, since only one country has ratified it, but it exerts a great influence on world trade. It is a multilateral trade treaty which embodies reciprocal commercial rights and obligations. Its aim is to reduce trade barriers between nations in an organized way and with the minimum of disruption. With its headquarters and secretariat in Geneva, the GATT is the main forum for multilateral trade questions, though it is not formally an international institution—nor is it exclusively European.

For many European countries, international trade is a vital factor in their economic development. The 'Tokyo Round' talks, or multilateral trade negotiations (MTN) as they are called, which were completed in Geneva in the Spring of 1979, were the most comprehensive ever held and comprise the European Community, the US, Japan, and some seventy other participants. The effect of the agreement will be to reduce tariffs by an average of 25 to 30 per cent over the next eight years. The aim was to reduce barriers and distortions to the flow of international commerce, and the outcome will determine whether the momentum towards freer trade which has more or less prevailed for the past 30 years, can be continued. For workers in Bradford, Brussels, or Bordeaux, especially if they are employed in industries which are export orientated, the agreement on the 'Tokyo Round' will have a real bearing on their future.

But developing countries form two thirds of GATT members, 102 of them attending the GATT Conference in Tokyo in 1973. The 'Third World' is an unofficial designation for all the 'emerging' nations of the world. Underdeveloped and 'backward' by Western standards, they represent much of the population and resources of the world. Their power and influence grows daily and the US, Russia, China, and the EEC are battling for influence in the Third World. The Lome Convention, which was signed in February 1975, gives more than fifty African, Caribbean and Pacific states a special relationship with the European Community. These 'ACP' countries include the whole of independent black Africa and have a combined population of

270 million. The special relationship gives these countries trade with, as well as aid from, the Community.

On a much bigger scale the GATT is tackling the same basic arguments about trading relationships. The main argument between the West and the Third World in GATT negotiations relates to reciprocal customs taxes. The fact is that the poorer nations do not want reciprocity to act to their detriment. They want to be able to tax their imports from rich nations, which in turn should permit imports of goods from Third World countries at low rates of tax. This they feel would be fairer than equal rates of tax, as it improves the ability of poor countries to compete with the highly developed nations.

The technical agreement which embodies the GATT consists of four basic provisions:

1. *Non-discrimination.* Through the GATT's 'most favoured nation' clause (MFN), each country's negotiated concessions apply equally to all signatories. Any concession made to one country must be extended to all. There are exceptions stipulated, involving generalized tariff preferences extended by industrialized countries to developing countries, customs unions, and free trade areas.
2. *Tariff protection.* Tariffs, not quotas, are the approved means of protecting domestic industries from foreign competition.
3. *Consultation.* Existing and potential trade disputes should be submitted to consultation.
4. *A framework.* A forum is provided for holding periodic negotiations to reduce trade barriers and codify the results in a legal instrument.

The first four rounds of GATT tariff–cutting negotiations took place in 1947, 1949, 1950–51 and 1955–56. All dealt overwhelmingly with tariffs, and all were dominated by the US policy of fostering economic recovery and cooperation in Western Europe. 'The Dillon Round' of 1960–62 followed the establishment of the EEC in 1958 and proved that the Community's internal trade liberalization could be squared with its external commitment to the further growth of international trade as a whole. The 'Kennedy Round' of talks were concluded in 1967 and included an anti–dumping code, substantial tariff reductions on a wide range of industrial goods, and new arrangements for agriculture. The scope of the seventh round of multilateral trade negotiations was outlined in the 1973 'Tokyo Declaration' and approved by trade ministers from 100 countries. It said that the object was 'to achieve the expansion and ever greater liberalization of world trade and improvement in the standard of living and welfare of the people of the world—through the progressive dismantling of obstacles to trade and the improvement of the international framework for the conduct of world trade'. The phased reduction of tariffs embodied in the 'Tokyo Round' agreement reached in 1979, is certainly a substantial step in this direction.

All these extra Euro–activities may seem, and in some ways are, a far cry from the real world of work. But decisions about international trading patterns can be crucial in deciding the future of a Yorkshire textile firm or a Midlands car factory. In the same way, the social responsibilities prescribed for multinationals by the ILO or OECD can affect the industrial relations climate in a large organization. Bodies like the ones which have been briefly described help to set the parameters within which industrial relations are practised.

Part 2
Industrial relations institutions: trade unions and employers

6. ETUC and UNICE—the parent bodies

ETUC

Modern British trade unions grew out of the Industrial Revolution, which came later in other countries. British unions saw the Labour Party as their political arm, whereas in other countries of the European Community the political parties—Socialists and Communists—formed the unions. The church also played a less significant role in Britain (which had its Reformation in the sixteenth century) than in Continental countries, where it formed Christian unions to help in guiding the industrial as well as the spiritual life of the industrial population. Compared with other member states of the Community, the Communist Party is less important in British trade unionism—though extremely active—and there is no equivalent to the situation in France and Italy, where the Communists control the two largest trade union confederations. This historical experience has led to Continental unions being more politically active—indeed, political forces in their own right.

The parent trade union organization for Europe is the European Trade Union Confederation (ETUC) which was set up in February 1973, by merging the European Confederation of Free Trade Unions (ECFTU), with the EFTA Trade Union Committee. The founding members were OGB: Austria; FGTB: Belgium; LO: Denmark; SAK: Finland; TOC: Finland; FO: France; DGB: Germany; TUC: Britain; AI: Ireland; CISL: Italy; UIL: Italy; CGTL: Luxembourg; NVV: Netherlands; LO: Norway; LO: Sweden; TCO: Sweden; SGB: Switzerland; and the UGT of Spain. The basic problem which faced the ETUC at that time (and it is still not solved) was the problem of different patterns of trade unionism and the diversity of national trade union economic and political interests. Each national trade union centre exists within a distinct national culture. Traditions, history, size, and structures all vary considerably, but each national trade union organization also differs in its role, power, and objectives.

For example, Scandinavian unions are well–organized, enjoy great status and influence, and can usually realize their aims without massive social conflict and dependency on government. German trade unions are less densely organized, but firmly established and logically structured. They have outstanding financial strength and exert powerful influence through participative systems on the private and public sectors of industry. The French unions are less well–organized and financially weak, relying more on political pressures on governments than on the exercise of bargaining power at the workplace. Belgian and British unions are well–organized; they have less financial strength than the German or Scandinavian unions, but possess considerable bargaining strength. They both have strong political influence but vary in their organizational patterns. Trade union membership, too, varies between countries, industries, and professions. Belgium and Denmark have the highest ratio of unionized workers, well over sixty per cent, and traditions of firm discipline and high fee paying. France and Italy have the poorest records, both in terms of fee paying and membership density (probably less than twenty–five per cent in each country).

These average figures however, mask wide variations. For instance, in France trade unionism is high among teachers (90 per cent), electrical power workers, the gas industry, and the public sector, but weak in textiles and building. In Belgium, textile trade union membership is as high as 85 per cent. There are other basic differences too. Most continental unions are willing to work within a legal framework, seeing the law as a protection, whereas in Britain trade unions see it as a clamp. In Britain and Ireland, wage negotiations are usually carried on at factory level with shop stewards playing a prominent part. In Denmark and the Netherlands, bargaining is conducted through a centralized framework involving governments, employers, and unions. In most continental countries works councils are found, which are elected by all the employees, whether or not they belong to trade unions.

These diversities explain why European trade unionists took so long in forming an organization commensurate with their numerical strength. There were six main influences prompting the formation of the ETUC. First, economic integration, not only in the European Community, but throughout Europe, made it important to develop a counterweight to the giant multinational companies straddling the Continent. Mergers between firms had been given an extra impetus by the establishment of a customs union and the gradual abolition of tariff barriers. While not objecting to the existence of multinational companies as an inevitable trend in a Community which was becoming increasingly integrated, trade unions were aware of the potential problems posed for them by the flood of mergers and the growth in size and geographical scope of many firms. The possibility of these large industrial units transferring production and research activities arbitrarily from one country to another was seen as a challenge to the trade union movement.

Hence the concern of the ETUC for central measures was, and still is, primarily related to job security, working conditions, and participation in management decision–taking. A second influence on the formation of the ETUC was the need to take full advantage of the provisions written into the constitution of the European Community which provide for consultation with the trade unions. Although the ETUC covers a much wider area than the Community, it was clear that a coordinated approach by trade unions to Community proposals would enhance their power and influence. A third factor was the strength of the employers' organizations which had developed at the level of the European Community for the pursuance of their interests and the operations of multinational companies. UNICE and COPA (the management organizations) had established central organizations before the accession in 1973. They could speak to the Community institutions with one voice for their respective sectors, whereas the unions had three or four organizations representing workers' interests at European level. Moreover, UNICE was much better placed financially than the trade union organizations.

A fourth influence concerned Community policies in the field of agriculture and the free movement of labour. For example, the impact of the CAP prompted unions to consolidate their efforts, at European level, to influence the various Community institutions to initiate and implement relevant policies, and financial assistance, to provide vocational training and in some cases unemployment benefits for displaced agricultural workers who had to find employment in industry. The geographic enlargement of the Community from six to nine countries was the fifth pressure having an impact on the formation of the ETUC. A sixth dimension was that a new organization would give a golden opportunity for ending the political and ideological divisions of European trade unions. While these goals have not yet been fully realized, there are now 31 national trade union centres in 18 member countries of the ETUC, covering a total membership of 40 million. While all the founding members were affiliated to the International Confederation of Free Trade Unions (ICFTU), the present members include the Christian trade union national centres in Western Europe and the Irish TUC, all of whom were affiliated in 1974. Shortly afterwards, the Italian CGIL, which is Communist/Socialist in orientation, was accepted into membership. The only national trade union centre not in the ETUC at present is the Communist CGT of France and they are discussing the possibility of affiliation.

The British TUC's role in the creation of the ETUC and its attitude towards the European Community would make an interesting study. For the moment, the relevant points are that the TUC saw the need to bring the European Community and EFTA trade unions together in the early 'seventies, as it became clear that Edward Heath would take Britain into Europe after the removal of General de Gaulle's opposition. At that time the TUC was bitterly hostile to entry into the Community and its response, therefore, was to press for the widening of the base of European trade unions. It also suited the mood of the TUC General Council at that time, which was to achieve a closer relationship between the Communist–led unions in Western and Eastern Europe as a means of strengthening the Socialist forces in the capitalist countries of Europe. The dropping of the distinguishing word 'free' from the title of the new organization, and pressure from the British TUC and the Belgian FGTB for the organization to be based on invitations to the European affiliates of the ICFTU (Social Democratic), WCL (Christian), and WFTU (Communist), eventually made it possible for a widely–based ETUC to be formed, though not without hard arguments.

Victor Feather, General Secretary of the TUC in 1973, was appointed first President, no doubt to persuade the TUC to drop its opposition to the European Community; but though he was a convinced European, Lord Feather could not convince the TUC General Council that it should withdraw its boycott of all the European Community institutions after Britain's entry. At that time Jack Jones was chairman of the TUC's International Committee, and his strong anti–market views were based on his profound belief that a greater European unity should be won on the basis of Socialist principles, rather than the free market principles implicit in the Treaty of Rome. Until the referendum in 1975 confirmed British entry into the European Community, the TUC maintained its boycott of all Community institutions and caused considerable embarrassment to the ETUC by depriving it of its full quota of committee delegation members. Since 1975, however, the TUC has participated to the limit of its resources in the work of the ETUC and the various Community bodies.

Since its formation the main strength of the ETUC has been in its relationships with the European Community and with the European Commission in particular, with which it has close and comprehensive links. The ETUC favours the creation of industrial committees, with group unions in particular industries to deal with problems of particular sectors. There are at present 12 of these, covering the metal industry, mining, textiles, chemicals, food, agriculture, construction, entertainment, post and telegraphs, transport, clerical workers, and teachers. The role of these committees is still evolving, but already they have given certain industries a specific European dimension and are seen by the ETUC as a key element in the European structure of trade unionism.

Decision–making procedures are simple and effective, majority decisions being allowed in Congress, which meets every three years, and in the Executive Committee, which meets six times each year. This majority voting is in itself an indicator of progress. While unanimity is required on vital issues in the ETUC, the majority decision–making idea is regarded as being necessary in order to reach 'progressive' decisions which will serve the long–term interests of the trade unions in general. This is a gradual way of shifting power from the national to the Community trade union level and distinguishes the ETUC from UNICE and COCCEE which still maintain unanimity in their decision–making. One of the outstanding cases where a majority decision was reached in the ETUC Executive Committee was the issue of workers' participation on the management boards of firms, especially with regard to the statute of the so–called 'European Company'.

Since its inception the ETUC has been directly concerned with the problems created by multinationals. Its strategy is to achieve:

1. an international code of regulations and laws in the individual countries that will guarantee that the unions are able to obtain the information they feel is essential if they are to bargain effectively;
2. to have the right to participate directly, through representation on appropriate organs of managerial control and on consulting bodies such as works councils, at both international and national levels;
3. to support the efforts of its industry committees to persuade multi-national enterprises to agree to consultation and collective bargaining at European level.

These objectives have in general been strongly supported by affiliates, despite conflicts of opinion as to the roles of participation and collective bargaining at the European level.

The significance of these principles is that they are enabling the ETUC to make a contribution to the evolution of a European system of industrial relations. To do this effectively, however, it must maintain and develop a permanent working relationship with Community institutions and multi-national companies, and keep a tight control over the many arguments and contradictions which are bound to beset an organization with such a wide spectrum of political and industrial beliefs. The ETUC undoubtedly has the muscle in terms of membership, but with improved organization and more political unity it can punch its full weight even more effectively.

UNICE

The Union of Industries of the European Community (UNICE) was set up in March 1958 when the Treaty of Rome came into force. The national central federations of industry felt the need to form an organization which could represent them as a whole at community level and within which the general problems raised by the implementation of the Treaty of Rome could be discussed. UNICE in fact comprises the central industrial federations of the nine countries of the European Community and, as Greece is an associate member of the Community, the Federation of Greek Industry has also been associated with UNICE since 1962.

According to its rules, the aims of UNICE are:

1. to encourage and foster the spirit and links of solidarity among its members;
2. to encourage the elaboration of an industrial policy in a European spirit;
3. to be the official spokesman of the industries of the member countries *vis-à-vis* the common market institutions, for all problems of general interest, or related to matters of principle, concerning the policy of the central federations of industry;
4. to represent European industry *vis-à-vis* the business organizations of Third World countries.

UNICE has been considered from the start as the spokesman of industry for all questions on which the Commission wishes to collect the authorized opinion of industrialists. The Commission consults periodically with UNICE on the economic situation in the European Community. The social field is naturally one in which UNICE has been in frequent contact with the Commission—usually alongside ETUC representatives. This work has encouraged UNICE to strengthen its links with organizations of non-industrial employers, and has led to the formation of an employers' liaison committee consisting of UNICE and several bodies with formidable titles: COCCEE (Committee of Trade Organizations of EEC Countries), CEA (European Assurance Committee), UACEE (EEC Craftsmen's Union), COPA (Agricultural and Professional Organizations Committee), and CEEP (European Centre of Public Enterprises), although not members of the liaison Committee, also take part in the consultations held by the Commission in the social field. Despite the cumbersome appearance of this body, it does valuable work.

UNICE has perhaps less frequent contacts with the Council and the European Parliament, though here other influences are at work. For example, national federations like the British CBI have close contacts with their government's permanent representatives in Brussels. They follow the work of the various Council groups and ensure that they take the interests of industry into consideration. Contacts with the European Parliament are kept up by national federations of employers through their specialized departments, and the Parliament is also told of positions taken by UNICE. Perhaps the closest and most practical links are between UNICE and the Economic and Social Committee, which is the only Community organization in which the private sector of industry is represented by virtue of the provisions of the Treaty of Rome. Since 1962, UNICE has provided the secretariat for the employers' section of the Economic and Social Committee and it acts as coordinator and provider of information.

The Council of Presidents is the decision-making body of UNICE and meets every two months. It comprises the presidents of the central federations of industry affiliated to UNICE. The Executive Committee prepares the work of the Council and meets five or six times a year. It also surveys general trends in the European Community and prepares UNICE statements on Commission activities. The general secretariat, and committees consisting of permanent delegates and experts, facilitate these tasks. In fact there are over thirty committees of experts dealing with issues such as regional policy, environment, competition, tax problems, and industrial relations. In recent years the number of meetings held by various UNICE bodies has averaged about two hundred and fifty a year. UNICE contends that it performs three important functions. First, it ensures that the views of industry are heeded by the European Community institutions. Secondly, UNICE seeks to promote understanding of European problems and encourages employers in different member states to think and act in a way which takes into account the existence of the Community. Thirdly, UNICE represents European industry in relation to Third World business organizations, particularly in GATT conferences, and has close contacts with the OECD, ILO, UNCTAD and WIPO.

UNICE argues that it does not consciously play a political role, but from time to time when the Community has faced difficult industrial problems (and this has been all too frequent in recent years) it has spoken out publicly in favour of a European approach to problems, believing that tariffs and economic union are both necessary. In general UNICE and its national federations are in favour of non–intervention in the economy. They realize, however, that planned measures which may have a restricting effect on industry in the Community and the national field, will prove necessary if technology is to evolve in a way which will be beneficial to the whole Community. This point applies particularly to regional disparities and the severe difficulties faced by certain industries, such as steel, shipbuilding, footwear, or textiles.

While recognizing the coordinating role of the Community's policies, UNICE believes that the final responsibility for industrial development should rest on the freedom of choice and decisions of industrial management. This emphasis on a strong competitive structure has been maintained throughout the situation created by the energy crisis and the relative shortage of raw materials. UNICE, therefore, is a European forum where employers can get to grips with inflation and economic disarray within the framework of the Community by working towards the objectives of the Treaty of Rome.

The alphabetical chaos of names which has pervaded this chapter has over the years also muddled Europe. The European unions, more than the employers, have suffered from religious and ideological wars, culminating in the cold war. As Harm Buiter, former General Secretary of the ICFTU, has pertinently observed: 'In the Latin countries trade unionism is a movement

61

and not an organization. In the well–established democracies there needs to be more of a movement, as there needs to be a little more organization elsewhere.' The northern democracies of Europe have unions which are virtually part of the fabric of government. In Britain, for example, the TUC, the first organized movement founded in 1868, helped to give birth to the Labour Party and has since continued to work within a framework of parliamentary democracy. In Germany, after 1890, the German unions established a solid structure with great respect for the new state; events gave them a better, more national structure after the last war. Sweden shows a similar trend, with the Workers' Confederation profiting from later industrialization and devising a disciplined hard-bargaining front which is now a matter of envy in Europe.

In the southern democracies, trade union revolution and communism seemed much more attractive, and the French unions toyed with anarchism and syndicalism. After the Second World War the Communist and Catholic unions worked together for a time, but then drew apart and the socialists in the Communist CGT split off to form the *Force Ouvrière,* smaller than the CGT and predominantly white-collar in composition. French trade union membership is not more than three million—less than a third of the British. A similar story can be told about Italy, where after the last war an attempt was made to set up a non–political trade union federation, the CGIL, with three separate general secretaries (Communist, Socialist and Christian Democrat). This new organization soon broke down into the UIL (Socialist), CISL (Catholic) and the CGIL (Communist). The European Community brought new problems. The communist unions opposed it from the beginning as a capitalist conspiracy leading to the ruin of the working class. When this did not happen, the Italian CGIL began to come to terms with it. This new mood culminated in their affiliation to the ETUC.

Because the TUC is the biggest and most powerful trade union organization, its entry into the ETUC was expected to stiffen the sinews of European trade unionism. To some extent this has happened, but for three reasons the expected fireworks have not materialized. The formation of the ETUC was quickly followed by the oil crisis and severe unemployment, which fully occupied the ETUC affiliates in their own countries. Secondly, the TUC did not lift its boycott on Community institutions until 1975, thus curtailing the effectiveness of the ETUC's contacts with the European Commission. Thirdly, the TUC is only just shaking off its post–referendum hangover towards the European Community. British trade unionists serve on the numerous committees attached to the Community's institutions and do a workmanlike job, but there is something missing. Partly, this seems due to the TUC's wish to operate at European level through the ETUC, which is broader based, than through the various Community institutions, which still give many British trade unionists ideological hiccups. Furthermore, there is a staffing problem, as the implications of a full TUC manning of committees in the European Community means about forty or fifty senior British trade unionists of national officer calibre spending around forty or fifty days a year in Brussels or Luxembourg.

But while technocrats, bankers, and tycoons are operating on an increasingly European scale, and the transnational corporations are co-ordinating their factories and markets across frontiers, the trade unions need to punch their full weight in order to be an effective counterbalancing force. The unions probably feel they are punching at a jelly most of the time, as they are unable to grapple with the Community as they would one of their own national parliaments. Until June 1979 there was no proper parliament, simply a mysterious dialogue between bureaucrats and politicians. Despite their shortcomings, however, the ETUC (and UNICE) are the parent bodies in their field in the European Community and destined to play a major role in the evolution of European industrial relations. They have the 'ear' of the Commission and the president at any time when they feel strongly about things, and they are consulted on all important issues before decisions are taken.

UNICE is a competent, logically structured body covering the 'nine' though lacking somewhat in political 'clout'. This is partly due to its own inhibitions about publicizing its problems. The ETUC is bigger and politically stronger, but its influence is to some extent diluted by the need to find a consensus among its affiliates, who come from 18 countries. Both the ETUC and UNICE have given consistent support to the Community concept, and are achieving a good measure of coordination at the Brussels level for the limited though important functions they perform there. They deserve to be, and indeed eventually will be, more than the powerful lobby they presently constitute. So far as the unions are concerned their real strength is still at local and national level, as unions are in essence bargaining instruments. For this reason the ETUC cannot maximize its influence at Community level until such time as collective bargaining assumes a Euro-dimension and unions and employers have adapted their organizational structures to carry it out at that level. Those who are disturbed by these possible trends can relax—for a time—as the wide variations in wage and fringe benefit levels in the Community will ensure the slow emergence of Euro–bargaining.

7. Industrial relations systems—take your pick

To attempt even a brief summary of the industrial relations situation in each community country is like trying to sail the Queen Elizabeth II up the Leeds and Liverpool canal! There is far too much material and not enough space. Different national histories and cultures have produced a multicoloured patchwork of collective bargaining arrangements in the European Community, thus making meaningful comparisons hazardous. Nevertheless, this chapter attempts to give the broad outlines. Reference was made in Chapter 1 to the existence of three patterns of industrial relations in the European Community. The German system with tight discipline, codetermination, and industrial trade unionism; the British system, strongly emphasizing voluntarism but with conflicting rather than cooperative working methods; and the Benelux systems of joint consultative committees concentrating on job security, information, and production. Within these mainstream trends are many individual variations.

France

French industrial relations reflect class–conflict ideologies. Collective bargaining is regulated by a law dating from 1950, amended in 1971. Since then a labour code has been developed, on which industrial relations are based. There is a tradition of state intervention, both in disputes' settlement and in the regulation of working conditions by protective legislation. The original law identified the industry as the principal level at which agreements were to be negotiated, but the amendments facilitated agreements both at company and national level. The main employers' organizations include the CNPF (the National Council of French Employers); the CGPME (the General Confederation of Small and Medium–sized Employers); Enterprise and Progress (a small group of CNPF members, describing themselves as 'progressive'); and the CJD (the Centre for Young Managers).

The main trade union bodies include the CGT (General Confederation of Labour) which is communist–led and claims over two million members; the CFDT (French Democratic Confederation of Labour); the CGTFO (the General Confederation of Labour Workers' Force); the FEN (the Federation

64

of National Education); and the CGC (the General Confederation of Supervisory Staffs). All parties in France believe that collective bargaining is in need of reform. Over four years ago the Sudreau Report on company reform stressed the need for changes. These are now being considered at ministerial level and are likely to affect information procedures, the content and scope of collective agreements, and the extent of trade union representation.

French trade union membership is very low; estimates vary from 18 to 25 per cent. Unions do not usually pay strike benefits and union officials are mainly part-time. There are probably three reasons for this weak situation. First, ideological divisions are a disincentive to recruitment. Secondly, the agricultural workers and large numbers of immigrant workers who have moved into industry are groups traditionally difficult to organize. Thirdly, there is a continuing paternalistic tradition, especially in small firms, where management prefers direct communication rather than union representation. Workers' representation is through four institutions with over-lapping competence, as they have been introduced at different times.

There are staff delegates, works committees, trade union sections, and health and safety committees. Works committees must be established in all enterprises employing more than 50 persons and the director of the plant or his deputy takes the chair. They are not bodies for negotiation, but have extensive information and consultative functions. They are designed to promote cooperation. The fragmented trade union structure has ruled out centralized incomes policies, though price controls have been used extensively since the 'fifties and planning contracts since 1963. National minimum wage rates have been enforced since 1952, and since the strikes of 1968 minimum rates are adjusted whenever prices rise over 2 per cent.

Luxembourg

Industrial relations in Luxembourg are highly institutionalized. Collective agreements are regulated by a law passed in 1965 and are legally binding on the parties. They are concluded for a minimum term of six months and for a maximum of three years. Industrial action is only permitted when a formal conciliation procedure has failed to reach a settlement—Luxembourg has enjoyed 25 years of industrial peace. Both employers and employees are represented at national level on the National Labour Council and the Economic and Social Council, which are responsible for planning economic and social development and government policy.

The main employers' organization is the Federation of Luxembourg industries, but the Steel Industry Employers' Association has a major role at national level, due to the predominance of the steel industry in the country.

65

Trade unions are organized along industrial lines and are in two main federations: the CGT, which is socialist–oriented and the Christian LCGB. There is also a small independent union of artisans and a non–political Federation of Private Sector Employers (FEP). Joint committees comprising equal representation of employers and employees were established in 1974. Their powers are primarily consultative on matters such as investment and production decisions. They have limited powers of decision–making on health and safety, transfers, and dismissals. Conciliation procedures are available and supervised by the National Conciliation Office. Wages are indexed and since 1974 one–third employee representation has been allowed on the councils of all public companies.

Denmark

A strong tradition of cooperation permeates Danish industrial relations. The emphasis is on voluntarism and legal regulation is at a minimum. Government agencies have been established by legislation, to be used in dispute settlement, and the state may intervene of its own accord where certain conditions apply. The system of collective bargaining is highly centralized, with the stress on voluntary collective agreements, which then become legally binding. There is a peace obligation on both sides for the duration of the agreement. The Danish Employers' Confederation comprises employers' associations and individual firms. Most trade unions are affiliated to the Danish Federation of Trade Unions (LO). A few unions, such as the Brewers' Union are not affiliated to the LO, nor are the three national federations: the Joint Council of Danish Public Servants and Salaried Employees, the Central Organization of Civil Servants, and the Joint Council of Danish Supervisory and Technical Officers.

Collective bargaining is strongly centralized and some 70 per cent of the workforce is unionized, partly reflecting the fact that unemployment benefit is administered by the unions. Collective agreements in Denmark are negotiated at national level by the Danish Federation of Unions, and relate to general matters (minimum wages, holidays, insurance benefits, etc.) as well as problems specific to individual industrial sectors (training, safety, etc). In the event of conflict, the Minister of Labour appoints mediators in an attempt to help the parties to reach agreement. These mediators are empowered temporarily to suspend strikes or other forms of industrial action. Two years is the normal period for general and industry agreements. Cooperation committees must be established in enterprises with 50 or more employees. These have the right to information, the right of 'co–influence', and the right of codetermination.

Ireland

Collective agreements are concluded at all levels but national collective bargaining predominates. An interesting feature of Irish industrial relations is the recent development of the Employer Labour Conference and the associated wage round. The conference is the arena for the negotiation of national agreements on wages, conditions, procedures on productivity, and other terms of employment. Plant and industry bargaining occurs independently of national agreements on a wide range of topics, including recruitment, training, and redundancy.

The main employers' organization is the Federated Union of Employers. The trade unions are not industry–based and both organization and membership often overlap between the UK, the Irish Republic, and Northern Ireland. The Irish Congress of trade unions (ICTU) is the main trade union organization. Works councils, with mainly advisory and consultative functions exist in about one–third of the smaller companies and about half of the bigger companies. These councils have equal representation and are chaired by management representatives. The councils are generally felt to complement effectively the collective bargaining process. Worker representation does not take place in the private sector, though it is not prohibited by law. Individual trade unionists have been appointed to sit on nationalized boards, and the government has recently introduced legislation covering certain commercial public enterprises to allow one–third worker representation on their governing bodies.

Germany

Industrial relations in West Germany take place within a strong legal framework. The unified trade union system and the codeterminational concept were introduced after the war as a bulwark against the misuse and concentration of economic power. Collective bargaining takes place primarily between unions and employers on an industry basis and by region of the country. The agreements are legally enforceable. A key feature of the system is the prevalence of the 'social partnership ideology'—an acceptance of the role of both parties within the social and economic order and the balancing of their interests through various negotiation procedures. Works councils are elected in all factories with five or more employees. Management is not represented in these works councils, which have consultative and codeterminational rights.

The right to joint consultation includes safety regulations, construction equipment, manpower and production, planning, and training arrangements. Although such decisions are still effective in the absence of works council approval, the council must be given the chance to give its views, and

67

an attempt must be made to reach agreement. Codetermination rights for the works councils mean that any proposal covered by codetermination has no effect without works council approval. Without such approval the issue is decided by an arbitration committee. The subjects embraced by codetermination are extensive and include social welfare, personnel policies, and a range of economic issues. Companies with over a hundred employees must also form an economic committee of the works council, to facilitate discussions between the employers and the works council and to ensure that economic information is passed on to the council.

The main body of West German Employers is the Federal Association of German Employers (BDA) which represents 800 industry associates. Most of them are grouped in the two main affiliated organizations, the state confederations and the main professional confederations. All branches of the economy are represented, though the iron and steel industry trade associations are not members because of the different systems of codetermination. The German Trade Union Federation (DGB) comprises 16 unions representing nearly 8 million members out of a total of 9 million trade unionists. The industrial unions in the DGB aim to recruit all personnel into a single union, including blue and white–collar workers, so inter–union competition is rare. The unions have autonomous bargaining power. There are a few unaffiliated unions, such as the German Salaried Employees (DAG), the German Civil Servants Union (DB), the Christian Trade Union Federation (CGB), and the Union of Police (GDP).

Worker participation at board level is basically governed by two pieces of legislation, the Codetermination Act (1951) which applies to the coal, iron, and steel industries and the Works Constitution Act (1952) which is applicable to joint–stock companies with more than 500 employees. Both acts give a compulsory two–tier structure of supervisory and management boards, with varying provisions for employee representation on the supervisory board: parity representation for 'codetermination' firms and one–third in 'works constitution' firms. A third determinant is the controversial 1976 Co-determination Act, which gives its shareholders and workers' nominees an equal number of seats on the supervisory boards of companies employing more than 2000 people. Although its constitutional propriety has been challenged, it is now accepted by employers and trade unions. Collective bargaining in West-Germany begins at national level with 'framework' agreements covering subjects like hours of work, shift premiums, overtime rates, and other general issues. These agreements often run for three or four years. Wage levels are usually negotiated annually at industrial or regional level.

Any elaboration of these issues at plant level is the responsibility of the works council and management, but the union has no negotiating role within the enterprise. Arbitration procedures are available to resolve disputes which might arise. In the larger firms 'works trustmen' or 'union trustmen' are elected by secret ballot. These persons have the right to consult with management over personnel and social matters and act as intermediaries between shop–floor management and the works council. Works councillors cannot initiate strike action. This can only be done legally by the official union after 75 per cent have voted for a strike in a secret ballot. The West German industrial relations system is summed up by the 1952 Works Constitution Act, which says simply: 'the employer and the works council shall work together in a spirit of mutual trust—for the good of the undertaking and its employees, having regard to the interest of the community.'

Italy

The impact of rapid postwar industrialization is reflected in Italian industrial relations. Regional problems were linked in the South with a quasi–feudal structure, and gave rise to class conflict which was intensified by wartime resistance and collaboration experiences. Traditional industrial relations structures have been challenged and have not yet settled down. Nationally–based collective bargaining has been pre–eminent during most of the post–war period, though the balance is beginning to tilt towards plant bargaining. The three levels of bargaining are general, industry–wide, or company–based. General contracts are agreed separately between each of the major unions and employers' federations on items of general importance. The main collective agreements are concluded at industry level and are concerned with establishing trade union rights, basic rates of pay, and conditions of employment. Plant bargaining was comparatively unimportant and restricted to issues like production bonuses. During the 'seventies, however, plant bargaining has widened to cover investment policy, work allocation, housing, and welfare outside the enterprise.

There are two main employers bodies: Confindustria, representing the private sector employers, and Intersend, which covers employers in firms where the state has a majority shareholding. Italian trade unions are organized on an industrial basis. They emerged from state control in 1944 in a unified form, which reflected the prevailing political unity; but the political conflicts of the cold–war period split them into three main groups in 1948. The CGIL (General Confederation of Labour) is the largest, being predominantly Communist and Marxist in approach, though it has recently been allowed to affiliate to the ETUC, which is non–communist. The CISL (Confederation of Workers' Unions) caters for large numbers of Christian Democrats and Catholics, and the UIL (the Italian Union of Labour) is strongest in the professional and white–collar area. Works committees were

69

set up after the war in many firms, for the purpose of promoting cooperation and understanding between workers and management. They are now largely moribund, the unions having felt that such committees would either be prone to company control or would assume powers the unions did not have.

Since the industrial disputes in 1968–69, 'factory councils' have emerged and become widespread at company level. These councils are bodies made up of homogeneous groups of workers, defined on the basis of production units or occupational categories. All employers in such a group, whether union members or not, vote for a shop steward, accountable to the group and subject to recall by it at any time. The shop stewards, elected by each group, then combine to form a factory council. The term 'shop steward' is not synonymous in meaning with its British counterpart, since in Italy he is elected by both union and non–union employees, and is responsible to both. These factory councils resolve differences and negotiate agreements at plant level over a wide range of issues, including pay and manning levels, transfers and promotions, work organization, and vocational training.

They have no direct access to union funds, and call for voluntary collections when the need arises. They work on the basis that relations with management must be based on conflict and that the authority to negotiate and conclude agreements must always be underpinned by the support of all employees. The factory councils also operate in state–owned industries and to some extent in the public services. Unions and employers are generally opposed to employee representation at board level in the private sector, though individual trade unionists sit on the supervisory boards of one or two nationalized industries. The emphasis seems to be not on participation, but on controlled confrontation through a collective bargaining system which ranges over all employment issues and may even extend to social issues outside the factory.

Netherlands

A strong commitment to cooperation between unions and employers, and a highly centralized bargaining system are the two main strands in the Dutch industrial relations system. These close relationships grew during the wartime occupation, despite the religious and political pluralisms which marked both trade union and employers' organizations. A low level of industrial conflict and extensive social progress have also been linked with these factors. Under Dutch law, collective agreements are legally binding and can be extended by law to cover firms not party to the original nego-tiations. The agreements may be concluded at industry or company level. Though there is a tradition of centralized bargaining, the tendency for industrial settlements to be augmented by company level bargaining has become increasingly common in years when there is no central agreement to be concluded and no statutory incomes policy. Nevertheless, a national minimum wage is jointly negotiated and there is automatic wage indexing. The Association of Netherlands Enterprises (VNO) is the main employers' organization. The religiously based employers' organizations retain their separate identity but cooperate in the Federation of Catholic and Protestant Employers (FCWV). Trade unions are organized into three main federations: the Netherlands Federation of Trade Unions (NVV), which is social democratic; the Netherlands Catholic Trade Union Federation (NKV); and the Protestant National Trade Union Federation (CNV). The NVV and NKV are working towards a merger, which they intend to complete by January 1982.

The Foundation of Labour is a corporate body of employers' and trade union organizations, which emerged from the occupation. It provides a platform for discussion at national level and plays a major role in incomes policy. Several of the original functions of the Foundation were taken over by the Social and Economic Council (SEC), which was created in 1950. The SEC has tripartite representation (trade unions, employers, and those appointed by the Crown). Its primary duty is to serve as a standing advisory body to various government ministries, who must seek the advice of the SEC before carrying out measures of economic or social importance. The SEC may also act or advise on its own initiative, though cases of this are rare. Works councils in Holland were established by law in 1950 and given wider powers in 1971. A works council must be set up in any enterprise with 100 or more employees and consists of the manager of the enterprise and other members elected by the employees from their own ranks. The main rights of the works council are to be informed and consulted on a wide range of issues, but it also has rights of codetermination on matters immediately affecting employees, such as safety and health measures, work schedules, vacations, and the introduction of pension–planning, profit–sharing, and savings programmes. Works councils also have a say on appointments to supervisory boards, which were made compulsory by an Act of 1971 for companies with capital and reserves of £$1\frac{1}{2}$ million and at least 100 employees.

Members of the supervisory boards must be independent of both employee and shareholder interests. In particular, no official of the trade union which has the appropriate negotiating rights and no employee of the company may sit on the supervisory board. The first supervisory boards were appointed in 1971 by the annual meetings of shareholders. Vacancies are filled by seeking nominations from works councils, the shareholders' annual meeting, the executive board, and the supervisory board itself. The election or cooption is made by the existing members of the supervisory

71

board, though the works council and shareholders' meeting may object to a nomination on the grounds of the nominee's unsuitability, or the unbalanced composition of the board. In short, although the Dutch system of participation precludes employee representation at board level, it does ensure that the final composition of the supervisory board is acceptable to both employee and shareholder interests.

Belgium

Belgian industrial relations are marked by a spirit of practical cooperation. The unions and employers have collaborated closely on industrial relations matters during the post–war years. A Pact of Social Solidarity was signed towards the end of the Second World War as a basis for industrial reforms. A national agreement on 'Social Programming' was signed in 1960, establishing a joint programme for social advancement in industry at plant level, with this type of bargaining gradually assuming more importance. The two sides of industry are involved at national level in four main ways. First, administratively, through the management of the social security system. Secondly, they are involved in 'social programming': the regulation of agreements at inter–industry level, which covers issues like pensions, holidays, and works councils, and can be made binding on all employers by Royal Decree. Thirdly, the unions and employers participate in an advisory role on a number of government bodies dealing with social and economic issues.

Fourthly, both sides are represented on the CNT (National Council of Labour), which has wide powers. This body is consulted by government on legislative proposals in the industrial relations field. The CNT also concludes collective agreements made binding by Royal Decree on the private sector of industry. The main employers' organization is the Federation of Belgian Enterprises, comprising some 48 sectoral affiliates covering most branches of economic life. The three main unions are the CSC (the Confederation of Christian Unions), the FGTB (Belgian General Federation of Labour), and the CGSLB (the General Centre of Belgian Liberal Unions). Only these three qualify as 'the most representative trade union organizations' and therefore qualify for recognition by the government and employers' associates. The main focus of collective bargaining is at industry level in joint committees. There are 88 of these at present, covering practically every worker in the country. They have an equal number of employer and union representatives, with an independent chairman appointed by the Crown. The committees can unanimously request that Royal Orders be issued giving binding force to their decisions. Within the company, employees participate through three overlapping institutions: the works councils, the safety and health committees, and the union delegations, this duplication reflecting a compromise between the conflicting views of the major unions.

Works councils operate in firms employing 150 people or more. They do not exist in the civil service or nationalized industries, except for the railways, where special arrangements apply. The councils have three main functions: a consultative and advisory role, the right of codetermination on certain issues, and the right to receive information. The chairman of the works council is the head of the undertaking and he may appoint further members from the supervisory personnel, though these may not exceed the number of employees on the council. An employee is secretary to the works council. The councils have the right of codetermination on work rules relating to hours of work, holidays, and welfare matters. If necessary, disputes on those points can be resolved by a conciliator from the Ministry of Labour. Trade union views on the works councils are ambivalent, some trade unionists feeling that the safety and health committees offer greater scope for negotiation, particularly in the iron and steel industry where these issues are of major importance.

The union delegation, which is a formal body representing all three main union organizations at plant level, is the usual channel for dealing with employment problems and individual grievances. The delegates, however, have no power to negotiate on general issues like wages or holidays. These must be referred to their union officials, but they can and do negotiate productivity bonuses or early–retirement provisions. A national minimum wage is applicable in Belgium and there are 'no–strike' or 'peace' clauses in many agreements. For example, in the metalworking industry the unions undertake to prevent unofficial strikes, and to get members back to work within three days should such a stoppage occur. If it continues, no benefit is paid by the union. To help enforce these 'peace' clauses, most employers pay unions or their members a lump sum each year, usually about 1 per cent of average earnings. A proportion of the payment is withheld if the no–strike provision is broken.

United Kingdom

British industrial relations appear to have three main characteristics. First, the legal framework is minimal compared with other European countries. Great emphasis is placed on voluntary agreement; though in recent years legislation generally favourable to unions has been enacted, especially in the field of employment law, some of it being a *quid-pro-quo* for wage restraint during the period of the Social Contract (1975–78). Major efforts to revise the system of industrial relations were launched in the late 'sixties by the then Labour Government. The Royal Commission on Industrial Relations, the Donovan Commission, gave its report in 1968, and the Government issued its White Paper 'In Place of Strife' in 1969, which incorporated many of the Donovan recommendations, including the use of ballots and measures to reduce the frequency of unofficial strikes. This package met intense union opposition and was rejected by a special conference. A further attempt to subject British industrial relations to the rule of law was made by the Conservative Government in 1971, with the Industrial Relations Act. This also failed, following massive trade union resistance and much of it was repealed by the 1974 Labour Government.

The second main characteristic of British industrial relations is its decentralization. In industry, the plant or factory is often the main focus of negotiations on working conditions. National agreements are made between employers' associations and trade unions, but actual wages paid at the plant level are often considerably higher—sometimes 30 or 40 per cent more than the national agreement. The third distinguishing feature is the increased number of shop stewards and their enlarged bargaining role; there are approximately 300 000 of them in the UK. While the traditional pattern of national agreements had inhibited shop–floor activity, postwar conditions proved favourable for workgroup pressures and shop stewards assumed numerous, though informal bargaining rights on issues like overtime, labour utilization, discipline, incentive schemes, etc. Their role is often imperfectly defined and a further complication is the multi–union situation in factories and the inadequacy of inter–union institutions at that level. The informality of the shop steward system is its strength—and weakness. Unofficial strikes are frequent, costly, and often devastating if key workers are involved and the stoppage prevents thousands of others working.

This problem is largely avoided on the Continent by legally binding agreements and the almost universal presence in other countries in Europe of works councils. Most British employers are organized in the CBI (Confederation of British Industry), either directly or indirectly. The CBI has two hundred trade or employers' associations as affiliates. The CBI does not engage in collective bargaining. This is a task for the separate affiliated associations, though in practice members of particular employers' associations are free to negotiate locally with their employees. The associations assist their members in collective bargaining on working conditions and in the adjustment of grievances. The sole national centre for trade unions is the TUC (Trades Union Congress), with an affiliated membership of almost twelve million. Density of trade union organization varies from trade to trade, from 12 per cent in distribution to almost 100 per cent in coal mining. The TUC has no authority to conclude collective agreements. It plays a primarily coordinating and advisory role and the decisions of the TUC General Council are not binding on the member unions.

Equally, the CBI is given fewer powers by its members than most of its sister organizations in the rest of Europe.

Collective agreements may be made at industry, company, and plant level. Since the 'fifties, plant bargaining in manufacturing industry has been growing in importance, productivity bargaining having provided some of the impetus. Successive phases of incomes policy, of a statutory or voluntary kind, added to the devolution of power to shop stewards, have diminished the role and influence of many full–time officials.

A balancing trend, however, has been provided by legislation during the 'seventies, giving statutory protection against unfair dismissal. The skill developed by the more sophisticated trade unions in representing their members has been noticeable. Union legal departments have expanded greatly and full–time officers have acquired considerable expertise in arguing about unfair dismissals. The 'closed shop' is estimated to cover 5 million of Britain's 12 million trade unionists. As a concept it remains peculiarly British and intensely controversial. Worker participation is also proving to be a controversial concept in Britain. The recent Bullock Report attracted stiff opposition from the CBI and subsequent proposals also had a rough ride. Moreover, a number of large unions are unenthusiastic about employee directors and hold differing views about lower level participation, though individual trade unionists serve on nationalized boards. With 480 trade unions and more than 500 employers' organizations, British industrial relations present a happy chaos: ingenious bargaining systems, bitter demarcation disputes, and strong, often ruthless pressures on governments.

8. International trade unions—punching their full weight?

International trade unionism has generally had more bark than bite. Mark Twain once said that Adam and Eve had many advantages, the main one being that they escaped teething. No such bonus of instant maturity has been enjoyed by worldwide federations of trade unions, which have had a long though not very successful history. The founding of the International Confederation of Free Trade Unions (ICFTU) in December 1949 marked the culmination of efforts stretching over a hundred years to build an effective international workers' organization. With 122 affiliates, for the most part national trade union federations, giving a total of 60 million members in 90 countries located in all 5 continents, the ICFTU has enormous potential power. It groups together Britain's TUC, the Canadian CLC, the German DGB, the CIO of Liberia, the Malaysian TUC, and the Mexican CTM. In some countries more than one national trade union centre is affiliated to the ICFTU, for instance, in Sweden, India, Italy, and Finland.

From its early days the labour movement has placed great stress on internationalism. Moral fervour has always been great, but organizational support has been variable and sometimes weak. But the truth is that it is difficult for internationalism and the ideal of international trade union brotherhood to have real significance for workers who feel their immediate economic problems are inextricably bound up with the affairs of their own nation and their own trade union. There are also other factors which blunt the cutting edge of trade unions at international level. Modern countries are a multi–coloured patchwork of histories, cultures, and institutions. Britain has the oldest and most complicated trade union structure, but Continental unions have their intricacies too. For sheer size, the British trade union movement is outstanding in Europe, but it is by no means the strongest in proportionate terms. Moreover, the influence of the TUC on the Labour Government after 1974 pales when compared to the longevity of Social Democratic governments in Sweden, with which the LO has close links.

Nor has the TUC any rival centres of trade union power like Belgium, France, Italy, and the Netherlands. These last four countries, like Denmark, Germany, and Sweden, also have separate minority confederations for white–collar workers or civil servants, or both. But alongside the growing strength of the ICFTU, two other important developments are underlining the relevance of international trade unionism—the growing unification of the European economy prompted by the European Community, and the increasing power and influence of the multinational companies. The different and sometimes absurd patterns of existing trade union organization are often divided before corporate economic interests on the national plane and are becoming increasingly ineffective. The multinational company can plan investment, allocate markets to plants, fix prices, and coordinate policies on collective bargaining, all on the same European scale. To respond to this trade unions need to coordinate the views of at least five or six trade union confederations, sometimes as many as ten or twelve, before they can present a common front. This obviously takes time and when the policy has been devised the situation has sometimes changed appreciably.

The logical next steps are inescapable though they may make national trade union leaders squirm. The justification for union organization at national level has been the existence and relevance of the nation state as an arena within which industrial and political decisions affecting workers take place. As the barriers to trade and industrial development within the European community come down, with the customs union, coordinated company laws, and labour legislation—and in particular, the introduction of a unified currency system, which seems probable in the 1980's—the role of national trade unions will be drastically changed. Before looking at the various options, however, the background to the international labour movement should be viewed more closely, together with the functions of the ICFTU.

The difficulty of developing international trade unionism is obvious if one looks at the conflicting views of national trade union centres. Trade unions in different countries were born and nurtured in varied conditions and developed their own philosophy and tactics, thus making collaboration at international level a sensitive and uncertain business. Before the First World War the trade union movement showed four main trends:

1. *Original trade unionism* was essentially Anglo–Saxon inspired and derived its name from trade union organization in Great Britain and the TUC (founded in 1868). The trade union was seen as a body of exclusively professional character. Its tasks were concerned with economic problems affecting the workers. Unlike movements which took their inspiration from Marxism, it did not consider the class struggle as the fundamental point of Labour policy. To improve working conditions it relied much on the help of the middle class, inside and outside Parliament, which had grasped the usefulness of a gradual improvement of the workers' situation. Trade unions took an active part in creating the Labour Party in 1901 and, after the Second World War, became the driving force behind the introduction and implementation of various schemes for nationalization. Historians have divided this evolution into

two phases which they call 'old unionism', where trade unions are based on crafts and 'new unionism' where it is based on industry.

2. *Anarcho–syndicalism* is basically of Latin origin and finds its expression in the Charter of Amiens (1906). It is a class–war movement based on the belief that the destruction of the capitalist system is the most effective way of defending the interests of the working class. This form of trade unionism has supporters in France, Spain, Argentine, Mexico, Sweden, and the Netherlands.

3. *Social democratic trade unionism* was the third current feeding the trade union movement in the early twentieth century. It was especially strong where powerful Social Democratic parties existed—for example, in Germany, Austria, Belgium, the Netherlands, Scandinavia, Eastern Europe, and Switzerland. The party and the union shared the work, the former looking at problems concerning the labour movement from the political angle and the latter taking care of purely economic questions. In France this form of trade unionism was represented by the 'possibilists' and in Britain by the Fabians. In short, each of these three trends was defined by its position *vis-à-vis* the political organizations—original trade unionism advocated an inactive role in the political struggle; anarcho–syndicalism proclaimed the supremacy of the trade unions over the state; and Social Democratic trade unions stressed the equality of the trade union and the political party.

4. *Christian trade unionism.* The fourth trend was based on a completely different ideology, developed in the last years of the nineteenth century and the beginning of the twentieth century, namely, the Christian trade union movement. This movement took shape following the Papal Encyclical 'Perum Novarum' (1891) which laid down the economic and social policy of the Christian world. It stated that economic and social life implied collaboration between all people and rejected violence and the class struggle, whether from the employers' or the workers' side. In brief, the declaration laid down that all relations between individuals and classes of people must be directed and governed by Christian notions of justice and charity. The Christian trade unions had a double effect on the labour movement—they attracted workers who could not accept the other trade union ideologies, but they also split the working class and led to trade union pluralism in many countries.

Up to 1901 the only international ties between trade unions were the international trade secretariats. These organizations established trade union organizational links within the same trade in different countries. Some of these early industrial internationals were the hatters (Paris 1889); the tobacco workers (Antwerp 1889); the miners (Manchester 1890); the metal-workers (Brussels 1891); the brewery workers (Berlin 1896). On the eve of the First World War there were 33 of these international trade secretariats. Their main work consisted of compiling statistics and legal documentation. During strike periods they prevented the transfer of substitute manpower and organized financial aid. These international secretariats were, however, under socialist influence and soon saw the value of unity amongst all workers. In 1901, largely due to pressures from German trade unions, the International Federation of Trade Unions (IFTU) was formed. Just before the First World War broke out the French trade unions pressed the IFTU to call an international general strike to prevent any outbreak of hostilities.

The IFTU referred the matter to the International Socialist Congress, but meanwhile workers in the various countries rallied to their national colours and the IFTU folded up. Efforts were made during the war to maintain contact between the trade union national centres. While patriotic instincts blurred the ideal of internationalism during the war, the war effort gave the working class an awareness of its force and its importance in the life of the nation and enabled trade unions, after the war, to present with greater authority their claims to contribute to the elaboration of the peace. At a conference in Leeds (Great Britain) in 1916, attended by trade unionists from non–occupied countries in Europe, it was decided that any peace treaty should place the working class beyond the reach of international capitalistic competition and ensure for it minimum moral and material rights—the right to work; the right to migrate; the right to social insurance, hygienic working conditions, and industrial safety.

International trade unionism, suffering the—after effects of war, was evolving hesitantly. The four ideological currents by which it had been actuated up to 1918 continued their influence, but a new force emerged—the Red Trade Union International, organized by the new Communist government in Russia. This body came into immediate conflict with the IFTU, which had been revived in 1919. With a membership of 18 million in 14 countries the mission of the IFTU was to:

1. bring about the unity of the working class by developing ties between the trade union organizations of all countries;
2. organize International Trade Secretariats (ITSs) in the area covered by the IFTU;
3. uphold the interests and efforts of trade unions in all countries, both nationally and internationally;
4. promote the progress of international social legislation;
5. foster workers' education;
6. avert all wars and combat reaction.

The IFTU was a federation of national trade union centres, the ITSs coexisting as autonomous bodies. The Red Trade Union International (RTUI) proposed to organize workers in different countries to overthrow capitalism, establish the dictatorship of the proletariat, and oppose trade union reform. These brief historical references are simply landmarks down the main track of trade union development and show clearly why international trade unionism is still full of sensitivities. Between the wars, national differences combined with ideological disputes to weaken any resolution there might have been in the face of a world slump and the rise of national socialism. Free trade unions were brutally suppressed in Germany, Italy, and Spain in the 'thirties and by 1939 there was little semblance of international trade unionism. Meanwhile, the Christian trade unionists had been busy during all these years. An International Secretariat had been formed in 1908 and in 1920 the IFCTU (the Internation Federation of Christian Trade Unions) was created. At that point the new organization covered 10 countries and $3\frac{1}{2}$ million workers. Its principles were 'to uphold the Christian doctrine and its ideals of justice, charity and fraternity'. It decided in favour of 'the systematic collaboration of the classes' and condemned any liberal, socialist, or communist regime.

The Second World War brought a new phase in the evolution of the international trade union movement. Trade union work still continued, albeit at a slower pace. The IFTU Secretariat was transferred from Paris to London and, in addition to clandestine movements, Anglo–French, Anglo–American and even Anglo–Soviet trade union committees were set up in order to intensify the war effort. An attempt to build an Anglo–American–Soviet trade union committee failed, a setback which foretold the difficulties which were to arise later in the World Federation of Trade Unions. Moreover, the Soviet Trade Unions declined to join the old IFTU, which it was hoped to rebuild after the war. In 1943, the British unions asked their General Council to consider calling a world conference of trade unionists from all countries. This was held in February 1945 in London and known as the World Trade Union Conference. It led to the creation in the autumn of that year of the World Federation of Trade Unions (WFTU). This merger, however, had been achieved in the postwar spirit of idealism and the unity, unfortunately, turned out to be nominal. As the Cold War set in, the ideological differences deepened and the refusal of the Communist bloc to have anything to do with Marshall Aid was the occasion for Western trade unions to withdraw from the WFTU. In 1949, after a rapid succession of withdrawals from the WFTU, the non–Communist trade union federations felt it was essential to form a new international to deal with the many pressing problems arising at world level, and the ICFTU (International Confederation of Free Trade Unions) was born.

The brief glance into history shows how the European labour movement has been the cockpit for political intrigues. Of the four streams of trade union activity previously examined, three have crystallized into world trade union organizations—the Communist WFTU set up in 1945, the social democratic ICFTU, created in 1949, and the Christian WCL (World Confederation of Labour) formed in 1950. Despite the apparent rigidity of these divisions, things are not quite what they seem. The Italian Catholic CISL, for instance, is a member of the ICFTU. The CFDT (the French Democratic Federation of Labour) has gradually distanced itself from the Church and now advocates a movement towards a democratic socialist society, though still remaining a member of the Christian WCL. The FO (*Force Ouvrière*) in France follows the French syndicalist tradition, which is committed to complete independence from all political parties, though it affiliates to the ICFTU. The great bulk of the membership of the WFTU comes from within the Soviet bloc, though it has important Communist affiliates in France and Italy. In the past the WFTU has adhered strictly to the Communist party line, but now that the French and Italian Communist parties have declared their independence of Soviet policy, there may be a different set of implications. As both countries are members of the European Community, there could be important consequences for trade union unity on the way. In Holland there is a great deal of cooperation between Catholic and socialist unions. Furthermore, some British trade union leaders pay frequent visits to the Soviet Union and observers from that country attend the Trades Union Congress regularly. In short, there is clearly an international conscience within the trade union movement which is trying to find adequate expression. German workers have supported British workers in disputes with the Ford Company and British workers have supported workers in the General Electric Company of America, as well as Californian grape–pickers. These isolated cases are not sufficient to make world trade union organizations influential in the practical field of industrial relations, but they show that trade union idealism still burns strongly and can occasionally be mobilized for international cooperation.

So the various strands which we have traced in the international trade union movement eventually produced three world federations, each with well–defined political or religious principles. Although this division blunts the effectiveness of trade unionism at world level, it could have been much worse. In general, the unions have refused to get fully involved in high–level power politics. Utopian Socialist doctrines have had a long history in European thought and although the workingmen's international association, known as the First International, set up in London in 1864, inspired terror in the hearts of many governments, its physical support, especially from trade unions, was limited and its effective existence ended in 1876.

In 1889, at a Paris Conference held on the 100th anniversary of the French Revolution, a Second International was formed, linking many socialist organizations round the world and involving many trade unions.

Several congresses of this International took place but the general discussion often proved inadequate for the specific industrial needs of trade union groups participating. In 1896, Tom Mann and James Sexton established an International Federation of Ship, Dock and River Workers, with the aim of preventing the labour force in one port being used to undermine the working conditions achieved in another. This transport workers' initiative was significant because it involved unskilled workers. International organizations had developed amongst skilled workers some years previously— cigar makers, shoemakers, and hat workers, for instance. The miners followed in 1890, glassworkers and printworkers in 1892, tailors and metal workers in 1893, and textile workers in 1894. By 1914 28 trade–based internationals (later to be called ITSs—International Trade Secretariats), were in operation.

So the seeds of international trade unionism began to take root during the period of the Second International, via the trade–based internationals and the IFTU. After the Russian Revolution in 1917, the Third (Communist) International was launched, listing among its 21 conditions for admission the strategy of organizing revolutionary trade unions, whose mission was to struggle by every means against so–called 'reformist' trade union leaders. The Red Trade Union International, set up in 1921, pursued the same ruthless philosophy and compelled trade unions to reconsider their principles. By the time the ICFTU was formed in 1949, international trade unionism had been truly tested in the furnace of events and two of the three world international trade organizations, the ICFTU and WCL, had decided on the basis of experience not to get too closely and directly involved in politics. The ICFTU's policy is defined by a democratic congress which meets every four years and at which all affiliates are represented. Congress elects an Executive Board comprising 29 members representing the different areas of the world, which meets twice a year and directs the activities of the Confederation between Congresses. It elects the President and Vice-Presidents of the ICFTU.

The ICFTU Secretariat in Brussels is headed by the General Secretary, who is elected by Congress. He is responsible for the administration and keeping contact with affiliated organizations. There are also permanent ICFTU offices in Geneva, New York, Tokyo, Djakarta, New Delhi, and Mexico City, and ICFTU field staff work in different parts of the world. In order to give active assistance to the development of trade unions in the Third World, the ICFTU has established regional organizations, each formed by affiliates in the continent involved. They enjoy a wide measure of autonomy, having their own executives, presidents, secretaries, and offices. These organizations are:

ARO The Asian Regional Organization, which has its headquarters in New

Delhi, India.

AFRO The African Regional Organization, which operates at present from Freetown, Sierra Leone, and also has a research centre located in Nairobi.

ORIT The Inter–American Regional Organization of Workers, with headquarters in Mexico City.

The European Trade Union Confederation (ETUC) was set up in February 1973, by merging the European Confederation of Free Trade Unions (ECFTU) into the EEC, with the EFTA Trade Union Committee. Founded by 13 ICFTU affiliates, the ETUC has since been joined by a number of other European national centres. Its constitution enshrines the ICFTU's principles and there is close cooperation between the two organizations, based on a mutually agreed division of labour. While the ICFTU is based on national centres, the 16 International Trade Secretariats (ITS) associated with it group national unions of a particular trade or industry at the international level. These autonomous federations—many with a history dating back to the last century—make up the industrial wing of the international trade union movement. The ICFTU maintains close working relations with them, acting as their spokesman in international bodies and cooperating with them in educational and organizing activities in the Third World. These ITSs are as follows:

1. The International Federation of Building and Woodworkers (IFBWW)
2. The International Federation of Commercial, Clerical, and Technical Employees (FIET)
3. The Universal Alliance of Diamond Workers (UADW)
4. The International Secretariat of Entertainment Trade Unions (ISETU)
5. The International Union of Food and Allied Workers (IUF)
6. The International Federation of Chemical and General Workers (ICF)
7. The International Metalworkers' Federation (IMF)
8. The Miners' International Federation (MIF)
9. The International Federation of Petroleum and Chemical Workers (IFPCW)
10. The International Federation of Plantation, Agricultural, and Allied Workers (IFPAAW)
11. The Postal, Telegraph, and Telephone International (PTTI)
12. The Public Services International (PSI)
13. The International Federation of Free Teachers' Unions (IFFTU)
14. The International Textile, Garment, and Leatherworkers' Federation (ITGLWF)
15. The International Transport Workers' Federation (ITF)
16. The International Graphical Federation (IGF).

The ICFTU acts as a forum and a clearing–house for the exchange of views and experiences between national trade union movements, to coordinate their efforts and to work out common strategies to defend and promote the workers' interests. From time to time it convenes world trade union conferences to deal with specific problems—inflation, employment, trade union action, the second development decade, and multinational companies. Moreover, the ICFTU is recognized as the spokesman of the world's workers, both in international conferences and in the United Nations and its special agencies, such as UNCTAD, UNESCO, and FAO and intergovernmental bodies like the World Monetary Fund, the OECD, GATT, IMCO, IAEA. It uses these and other gatherings to ensure that no decisions are taken on purely political and economic grounds which might adversely affect the welfare of the working class. The rift between the ICFTU and the Russian–dominated WFTU remains wide, for obvious reasons, though the WCL (formerly the International Federation of Christian Trade Unions) and the ICFTU are moving steadily towards a common front, especially on European issues. The strength of the ICFTU is its determination to be free and independent of external pressures, especially political domination. Its weakness is the absence of the American AFL/CIO (American Federation of Labour and Congress of Industrial Organizations). This body withdrew from the ICFTU in 1969 after disagreements on a number of issues, one of which was the contacts being made at that time with unions in Eastern Europe by the TUC and DGB. Another issue was the jurisdictional conflict between the ICFTU and labour educational programmes being mounted in developing countries by the AFL/CIO and US State Department.

Whatever the merits of the arguments, there is an urgent need for the AFL/CIO to rejoin the ICFTU, both in terms of finance (it supplied one–quarter of the affiliation fees paid to the ICFTU) and to permit international trade unionism to provide an effective counterbalance to multinational corporations. On the assumption that this happens soon, though it may well have to wait for a change of leadership in the AFL/CIO, one might anticipate two main lines of development in international trade unionism. First, national unions may group into something resembling the ITSs, though with more power. For example, they might levy funds on their own account and begin to conduct negotiations on specifically defined matters at global and European level. They could then talk positively and powerfully to the European Commission and to multinational companies in Europe. The key point is that this would raise the unions to the same level of organizational integration as their adversaries. In fact, an 'International Industrial Union' of this type would be able to deploy Europe–wide resources not only against multinational firms but against an employer operating in a single territory. There are clearly big advantages awaiting those unions which can find ways of overcoming outdated divisions of a political and ideological kind and can organize at the level which the working of the economy demands.

The second trend might be for more collective bargaining to take place above and below the national level in the member states of the Community. National unions and national confederations would become more involved with subjects which remain the competence of national governments—social security, safety, taxation, employment policy, etc., where workers need direct and effective representation. Plant bargaining may assume far greater dimensions and, alongside the European framework of bargaining previously described, may develop new areas not exclusively demarcated by national boundaries within which bargaining could occur. Adjoining regions of Holland and Belgium, or Belgium and France, or Luxembourg, France, and Germany, might be brought into a natural bargaining net defined by industrial or economic similarity. If all this has a sinister ring to employers, it should be remembered that collective bargaining can only be effective if it reflects the actual industrial situation. The growing interdependence of nation states and the widening influence of multinational companies, make international trade unionism and wider bargaining patterns desirable and necessary.

9. Multinational companies—boon or bane?

Is the multinational company an instrument of economic imperialism, or a beneficial carrier of advanced management, science, and technology? Most people roundly denounce or stoutly defend multinational companies, which are in themselves a rueful commentary on modern democratic society—a sort of sad barometer of its strength and weaknesses. They reflect man's technological ingenuity, the ruthlessness of the boardroom power game, the inability of national governments to cope adequately with international business problems, and the need to relate the profit motive more closely to social responsibility.

In part their future is linked to what could be the economic and political battle of the decade—the drive for prosperity and a new economic order by the poorer nations. One of the key goals of the developing nations, as stated in UN declarations, is to raise their share of the industrial world's output from 7 per cent today to 25 per cent by the year 2000. At present it is estimated that multinationals account for 20 per cent of all industrial output (excluding the Soviet Union and China), 50 per cent of international trade, and up to 70 per cent of private technology. To change this structure, therefore, means great risks for multinationals, or great opportunities.

But to denounce multinationals in general is as unrealistic as presenting them as benign institutions devotedly working for the public good. The truth is probably between these two positions. They bring considerable benefits to society, and create a plethora of problems. They are a pertinent example of the gap between man's technological brilliance and society's ramshackle social machinery. In a nutshell, multinationals have been trapped by the speed of their own advance. They have far outdistanced their running mates, governments and trade unions, who have to work in a more ponderous, participative—some would say devious—way. Multinationals now stand exposed to criticisms, often trenchant, based on a mixture of fact and misunderstanding.

In a wider sense too industry and society are on a collision course, due to the inherent conflict between nationalism, with its inward–looking concepts, and industrialism, with its global implications. This incompatibility between political and economic life has produced two wars during this century and motivated bodies like the UN, the ILO, the OECD, and the

European Community—organizations not just idealistically conceived, but rooted in a practical awareness of the problem. 'Witch-hunting' or 'white-washing' multinationals is a dangerous and self–defeating process. It merely adds to the emotional climate of a debate which is already highly politicized, even though the UN has recently admitted that the big corporations offer the best chance, if properly harnessed, of spreading knowledge, technology, and industry to developing countries.

It may seem arrogant, but someone has to try to assemble the pieces of this social jigsaw, a puzzle created by the cumulative effect on industry of science, war, education, poverty, and technology. The European Community is working hard to forge a new framework of social responsibility within which large firms will operate. A code of conduct was approved by the OECD in 1976 and the ILO has produced a 'Tripartite Declaration of Principles concerning Multinational Enterprises and Social Policy' (November 1977). This declaration concerns the social aspects of multinational operations and some points are for inclusion in the UN's more general code of conduct for multinationals, which is currently being devised.

All this indicates the close scrutiny to which multinationals are being subjected throughout the world. Various measures are afoot in the European Commission. In 1977 the European Parliament voted in favour of a proposal that 'binding and legally enforceable terms must be laid down for international undertakings and a framework for their activities defined in one or more international agreements'. Nevertheless, the decision to construct such a framework does not rest with Parliament but with the Commission and the Council of Ministers. In fact over thirty measures which directly or indirectly concern multinational companies are at various stages in the Community's legislative pipeline. Some have already been approved by the Council of Ministers.

The public interest

TAX PROBLEMS

1. Directive on parent companies and subsidiaries
2. Directive on mergers, divisions, and contributions of assets
3. Work in the field of international tax evasion and avoidance
4. Community regulation of transfer prices and licence fees

SECURITY OF SUPPLY

5. Work in the field of energy and raw materials

MONETARY PROBLEMS

  6. Work concerning speculative short–term capital movements
  7. Improving statistics in the field of international financial flows

OUTBIDDING IN AID BY PUBLIC AUTHORITIES

  8. Coordination of national and regional aids

PROTECTION OF SHAREHOLDERS AND THIRD PARTIES

  9. Proposed directive concerning law relating to groups of companies
10. Proposed directive on liability for defective products

The interests of workers

SECURITY OF EMPLOYMENT

11. Directive on collective redundancies
12. Directive on acquired rights of workers
13. Directive on national laws relating to mergers
14. Directive on insolvency procedures

CONDITIONS OF EMPLOYMENT

15. Joint Committees (eight in existence, many more in prospect)
16. Proposed regulation on Statute for European Companies
17. Proposed fifth directive on company structure, including employee participation
18. Harmonization of labour law, giving participation in works council of parent company for employees of group subsidiaries
19. Suitable representation of the interests of employees of public limited liability companies
20. Measures to limit overtime

The maintenance of competition

21. Regulation providing for the compulsory prior notification of mergers
22. Active surveillance of oligopoly situations

88

Methods of purchase of undertakings

23. Community rules on takeover bids
24. Code of conduct for stock exchange
25. Rules regarding investment and takeover

Equality of conditions of reception

26. Bilateral negotiations on specific problems
27. Links with OECD on international investment and multinational companies
28. Work of the United Nations

Conditions of establishment of multinational companies in developing countries

29. The application of economic provisions
30. Application of EEC rules on transfer prices and licence fees
31. Development cooperation policy

Better provision of information

32. Annual Report on multinational companies
33. Fourth Directive concerning annual accounts
34. Seventh Directive concerning group accounts
35. Disclosure of information (preposals in preparation)

New activities

36. Consultation between Commission, member states, and the oil industry
37. Study of influence of foreign investment in the less favoured regions

This list is by no means comprehensive. If it seems stultifying it should be remembered that the Commission itself has to consult in detail with government, employers, and trade unions, both formally and informally, on all aspects of its work. The Commission is not opposed to multinational companies as such—indeed they are an obvious and integral part of the drive to increase the wealth of the Community and ensure its fairer distribution. But it does mean reminding such organizations that more power means more responsibility. Unless this is forthcoming then a blind and unyielding resistance to big firms as such will develop among workers, with a consequent deterioration in industrial relations. The European Community believes it can devise effective controls in this field as, unlike the UN, OECD, and the ILO, which have no legal powers to implement policies in member countries, the Community is a political organization with a system of laws and the institutional means to enforce them.

There are 'regulations', which are binding on member states; 'decisions', which are also binding, but with geographical selectivity; 'directives', which are binding but can be implemented flexibly; and 'recommendations' and 'opinions', which rely on the force of moral commitment. The Commission believes its legislative code for multinationals will form a coherent network, designed to give companies the autonomy and economic elbow–room they need to operate successfully, but within a new social and economic framework giving greater weight to the human aspects of business. But this social shield can only be a 'holding operation', for two important reasons.

First, getting Euro-laws passed in the Council of Ministers, where in practice unanimity is required, is a task of great complexity. Infinite patience is required to find the necessary consensus view and this means travelling at the speed of the slowest national ship, so to speak. As Benjamin Franklin once said: 'If laws are too gentle they are seldom obeyed—and if they are too severe, they are seldom executed'. Secondly, while setting a transnational legal framework for industrial operations is currently desirable, the longer–term, more democratic solution is for trade unions to organize their own counterweight to the size and power of multinational companies. At present, international trade unionism does not seem ready to act as a balancing force. Political arguments prevent the securing of complete unity of purpose. Moreover, there are still many internal arguments and difficulties concerning disparate comparative wage standards.

So a large part of the trade union movement persistently advocates measures on the part of the public authorities to control multinational companies on a national and international basis. Of growing importance, however, are the specialized international trade union bodies which cover a particular industry or groups of related industries. They are called **International Trade Secretariats (ITSs)**, bodies composed of national trade unions from given industries, which are associated with the International Confederation of Free Trade Unions (ICFTU). Some of these ITSs have been particularly active, especially those covering industries where multinational companies are much in evidence. They only have advisory powers at present, which somewhat blunts their cutting edge, though some ITSs have regional groups, which allows a greater concentration of effort.

Naturally, the multinational companies and employers generally are not enthusiastic about these activities, even with their political limitations. The multinational companies generally prefer to negotiate country by country with national unions and do not recognize in a formal sense the international 'company' union group as a basis for negotiations. On the other hand unions feel strongly about the power of a multinational company to shift production or operations, provisionally or permanently, from one country to another. Without concerted resistance by the trade unions this possibility can be a significant power factor in industrial relations, where the threat of production transfers, either direct or implicit, can weaken the union's position and reduce the effectiveness of strike action.

However frustrated multinational companies may feel about the trade union 'counterweight' argument and the swelling Community legislation, it is essential that they recognize three key issues:
1. The need for better communications
2. More effective management, well briefed in trade union history and techniques
3. The importance of a constructive response to social expectations.

It is often because of the failure to provide information, and lack of knowledge about plans and trends, that workers and their trade unions tend to see the dark side of multinationals rather than their positive social aspects, for example, the valuable contribution which they can make towards the economic and social goals of the Community. To complicate matters further, there is no legal definition for the term 'multinational enterprise', since each part or subsidiary of a company is a separate legal entity in the country in which it is located. But while lawyers search for definitions, the fact remains that of the 100 largest economic units in the world, about 50 of them are nation states. The others are the biggest of the world's 300 or so multinationals, which may in total produce about 15 per cent of the world's gross national product.

In Europe the impact of American multinational business has been on politically–mature societies, technologically–advanced economies, and socially–integrated peoples, proud of their nations' long histories of achievement. The physical presence, in Europe, of American corporations with thousands of American employees has been significant. Europeans have responded vigorously to this corporate invasion and governments have encouraged business mergers designed to create companies able to compete with the American giants. Research and development activities have been expanded substantially too. Many believe that the real 'gap' between European and American business management is managerial rather than technological. European countries are now taking positive steps to close this gap by setting up business schools and replacing nepotism by meritocracy when choosing leaders.

Another problem trade unionists feel strongly about is that multinational companies frequently seek to transfer the industrial relations and personnel policies and practices of the home country to the other countries in which they operate, or fail to conform to the practices of the host countries. Obviously, a foreign company that breaches locally–accepted standards is much more liable to criticism than is a local company acting in the same way. Employers agree that some errors have been made, but point out that multinational companies have sometimes been responsible for innovations in industrial relations practices that have generally been recognized as constructive, both in developing and in industrialized countries. The development of collective bargaining itself in some countries is an example. Moreover, the managerial staff of multinational companies are becoming increasingly international in outlook, as a result of specialized training programmes. This trend will clearly serve to diminish cultural tensions in industrial relations and personnel management, as internationally–minded managers can understand and avoid the dangers inherent in imposing alien practices on a local industrial operation.

All this illustrates the explosive and unsettled nature of most issues involving industrial relations in a multinational framework. Another ticklish point is the feasibility of centralized multinational collective bargaining. Many trade union organizations are advocating direct international collective bargaining between the central management of a multinational company and a trade union body representing its employees in several countries. Unions feel this would give access to the real locus of decision–making in multinational companies and induce an upward harmonization, at worldwide or regional level, of the employment conditions of the companies' workers. The unions also feel that such a bargaining style would give them greater leverage on company decisions concerning the transfer of production facilities or plant relocation. Employers are sceptical of the concept, arguing that disparate conditions and labour law practices in different countries where they operate preclude the possibility of establishing worldwide or even regional norms through international bargaining. It is also stressed that working conditions and wages upon which international bargaining may be sought are often subject to regulation through national legislation.

Indeed, in some countries statutory fringe benefits can amount to more than fifty per cent of wages, while in others legislation plays a minor role. Moreover trade unions may want to bargain internationally on issues that employers have traditionally felt were exclusive managerial prerogatives, such as investment and resource allocation. In short, it can be argued that the philosophical case for international collective bargaining has much to commend it, but at present the economic, political, and legislative problems make it extremely difficult to devise an agreed system. Even if these difficulties did not exist, there would probably be a great reluctance on the part of the multinational companies to accept these new dimensions for collective bargaining. In that case, however, the argument would be pertinent and agonizing, though untrammelled by all the other factors behind which, one suspects, some multinationals are sheltering.

It should not be forgotten that the European Commission has proposed legislation which covers this controversial point, in the form of a European Companies Statute. This will constitute the directly–applicable Community law under which enterprises which wish to engage in certain kinds of cross–frontier activity will be able, if they wish, to form a European Company and so adopt legal forms appropriate to the scale and require- ments of the European market in which they might wish to operate. Amongst its various provisions are two which are designed to help the employees of a European Company to influence the decision–making of the company in a number of ways. First, a European works council is to be formed in every European Company with establishments in more than one member state, which is to be responsible for representing the interests of all the employees of the company on matters which concern the company as a whole or concern several establishments. Secondly, the conditions of employment which are to apply to the employees of such a European Company may be regulated by European collective agreements, made between the company and the trade unions represented in its establish- ments. Multinational companies would do well to note that this legislation is pending though not necessarily imminent.

On balance, it seems clear that multinational companies are beneficial to society, though we have not yet devised the right framework of social responsibility within which they can best operate. The problem is that the debate about them has produced polarized fixed attitudes. The prolonged economic recession has also generated antagonisms to local jobs being con- trolled from another country. Despite the need for a basic framework of guiding laws, it is attitudes of mind which will really produce the successful industrial relations formula—a willingness on the part of the multinational company, its employees, and the host country to cooperate for their mutual benefit. The blunt truth is that the capacity of the various parties to co- operate will determine whether there is a basic legislative framework to guide multinational operations, or whether a more detailed code of behaviour will be developed by the lawyers and politicians.

If multinational companies feel a persecution complex developing, they should remember this and make sure their views are expressed with vigour and cogency. Meanwhile, the Commission will no doubt seem like a referee with a piercing whistle and a gimlet eye for infringements of the rules of the industrial game. The cynics may say that all this social responsibility is public relations eyewash, or altruism gone mad. All the evidence, however, points to the fact that it is the main vehicle for reconciling public and private morality with corporate good. As Adam Smith perceptively observed: 'Man is an animal that makes bargains; no other animal does this—no dog exchanges bones with another.' The outcome of this particular bargaining between private enterprise and social responsibility will have a significant bearing on the future of industrial society.

10. Euro–bargaining: ambitious dream or painful reality?

No subject is calculated to furrow the brows and raise the hackles of managers and trade union officers more than the prospect of Euro–bargaining; and yet its development seems inescapable, only the time scale is conjectural. There are three strong arguments to support this view. First, to be relevant and fair, collective bargaining must accurately reflect the elements in the industrial situation of which it is a part. 'I live in a very small house,' said Confucius, 'but my windows look out on a very large world.' He might have been describing the bargaining dilemma in Europe. The scale on which multinational companies operate, for instance, lifts them in various ways above the constraints of national bargaining. The fact that these companies are becoming increasingly aware of their wider social responsibilities is not a reason for opposing a more realistic bargaining framework. Commercial pressures can and do change managerial priorities. The matching of power with responsibility ought not to be left solely to the conscience of management, even though this might often suffice; it needs to be established and policed by a balancing force of trade union pressures operating on a comparable scale.

Second, Euro–bargaining is a logical consequence of the existence of the European Community, which in basic terms is concerned with developing the resources of its member states for the eventual benefit of everyone. The industrial implications of this policy include the customs union and the gradual coordination of company law systems, both measures being designed to facilitate the freer flow of trade throughout the Community and to maximize its wealth–producing potential. A whole new code of labour legislation is being constructed at European Community level. Directives on collective dismissals, acquired rights, insolvency, equal pay and equal opportunity for women in industry, are already established or in train. The controversial legislation on employee representation at board level is also well advanced. A collective agreements' register also exists at the Commission to facilitate international comparisons of industrial activities. In other words, new parameters are being set for industry in the Community. It would be naïve or foolish to believe that industrial relations can be kept permanently in a national context when these new international dimensions are being created for industry.

Whatever the difficulties, and they are clearly formidable, industrial relations procedures must be related to the scale of industrial operations in the area in which bargaining is taking place. Otherwise bargaining will lose its relevance and industrial leaders their credibility.

The third transnational influence is the network of joint committees serviced by the European Commission. These committees are bipartite, sectoral, and voluntary, and currently cover eight industrial sectors—coal, steel, sea fishing, agriculture, road transport, rail transport, footwear, and inland waterways. They discuss problems of common concern, learn from each other and exert a continuous and direct influence on the European Commission. More will be said about these joint committees later. It is clear, however, that they are one of the channels down which wider bargaining activities may eventually flow. Of course, there are genuine difficulties, as well as prejudices, slowing down the internationalization of bargaining systems.

Professor Herbert Northrup,[1] Director of the Industrial Research Unit at the University of Pennsylvania's Wharton School and a leading US industrial relations expert, believes that European collective bargaining is far from being just over the horizon. He argues that four factors hamper the evolution of cross–frontier bargaining:
1. Differences in labour law and practices between nations, even those knitted together in the European Community.
2. Management reluctance to enter into multinational regulations.
3. Trade union reluctance to yield part of their sovereignty to international groupings.
4. Lack of employee interest in the subject.

The Professor also contends that multinational bargaining, despite some trade union claims to the contrary, has not occurred outside the unique environment of Canada and the US, nor would it be a desirable development. He concedes, however, that some multinational companies have exchanged information with international labour groups and some have developed regular management/union interchanges on a multinational basis. The only one with a written agreement on the subject, he points out, is the French–based BSN–Gervais Danone glass group, which holds twice-yearly consultative meetings with union representatives from Belgium, Holland, France, Germany, and Austria, though negotiations on wages and conditions are outside the scope of such talks.

The Professor is unimpressed by the role played in industrial relations by the ITSs (International Trade Secretariats) set up, in theory, to counterbalance the multinational companies and believes that groupings within the European Trade Union Confederation appear better placed than most to

[1]*Labour Law Review,* July 1978.

move towards multinational bargaining. Even the most active of these, however, the EMF (European Metalworkers' Federation), which in July 1978 called for an incisive strategy towards multinational companies, has made little progress in cross–frontier bargaining as opposed to consultation and information exchange.

Management Centre Europe, which is based in Brussels, decided in 1978 to seek the views of management and workers in a number of multinationals on the subject of transnational bargaining. The verdict of those approached was unanimous—not in rejection of the concept, but in a somewhat entrenched lack of enthusiasm. Of the 15 multinational companies approached, only two were actively against transnational bargaining. Among the others, two paramount reasons were advanced to explain the marked lack of enthusiasm. First, the subsidiary company is usually integrated into the industrial relations environment of its host country and subject to the local management practices, with all the benefits and limitations this imposes on the total corporate structure and the local operation. Secondly, all 15 multinational companies approached, saw no great advantage in transnational bargaining for the improvement of either cash incentives or fringe benefits for their employees, as the priorities of union negotiators differed substantially from one country to another. It was also felt that the legislative framework within which these negotiations were increasingly conducted often made collective bargaining a somewhat automatic exercise.

The survey showed the corporate attitude to be sceptical towards transnational bargaining, the onus for any definite advance seeming to lie with the national trade union movements. Management Centre Europe also pointed out the other obstacle—that industry–level bargaining predominates in most western European countries, while bargaining with multinationals on an international scale must constitute bargaining at the enterprise or corporate headquarters level. Furthermore, the increasing control and interference exercised through legislation by many governments covers many areas of industrial relations. Transnational negotiations, therefore, might involve agreements which at any given point in time could infringe on the policies of some national governments, thus creating conflict between workers covered by the agreements and their governments. Differing views exist among national trade unions, though these mainly concern the issues which are felt to deserve cooperation, rather than the real concept of transnational bargaining. Many trade unions feel that the settling of industrial disputes is the activity most likely to develop by international cooperation between trade unions. Indeed, disputes in recent years involving seamen, dockers, and car workers, have spread through cooperation between international trade unions, though cooperation in work stoppages has usually

97

been to maximize the effects of on–going strikes, rather than to initiate new strikes.

The general union view is that their primary task is to unionize the plant or factory unit within their national boundaries, since the effectiveness of any form of concerted internal action depends on strong organization in the plants of the multinational enterprises, which are scattered over many countries and perhaps continents. Trade union officials in some countries also seem uncertain of the effects of transnational bargaining on their personal positions. Their internationalism is affected by the business cycle and tempered by power considerations. In short, if bargaining crosses national boundaries there must logically be a transfer of some power to the international bargaining group and perhaps from one official to another. This might account for the demand for tariffs, import quotas, and the exclusive use of national products during periods of recession. Many managers oppose the transnational bargaining concept as they see it as another level of power capable of shutting down the enterprise. They believe that the complicated nature of the bargaining arrangements makes a three–level structure inevitable—transnational negotiations, followed by national ones, and then local arrangements. They contend that unions and management would have difficulty assigning responsibilities and priorities for the three levels.

Charting a path through this jungle of controversy is not easy but it seems likely that transnational bargaining will develop in two quite separate ways. First, via multinational bargaining, with *ad hoc* groups of national unions in the same industrial sectors striking bargains with particular multinational companies. This trend has already started as quoted earlier (BSN—Gervais Danone Glass Group). The twice–yearly consultations are significant because they bring round the same multinational table unions from five different countries. Bargaining will at some stage blossom from these trans-national consultations, though slowly and via non–contentious topics such as safety, health, and training. Fringe benefits and wages come later as they are more controversial and need to be based on more experience and a firmer understanding. In theory, the ITSs (International Trade Secretariats) are a ready–made structure on which to build these activities, but so far their national affiliates have kept them on a tight rein, confining them mainly to advisory and publicity functions. The national union group approach may seem a more selective and effective way of dealing with a particular multi-national company, whereas the ITS would need to spread its efforts amongst all the multinationals in its particular field if internal difficulties are to be avoided.

Moreover, multinational bargaining is being pressed in another way. The ICFTU and the ETUC have asked the Council of Ministers in Brussels to support moves to call regular international conferences between multi-national companies, governments and trade unions. The idea has also been put to the UN Committee currently studying a proposal for a code of conduct for multinational companies. It appears that the unions wish to make progress towards some form of international bargaining with multi-national companies and see this as the first step.

The second type of transnational bargaining is possibly longer–term but even more exciting. It concerns bargaining at industry level, as distinct from one firm bargaining multinationally. This activity could properly be called Euro–bargaining and would be particularly suitable for laying down minimum standards of wages and working conditions for a specific industry across Europe. This clearly involves the joint committees of the European Commission, to which earlier reference was made. The 1973 enlargement of the Community produced an additional thrust for joint sectoral committees, due to the wider variety of economic activities and the more numerous divergencies in working conditions. The need for these committees will become even more apparent with the eventual accession of Greece, Portugal, and Spain to the Community.

The disparity between the living and working conditions of agricultural workers in these three countries, and elsewhere in the Community, will make the joint Committee for Agriculture an essential instrument for social improvement. The same could be said for other committees. The list of existing joint committees, which are bipartite, sectoral and voluntary, is given below, together with the year when they started to meet:

Coal   — 1955
Steel   — 1955
Agriculture   — 1963
Road transport   — 1965
Inland waterways   — 1967
Sea fishing   — 1968
Rail transport   — 1972
Footwear   — 1977

The coal, agriculture, and sea fishing committees have been given the 'statute' by the European Commission, which is simply a formalization of their terms of reference. It also permits the two sides of industry to place their own items on the agenda (called by the Commission 'the right of initiative'). The potential joint committees make a long list, but sectors where contacts are being made, either regularly or sporadically, include the following: civil aviation, shipbuilding, sea transport, public services, teaching, sugar, food, breweries, banks, insurance, distribution, construction, commercial travellers, and textiles. Talks in the first three groups mentioned are much further advanced than in the latter sectors. This is normal, as the process of launching the Committees is evolutionary and can be interrupted in a sector by political, industrial, or trade union problems. The committees, once started, meet once or twice a year in plenary session and would normally be about fifty strong, membership being divided between workers and employers in that particular industry throughout the Community. The committees' working groups study special questions and meet more frequently. The committees give a two–way flow of information and influence Commission proposals. They have a 'think tank' function too, and also permit specialized questions relating to their sector to receive a more detached and continuous process of study in a relaxed atmosphere.

Moving from this factual area into the realms of speculation about future trends, some exciting possibilities emerge. It seems clear that these committees may act as a launching pad towards some form of European collective bargaining, but only when they are ready for this activity. Understandably, neither unions nor employers are enthusiastic about the concept at present. Employers see themselves as being saddled with impossible commitments and punitive additions to labour costs, not to mention the threat of 'Euro-strikes' while unions are apprehensive about losing their hard–won autonomy. So employers generally are afraid of 'levelling–up agreements', while unions, especially in the richer European countries, do not enthuse about a possible 'levelling–down' process, which would in their eyes erode their favoured position.

There are two other arguments in favour of giving a European dimension to collective bargaining. It is felt by many to be morally wrong for gross and continuous disparities to exist between the wages and conditions of workers doing the same work but in different countries. Some variations will always exist, and reflect the historical and cultural differences and the varied economic backgrounds of the countries concerned, though blatant differences are hard to justify. Moreover, substantial differences in the wages and conditions between the same industries in different countries tend to make industrial relations systems abrasive in the country with the adverse conditions.

The problems are obvious and formidable. There are varied bargaining patterns and procedures within and between member states, which involve plant and national bargaining systems in different ratios. Furthermore, wage bargaining must be related to fringe–benefit bargaining, which is part of the overall cost of a collective agreement. Here again, the patterns vary in Community countries. Broadly speaking, the original six countries have given greater weight to the fringe element in bargaining than the three new countries. The same point could also be made about Sweden, Norway, Austria, and Switzerland. Another problem is that many European countries are practising wage restraint in one form or another, and seem likely to do so for the foreseeable future, thus emphasizing the problem created by wage differentials and making difficult the rational discussion of harmonized bargaining at local level. Euro–bargaining seems certain to come, but it will take time and will take the form initially of setting minimum standards at the international level. It is unlikely that much progress will be made until the present economic difficulties have moderated and in any case it will only happen if the employers and unions want it. Harmonized wage bargaining, like good industrial relations, cannot be imposed from above by national or international edict. It must evolve from mutual trust between all the parties concerned.

A significant background factor is the development of the European Collective Agreements Register, based in Luxembourg. It already covers 13 major industrial sectors and embraces at present more than 1500 collective agreements in those sectors. This exciting new project can provide access to a computerized information bank available at the Documentation Centre. Consideration is still being given to the administrative control of the Centre, though it is clear that the unions and employers at Euro–level will have a large part in this, in order to prevent misuse and abuse of the information. The 13 industries involved in the collective agreements register are listed below:

1. Iron and steel
2. Metal working
3. Textiles and clothing
4. Building
5. Chemicals
6. Petrochemicals
7. Food, drink, and tobacco
8. Printing and graphical art
9. Leather and footwear
10. Paper (production and processing)
11. Wood processing
12. Glass and glass processing
13. Extractive

So a European dimension is certainly being introduced so far as information in certain industries is concerned. The Commission's joint committees are an interesting new trend in the industrial relations scenario and their strength is in their voluntary nature. Some of them are already setting standards for their Euro–sectors in the field of safety and training, and fringe benefits are sometimes discussed. They are a valuable forum for discussing an industry's common problems in an international setting. If and when they wish to move into the Euro–dimension of setting standards for their sectors in the more controversial bargaining areas, they are well placed to do so. Transnational collective bargaining is therefore more than an ambitious dream; it is a fast–approaching reality. It is likely to take two broad forms, one a multinational type of bargaining, which will come first, certainly in the next few years. This bargaining will be probably done by multinational companies and national groups of unions in the appropriate sector, though it is also possible that strengthened ITSs may be asked to perform the same function. The persistent economic difficulties in Western Europe are likely to give a stimulus to this trend, as it is one way in which unions can hope to exercise greater influence on their industry's affairs and to win greater security for their members.

The other trend, phased back in time by the economic crisis, is towards European collective bargaining, but on an industry basis. Clearly crisis implications would make the introduction of this variation of transnational bargaining a hazardous business during the next few years. It must wait, therefore, for an easing of the economic problems currently afflicting Europe. When it comes, it will develop gradually in the non–controversial areas of industrial relations and the likeliest vehicles are the joint committees of the European Commission, or the industrial committees attached to the ETUC. Euro–bargaining may not be just over the horizon, but then the actual distance of the horizon depends on the elevation of the observer. From Brussels, the picture is fairly clear, though complicated. The Euro–dimension in collective bargaining will come in several stages: first by more detailed regulation of employment issues by Euro–laws; then by a gradual coordination of basic fringe benefits and working conditions; and in the longer term by an approach to minimum wage standards in industries at Euro–level. Multinational bargaining will be first on the scene, events forcing the pace. Euro–wide industry bargaining will follow later and more cautiously. Collective bargaining is an adaptive process, but changes have to be gradual and piecemeal. Industrial relations practitioners would do well to plan ahead on the basis of newer and wider involvements for their organizations.

Part 3
Industrial relations issues

11. Pension fund socialism—Europe's shopfloor shareholders

To what extent is equity capital in European industry owned by employee pension funds? The available evidence suggests that Europe's trade unions have only taken a thin slice of the corporate cake so far, but their appetite is growing. Trade unions are now sophisticated institutions, with investment portfolios, data banks, professional negotiating teams, and policy options which reach into every facet of modern society, from education to government foreign policy. Recurring economic crises during the past decade have bound members more closely to their organizations and caused management and governments (not without some misgivings) to look at ways of treating the trade unions as partners.

Trade unions are beginning to grasp the levers of power. Worker participation in management decision–taking is already a fact of life in several European countries and in others it seems simply a question of time. The implications and problems of 'pension fund socialism' have recently been studied by Peter Drucker in his book *The Unseen Revolution.* He argues that by 1985 at least 50 per cent of the equity capital of American business will be owned by employee pension funds. But demographics, social structures, and trade union realities vary between countries. The British National Association of Pension Funds, for instance, recently explained to the Wilson Committee that individual pension funds had very little power over British companies, since each fund had seldom more than 5 per cent of the shares. In other European countries, however, the trade unions are taking a commanding profile in corporate ownership.

In Sweden the LO is aiming to use co–ownership to reinforce participation by the direct influence on management which is at present in the hands of the owners of private capital. To this end the Swedish LO has called for companies to hand over between 20 and 30 per cent of pre–tax profits to special funds managed by the unions, either region by region or industry by industry. The workers would receive them in the form of a free issue of company shares. The most likely system would allow up to 20 per cent of the issued capital of each company to be voted by the local trade union, and the remainder to be voted by representatives throughout the industry. The idea is that the special funds should be administered centrally. Total control of the companies by central unions seems a possibility, though this seems to worry some Swedish workers who see the unions becoming increasingly remote and less easy to control.

105

These Swedish trends should be seen against the advanced background of social and labour legislation currently in existence. The idea of lobbying for legislation to force companies to hand over a slice of the profits in the name of participation is a short cut to corporate power, which will probably not be possible for some time anywhere except Sweden. But the thought of using existing union funds to establish a stronger voice in the boardroom is already spreading among trade union economists and researchers, especially in north–western Europe. The idea appears to have polarized the northern and the Latin trade union organizations in the same way as worker participation. The French see no reason for helping to manage a sick capitalist system. The Italian trade unions, too, feel that cooperating with management in any way will lose them rank–and–file support.

But traditionally French and Italian trade unions are highly politicized, with programmes of their own going much further ideologically than the traditionally pragmatic attitude of the postwar British, German, Dutch, and Scandinavian unions. In short, Latin trade union leaders seem more interested in ministerial portfolios than a voice on the board. If, however, one thinks of the impact unions might make on the ownership of company equity, on the basis of their economic strength, it becomes clear that the situation varies considerably in different European countries. The British stand about halfway in the scale between the rich Germans and Scandinavians and the poorly–funded French organizations. The latest available income figures for 88 TUC affiliated unions shows an annual income of about £95 million, most of this being membership dues from the affiliated unions. With a total expenditure of £76 million on administration, dispute benefit, sickness, and superannuation payments and other benefits, £20 million is left over for investment.

British unions hold assets totalling approximately £130 million, though not all of this is available for investment in the private sector. Thirty unions, each with a membership of over 50 000, hold fixed interest stocks (mostly in central and local government loans) of a market value approaching £51 million; 24 unions hold equities amounting to £20 million, mostly in private companies, and union–owned property adds up to £28 million. Finally, 25 unions hold some £13 million in loans to local authorities. The remaining assets are small and widely scattered. The German trade unions, in contrast, have assets of £1 billion, which gives them plenty of financial muscle to support their activities. Through their central organization, the DGB, they are already heavily involved in business. Interestingly, this is almost entirely by the use of their own 100 per cent–owned companies in direct competition with the private sector. In total, union firms employ more than 100 000 West Germans and are engaging at the moment in a programme of planned expansion.

With 16 DGB–controlled firms, union businesses have a powerful position in a number of sectors in the West German economy. They include a bank (the fourth biggest federally–based bank in the country); Germany's biggest home–construction group with annual profits of around £8 million; the largest life insurance company; building societies; a publishing house; a travel agency; and a retail cooperative chain founded in 1972, which is leading its private competitors with an annual turnover of £2 billion. The basis of this approach to business ownership by the DGB is to provide effective competition with the aim of steadying prices, and to give an example of the best possible working conditions and social policy, thus forcing private enterprise to follow its lead. Most of these profits are used for conventional trade union activity. The German unions have so far preferred to influence corporate policy by the example of their own well–run firms and by worker participation in the management of other industries. It would not take a big financial effort by the unions, however, to buy sufficient equity in key companies and key industrial sectors to gain decisive control; it seems bound to come.

On the same wavelength, the Swedish LO grouping holds about £6·5 billion in union funds, equivalent to 30 per cent of all the savings in the country. At the other end of the scale, the French trade unions are too poor to operate effectively in the market even if they wished to do so. The Communist CGT has an income, almost entirely from membership fees, of some £1·3 million per year. Out of this about 50 per cent goes in administration; propaganda costs (meetings, publicity, congresses, and recruitment) account for 20 per cent; while loans and subsidies to groups within the union network, and international liaison work, account for almost all the rest. The amount left for investment annually—in union property and real estate—is an insignificant £6000. The French unions maintain strongly that they have little in common with the reformist unions of Northern Europe. The CGT, in particular, seems interested more in political change than in coming to an agreement with capitalism.

A broadly similar position applies in Italy, though the present compromise between the country's Communist Party and the Christian Democratic Party is pushing militant Marxist trade unionists into logically untenable positions. A share in the government—even if only by right of veto—is one thing, but investment in the economy through private shareholding seems unthinkable to Italian trade unions at present. A considerable amount of cash is held by the Dutch unions, despite their comparatively small size (less than one and a half million members in the four central trade union organizations). Recently two of these bodies have agreed to merge—the NVV (the largest, with 618 000 members) and the Catholic NKV (with 405 000 members). Together, they hold investments and participations amounting to £8·3 million, mainly in collective investment funds, municipal loans, and union supported banks, but their portfolio in the private sector is still on a minor scale.

Turning from the practical aspects to the principle of joint ownership, it is important to consider its possible influence on attitudes at work and what conditions are needed to make it an effective motivator. In one sense it can be argued that nationalization is a kind of employee ownership in that, as a citizen, the worker is given a stake in the business. He owns it, together with other citizens, in a very real sense. In postwar years when a spate of nationalization occurred, it was often argued that nationalization would improve industrial relations, as workers would take a pride in ownership and seek to promote this new owner interest by making the industry prosperous and healthy. Sadly, these new links have proved too tenuous and controversial to affect personal behaviour in any startling way. It is also held that company pension schemes, which invest at least part of their funds in industrial and commercial shares, and trade union funds, which are also partly invested in free–enterprise industry, will make workers feel a sense of part–ownership.

The motivational effect of these developments has been negligible, probably because they have been presented as measures which were politically desirable or essential in terms of personal security. It is argued strongly by some employers that a worker's attitude to work is more likely to be influenced by owning shares in the company for which he works. On the other hand, workers have generally been reluctant to put their jobs and savings at risk in the same firm. This has understandably led to the view that this form of worker ownership is mainly of benefit to the firm. The initiative in this field, therefore, is not likely to come from individual workers—the onus is on the company to give a strong lead as, on balance, the company is the main beneficiary. The behavioural scientists have talked a lot about the need for workers to be self–directing and self–controlling, and the motivational value of this approach. Employee participation through the worker owning shares in the business which employs him represents an attempt to harness this form of motivation in a more general way, but within the confines of the company.

In the United States this form of worker participation has begun to take off in a big way. American companies have already registered 175 000 such schemes and new schemes are being started at the rate of 500 per week. The fact that there is no single prototype scheme has given rise to an active business consultancy in this field. It is not without significance that this approach to worker participation is most in evidence in the US—a country so committed to the free enterprise concept. In some respects Germany is the reverse of this with its participative systems working through its supervisory boards and formalized works councils. It seems to fit the uniform, disciplined way in which the Germans do things. But a number of laws have been passed by the German government, especially one in 1965, which encourage the formation of capital–accumulation schemes for workers. It was recently estimated that about fifteen million Germans are involved in about eight hundred and fifty of the schemes, almost all of them union negotiated.

From the available evidence, France is well up the worker–ownership league, though some distance behind the Americans. The French involvement in the idea is partly due to De Gaulle's interest in worker–ownership. Compulsory profit sharing was introduced in France for companies with 100 or more employees in 1967, but there was no stipulation that the money had to be invested in shares of the employing company. The asset cannot be realized by the worker for a period of five years and the exceptions are precisely given; they are marriage, dismissal, retirement, incapacity, or death of the worker or spouse. The average benefit to the worker of such schemes has been calculated at approximately two to three per cent of annual salary. The French government imaginatively introduced employee shareholding into Renault in December 1969, special shares being necessary as Renault is a nationalized industry. This system of workers holding shares in the company which employs them has since been extended to the nationalized banks and insurance companies, and the French taxation system appears to favour these schemes.

To be honest, there are genuine psychological difficulties in starting worker share–owning schemes and in particular ensuring their continuance. One way of doing this is through a scheme which retains the shares within a central fund until the employee retires. This delayed profit sharing is presented on the grounds that a worker gives his company his talents and time, but only part of this is reflected in the current earnings of the firm from which his current wages are paid—a proportion of his skill, time and effort is devoted to building up the future prosperity of the firm, and this is not easy to define. Only by establishing a long–range claim to the firm's earnings can the worker hope to get any benefit from this future prosperity to which he is currently contributing. From an industrial relations point of view it is this commitment to the future prosperity of the firm which is important and worth thinking about. It contributes to the overall sense of fair play and helps to build up the right climate in the firm.

This motivation–orientated policy on profit distribution concentrates the mind of the worker on the need to produce profit. This is controversial, as profit is still a term of opprobrium rather than a badge of honour in the minds of some workers and trade unions, especially in Britain. It is unlikely that the worker's attitude to profit will be changed (where it needs

109

changing) by preaching or exhortation. But to give the worker a vested interest in the prosperity of the firm, of which profit is a part—indeed the yardstick—is bound to give the worker a wider view. While these speculations are fascinating and highly relevant, the chill wind of official TUC disapproval of worker–shareholding is contained in the TUC publication on Industrial Democracy and is worth quoting, if only to show the extent of the difficulties to be overcome before worker–shareholding can really take off in Britain. The TUC view is:

Company based schemes of co–ownership and profit sharing are discredited. Trade union objections are threefold. First, such schemes do not in reality provide any real control over the managerial decisions. Many profit sharing schemes do not involve any common ownership principles in the sense of ownership implying control. Even if shares with voting rights are distributed this would have to be on a fairly massive scale before any real control was vested in the workers as shareholders. The reaction of most workpeople to this type of scheme is to regard the annual profit share out as no more and no less than a useful annual bonus. Second, there is no advantage to workpeople tying up their savings in the firm that employs them since this doubles the insecurity in such situations as Rolls Royce. The third general point about such schemes, however, is that they do little or nothing to reduce the degree of inequality of wealth and they do not include the public sector of industry. There may, indeed, be a role for the development of a form of capital sharing at national level, based on a national fund administered through the trade union movement. The 1972 Congress adopted a resolution calling on the General Council to investigate this whole area.[1]

The CBI in Britain took a less antagonistic, though still cautious, view when it stated recently:

We regard profit sharing arrangements, bonus schemes and the various other forms of incentive schemes including share purchase schemes as desirable in many circumstances, but they should not be made mandatory. We dislike a situation in which an individual other than a director has the bulk of his savings in the company that employs him.

Despite all these comments it seems clear that worker–participational systems of various kinds are here to stay and will form the basis for new motivational patterns in industrial society. Three stages of development can be traced. First, mass unemployment and economic adversity during the early part of the century imposed their own hard disciplines on the labour

1. 'Industrial Democracy', Interim Report by the TUC General Council to the 1973 TUC, paragraph 87.

force and traces of the bitterness these times engendered are still found in some industries. The second phase began about 1940, when jobs became more numerous than people to fill them, thus posing the need for a new understanding of work and the basis of human conduct at the workplace. The problem was how to motivate people in the absence of an economic whip. For the duration of the war, patriotism was the motivator, but postwar reconstruction magnified the problem, as a world scarcity of goods created a sellers' market and demand became enormous. It was not difficult to get work and unions saw no reason to abandon traditional ways of operating. Overmanning, restrictive practices, and rigid demarcation policies were maintained in Britain, though gradually modified in other European countries.

Labour shortages, however, led to tough collective bargaining, and good pay and fringe benefits together with improved working conditions became the order of the day. It is fair to say that most of these changes were long overdue anyway. The point is that unions quickly accepted them as a natural right and management conceded them (sometimes reluctantly) without any hope of rewards in terms of better motivation. Meanwhile, on the social front more young people received higher education and, being better educated, were not prepared to be as docile or deferential as their fathers. During the same period social welfare was being developed substantially, thus further emphasizing the need for positive rather than negative motivation. It was about 1960 when the third stage was reached in Britain and everyone began talking about the need to make work more challenging and to give workers more control over their working lives in general. The theory was that this personal involvement not only made the worker happier but increased his output.

During this period significant events were taking place in the same field in Germany, France, and Holland. The critical date in Germany was 1951–1952, when a resurgent Germany adopted worker participation in a highly legalistic form, and opened up an entirely new era in European industrial relations. But while this third stage of motivational experiments has worked pretty well for several European countries it has so far been a damp squib in Britain. The main reason is that British unions have a strong political objective and they do not hesitate to exercise political power. Prior to 1970, British unions were not very well–informed on worker participation as practised abroad. It was entry into the European Community and the prospect of having to come into line with continental practice which prompted the interest. But once aroused, this interest has been used by British unions not so much to motivate people as to increase union control of managements. In this sense the concept has gone sour, and this is not surprising. In all the continental countries where participation techniques

111

are practised successfully, the development has been gradual and commenced at shop–floor level. The Bullock Report attempted to build the house of participation from the roof downwards by beginning with trade unions on management boards. Although modifications have been made, the disastrous first effects have not been retrieved.

Putting it bluntly, the lesson to be learned from all these experiences is that no matter how technically competent a worker may be, if he is not motivated to work, either internally through work–sharing arrangements or externally through participation in decision–taking with management, he will not perform adequately. In short, however well you may train a worker, if he doesn't want to work he won't and what matters is making him want to give a good performance. Perhaps a fourth stage of the problem is now under way, as persistently high unemployment is once again putting workers very much on the defensive and wary of fancy theories which may in their view simply mask another way of working themselves out of a job. This is where worker share–ownership might square the circle, by encouraging the worker to keep the firm profitable thus enabling it to remain competitive, while guaranteeing him a share of the profits, preferably on a deferred basis, which gives added future security.

The future of worker participation in all its forms, together with pension fund socialism, is clearly as complicated as the current industrial picture. But two factors stand out. Unions are beginning to recognize the need for change. Many are working hard arranging to train their younger members and younger officials to assume more 'professional' roles, with courses in management strategy, economics, and business practice. At the same time, the new–style approach is attracting a number of bright young economists, lawyers, and statisticians, many of them motivated by a strong dislike for classical capitalism encouraged by the post–1968 university mood of militancy. Unions are increasingly interested in power and control. The task is to ensure that unions expand their responsibilities as well as any new authority they may win. Share ownership offers good prospects of inducing this sense of accountability and, if linked with soundly–based worker participation schemes, gives an excellent opportunity of combining radical change with social responsibility, to the benefit of industry and society.

12. Job enrichment—who wants it and why?

There is really no comparable pleasure to the feeling that you get on the way home after having done a successful day's work. If only we could find a way to give most people that feeling, Europe could dispense with the services of its statisticians and economic forecasters. Is job enrichment, then a firmly supported concept, reflecting social change and the widening gap between workers' expectations and the actual nature of work? Or is it simply a 'do–gooder's' fad, a tinsel–wrapped catch–phrase coined by academics, soon to be engulfed by the current harsh realities of unemployment?

The relationship between man and his work has long attracted the attention not only of psychologists, but (even before the advent of modern psychology) of philosophers, historians, and other scholars. There is more interest in the subject today than ever before and European countries are becoming increasingly concerned about the quality of life amongst their citizens and the human costs of economic growth and advances in technology. Even the writer Jerome K. Jerome has wittily declared that 'it is impossible to enjoy idling thoroughly unless one has plenty of work to do'.

The cynic can logically say that jobs must be available before they can be enriched, and with unemployment in the European Community running at 6 000 000, it is the quantity, not the quality of working life which should concern the policy makers. The physical conditions surrounding work understandably seem less important than material rewards when there is basic insecurity at work. The operation of incomes policies, which are being tried in one form or another in European countries, also keeps attention mainly on the pay packet. Who then really wants job enrichment—and why? Here is the first complication because in principle most people agree with the idea of making work more interesting and satisfying, just as most people accept the virtues of civilization, justice, or happiness.

But passive belief in ideals does not ensure their implementation. Concern shown about the quality of working life takes a negative form and is shown in disenchantment with existing arrangements, high rates of absenteeism and labour turnover, lower productivity, and deteriorating labour relations. The second complication lies in definitions. Samuel Butler said that a definition was 'the enclosing of the wilderness of an idea within a wall of words'. Practitioners of job enrichment have certainly strangled themselves with a string of different descriptions. Job enrichment, job improvement, job

113

satisfaction, work structuring, work humanization, and improving the quality of working life are but a few of the titles used. From Scandinavia come other mind–bending terms like 'socio–technics' or 'autonomous work–groups'.

There is some irony in the fact that these ideas from Norway and Sweden first originated in Britain at the Tavistock Institute, through studies of long–wall mining and cotton factory workers. The results were not taken up in Britain at the time but found a ready response in Norway and are now being presented to Britain as panaceas. Putting it bluntly, governments, researchers, and employers all seem enthusiastic about promoting job enrichment techniques, from a blend of altruistic and economic motives, whereas the trade unions are either lukewarm or indifferent to the subject. This explains the contradiction between massive front–line publicity for job enrichment and the slow response from workers, who see it as a manage-ment gimmick designed to boost profits or a luxury without meaning at a time of insecurity and unemployment.

These positive and negative aspects of job enrichment persist if we look at some of the specific activities in this field in different countries. On the positive side the Federal German Government are putting large sums into a Humanization of Working Life Programme. In Britain there is a Tripartite Steering Group on Job Satisfaction, a Work Research Unit, and a Government research programme. The Swedish Work Environment Fund and the French Fund for Improving Working Conditions are bodies designed to encourage action by individual companies and to subsidize practical improvements which are introduced. On a much wider front, the ILO has recently launched an international programme for the improve-ment of working conditions and environment (known as PIACT from its French acronym). On the legislative side, Britain adopted a general law on safety and health in 1974. Laws are also being passed, or are in preparation, in Finland, Sweden, Denmark, and Norway, concerning protection for workers and stressing the need to devise an overall policy to eliminate at their source all occupational hazards threatening the life or health of the workers.

This information makes it clear that concern for the quality of life at work has become a fundamental part of government programmes in Europe. President Giscard d'Estaing of France said not long ago: 'it is unnatural that in most of our countries environment policy does not cross the threshold of the factories and offices in which men—and nowadays more than thirty-seven per cent of women—spend a third of their adult life.' So, coming back to the negative aspect, people are becoming less and less prepared to accept economic efficiency as the sole reason for performing their work in conditions which may endanger their health or which they consider to be obstacles to self–fulfilment. Cultural and educational advances have bred new attitudes and, combined with the pressures of the consumer society, have made fragmented, repetitive, or monotonous jobs which leave no scope for individual initiative less and less acceptable, especially to the young.

There are new hazards to be taken into account nowadays too: the use of chemical substances, sometimes placed on the market without sufficiently appreciating their potential danger to the health of the workers or even of the neighbouring population; the replacement of muscular effort by nervous tension in work; and the problems created by the use of new technology, especially computers. In Western Europe millions of workers are tied to unpleasant, monotonous, tedious, or low–prestige jobs. It is as if the employment market were split into two, with one part marked by a combination of bad working conditions, exposure to various hazards, low pay, low skills, and inferior social status. It is also the sad though undeniable fact that certain underprivileged groups—the young, women, and immigrants—are being used as a labour reserve for unpleasant or tedious jobs.

In France there are laws and collective agreements defining unpleasant tasks. A law passed in 1975, concerning the lowering of retirement age for manual workers, explicitly lists the factors which entitle the workers to an earlier retirement after a qualifying period of service. These are: continuous or semi–continuous shift work; assembly line work; work as furnacemen; or, finally, outdoor work. At present in France there are thought to be more than two and a half million industrial workers, or about ten per cent of the labour force who fulfil these conditions. It is difficult to be precise in defining unpleasant or tedious jobs. The notion of unpleasantness relates to the physical and mental demands made on workers by jobs which are, for example, dangerous, strenuous, tiring, or dirty, or which involve working hours which are excessive, or exposure to noise, heat, or cold. In calling a job tedious one is thinking in psychological and social terms. The work is repetitive, uninteresting, monotonous, mediocre, carries little prestige, or is simply regarded as disagreeable. In Western Europe trends in the employment of foreign workers also have a bearing on the future of unpleasant jobs—immigration tends to perpetuate the tedious jobs and in many cases provides an excuse for not upgrading them. It is also the indicator of a shortage of national manpower for the less attractive types of employment.

The introduction of immigration controls has led to some rethinking on the part of planners in some countries as to how future immigration policy could be integrated with plans aimed at improving working conditions. The French Government is making provision in its economic plans for a vigorous policy of upgrading jobs, without which it is believed that French workers would refuse to do the jobs left vacant by foreign workers. Some Socialist countries have decided to pursue similar upgrading policies also.

115

The German Democratic Republic, for instance, has modified 300 000 jobs (about 7 per cent of the total) during the past three years. In the Soviet Union 28 million workers in manual occupations are due to be transferred to mechanized and automated jobs in industry between 1976 and 1980, and in Hungary it is estimated that between 1970 and 1985 there will be a 50 per cent reduction in non-manual jobs requiring no more than a primary education.

All this general activity in job enrichment right across Europe and embracing the whole political spectrum, indicates the momentum which has been generated to improve the quality of life at work. But in the industrial sense, when everyone is a 'duke', so to speak, who will want to be a 'dustman'? Here the social significance of all these activities becomes clear to the point of discomfort. There are two further complications. Not everyone wants to have their job or their working life enriched in the sense described. It may seem outrageous, but not everybody wants to be extended, challenged, made happy, or satisfied at work. They just want to 'get on with it'. In the official jargon, they have a tolerance for monotony and they are entitled to their opinion. These people tend to be mainly, though not exclusively, in manufacturing industry. Some weavers in the textile industry are perfectly happy with the repetitive nature of their work, as they can see the cloth being woven which is the end product of their efforts. The noise of the looms enables them to sing and shout without being overheard and they can think about other things while they are carrying out their routine tasks.[1]

The problem with monotony at work is that some people do like it, but they are probably a small proportion of the population. Their wishes should be respected. The other complication lies in the steadily changing patterns in the workforces of Western countries, which embrace the primary (extractive industries), secondary (manufacturing and construction), and tertiary (service) sectors of the economy. The service share of total employment in the Community rose from 30 per cent in 1960 to 45 per cent in 1975.[2] In no Community country does the tertiary or service sector now account for less than 35 per cent of all employment, and in some it is more than 50 per cent. Enriching the jobs of service workers, therefore, is part of the agenda society now faces. Paradoxically, workers and their organizations have shown comparatively little real interest in job enrichment schemes. There are several explanations for this surprising situation. First, job enrichment has not in general fulfilled the normal criteria for a bargaining objective. There is no clear consensus amongst workers as to how it may be obtained. The ways of attaining it are difficult to embody in contract terms; and the subject anyway relates to aspects of work which are traditionally

1. The author worked for several years as a weaver in a Bradford textile factory.
2. From Commission document 'Role of the Tertiary Sectors', May 1978, page 6.

management prerogatives and not closely related to traditional bargaining matters.

Secondly, workers often object that job enrichment schemes are a ruse by management to increase productivity. This is true in most cases, but it seems to be a legitimate objective to be as productive at work as possible. If this leads to higher rewards for those achieving it and in the process they discover that they are more satisfied by the work they do, that is surely a happy bonus. The instigator of change to improve jobs is usually the employer, because the trigger for most of the changes has been problems which were hitting and hurting management: absenteeism, industrial relations problems, recruitment difficulties, and low productivity. Even the most militant trade unionist sees the point about the value of a bigger economic 'cake' to share, and the importance of skill and effectiveness at work making workers worth more, and so increasing their bargaining strength. The negative fear of losing one's job is a poor motivator. It is much better to feel pride in a product and in being a member of an effective team; but this means efficiency, which in turn means everyone pulling their full weight and feeling their efforts are not being wasted. Pride in one's job sometimes evokes ingenuity too. The story is told of a woman working in a biscuit factory whose job was to see that no two chocolate biscuits rested against each other. When asked about the nature of her duties she said: 'I am responsible for every chocolate biscuit made by the company'.

A third reason for union caution towards improving jobs is that unions prefer to use their own consensus mechanism to identify discontent. They find the 'questionnaire' suspect and vaguely irritating, especially when it is suggested that it is a better way of assessing workers' needs than the union's own mechanism of discussion and representation. In fact the main difference between the 'questionnaire' and 'consensus' method relates to goals. The questionnaire aims at making the job fit the worker better, economic results always being kept in mind. Trade unions, on the other hand, seek a consensus on bargaining objectives. The two approaches are not always compatible, but once a consensus has been reached on whether the target should be better pay, more challenging jobs, or even higher productivity, the unions usually show themselves to be active and imaginative. As unions continue to demand and secure more of a joint say in industrial matters they will become more confident about avoiding what they sometimes see as management manipulation in the job enrichment field. The result could be more enthusiastic mutual experiments in this area, as in the case of several Swedish companies where it has become clear that such activity can pay off in terms both of higher productivity and more satisfying jobs.

One area where there is close cooperation between unions and management on the quality of working life is in the field of free time for rest and

117

leisure. This has a practical, slightly grim aspect in terms of the work–sharing ideas currently being examined by the European Commission and the trade unions and employers at Euro–level. More positively it involves examination of the dangers of excessive working hours, the problems of night work and shift work, work schedules related to individual preferences, and enlarging the choices available to workers between work, training, and leisure. For a long time the question of working time was considered from a quantitative angle—the number of hours worked—and was regulated uniformly for everyone in accordance with the needs of the company. Now it is seen that besides the quantitative dimension, which is still important since the shorter working week is still a basic union aim, there is another qualitative dimension. This is the need to find the most judicious distribution possible of the time devoted to work over the day, the week, the year—indeed over the working lifetime.

It is a question of working differently and better, of finding a balance between work, rest, and leisure which meets the needs of the individual and the community. In recent years creative ideas have blossomed freely; compression of the working day or week, flexible hours, part–time employment, and earlier retirement systems are the best known formulae. But two questions are dominating the discussions. The first is the issue of shift work, and more particularly night work. There are a number of conflicting considerations involved, since some people want such work prohibited or restricted because of its alleged adverse effect on the workers' health and family life; others stress its advantages from the point of view of job creation and improving the return on investments, or emphasize the need to revise the Convention prohibiting night work for women in industry, which they hold to be an obstacle to equality of treatment. The second question concerns the conditions under which a worker retires from work and whether he should give up all occupational activities. This is a particularly topical and important question not only from the point of view of employment policy—since the retirement of older workers is often put forward as a means of creating openings for the unemployed—but also for social security schemes, which might not be able to afford a reduction in the retirement age combined with the greater life expectancy which we now enjoy.

'Job enrichment' then is not just another phrase in the lexicon of work organizations. It is here to stay and should be studied and used although those who idealize it as the alchemy which transmutes failure into success in industry may well be disappointed. It is being planned and operated on a large scale by governments in Western Europe which have an eye not only on its potential economic benefits but on the political consequences of the frustration of the rising social expectations they have been instrumental in creating. The work being done in the ILO spans 139 countries. Its World

Employment Programme is aimed at promoting employment creation, while PIACT puts the emphasis on the quality of the employment created. The European Community's Dublin Foundation for the Improvement of the Working Environment is studying all the important aspects of job enrichment on behalf of the member states. It embarked on its first working programme in 1977, which includes an inventory of the most significant experiments in work reorganization in the nine member states. The Foundation is also studying the development of shift working in the Community and its related problems.

Trade union attitudes towards job enrichment remain mixed. When semi–autonomous work groups are introduced, for example, they can give workers a heightened sense of identity with colleagues and with the product the group is assembling. They also mean complex reorganization of payments systems, complicating the bargaining process, particularly if the work groups are of an experimental nature and only exist in part of a plant or company. Channels of authority and communication become less easy to define and in consequence trade union representation often undergoes a difficult adaptation period. In West Germany considerable interest was aroused by a regional strike of IG Metall in October 1973 over the humanization of work and worker participation. The strike achieved its aim of ensuring that works councils would have a major say in developments in this field, thus bringing the whole subject within the domain of collective bargaining. The DGB organized a conference on the subject in 1974, but the lack of real achievement in the various projects sponsored by the Government's research programme has not helped to maintain momentum. In France unions have tended to oppose humanization of work on doctrinaire grounds, but this view has been tempered by the need to come to terms with reality. This means that French unions often tacitly accept a final job enrichment scheme provided there are adequate guarantees ensuring rewards for any extension of workers' skills.

The Italian unions, on the other hand, have been active in improving the quality of working life. Agreements in the early 'seventies with employers such as Fiat and Olivetti paved the way for semi–autonomous work group experiments (or 'production islands') with flexible work cycles, use of robots, and job rotation. A more recent agreement at Pirelli was under negotiation for a year before being implemented and provided for continuous monitoring on a joint union/management basis. In Britain the TUC takes part in the tripartite quasi-Government Work Research Unit and generally takes a positive attitude towards developments in the field, without necessarily being a great innovator itself. The general lack of enthusiasm among British unions is linked, among other things, to the craft–based nature of many trade unions (and the problem of demarcation disputes in

119

work humanization schemes), the risk of upsetting existing collective bargaining structures, and a widely–felt *malaise* towards any innovations which might challenge the established shop steward system.

Given all these complexities, the following guidelines might be worth considering by those wishing to improve the quality of working life:

1. Working conditions which are clean, reasonably safe, and do not unduly endanger the health or safety of the worker or his family.

2. Employment which provides for continuity so that the worker feels reasonably secure about the future. Recognition of past service and performance, and early warning systems to alert workers to economic changes in the organization.

3. The right of all workers to organize themselves into unions or other bodies which have the task of representing workers. This right should apply equally to all and should include the right to refrain from membership.

4. Fair and equitable pay relationships and equal pay for equal work. Pay which is linked to responsibility and which recognizes and rewards service, skill, performance, and individual accomplishments.

5. Provision of an adequate and competitive package of employee benefits which reflects prevailing practice, integrated with national legislation, especially measures which protect the worker and his family in the event of illness, accident and death, and makes provision for his old age.

6. Personnel systems which consider individual workers as a growing, developing human asset; and provision for workers to compete for training, development recognition, and promotion.

7. Schemes to enable those who wish, to participate in management decision–taking, and to link this participation to the productive goals of the company.

8. A workplace climate which encourages openness, a sense of community, and personal equality, regardless of rank in the hierarchy. Teamwork and group cooperation across organization units.

9. The right to free speech, to privacy, to dissent, and to fair and equitable treatment at work, through a system which recognizes that a modern organization is a society in microcosm, entitling workers to the rights and privileges compatible with membership of a voluntary organization.

10. A balance between work and lifestyle. Work schedules, overtime, and career pressures should be equated with family, leisure, and recreational needs. Happy people are better workers.

These concepts set a high standard but they should be aimed at if job enrichment is to be taken seriously. The real message, however, is not in the baffling terminology of the subject or even in the desirable changes its application is bringing to the lives of ordinary people. The point is to see job enrichment strategically as one important piece of a vast new jigsaw of industrial Europe. Other parts of the picture still to be assembled are workers participation, a new work ethic, and fresh collective-bargaining patterns.

These are some of the waves in the fast–running tide of social and economic change induced by war, science, technology, education, and communications. The plain fact is that workers are increasingly expecting from their work not only a good income, but the opportunity to realize through their work some of man's higher needs, ranging from creativity to self–esteem. Some people may understandably feel that these goals are mainly abstract and high–falutin, but it is worth remembering that in the nineteenth century many campaigns were waged to secure respect for what at the time was called 'the dignity of the working man'. Job enrichment is simply a reinterpretation—a modern version of their worthwhile aims.

The ILO's constitution proclaims that 'labour is not a commodity', so reminding us that it is performed not by a machine but by a human being whose natural qualities need to be used and developed. Although the trend is towards a reduction in working time, work still occupies a central place in man's existence. It is not simply a means of earning a living—it is also the vehicle through which he should be able to express his creativity. As Maxim Gorky said: 'When work is a pleasure, life is a joy! When work is a duty, life is slavery'. The growing reaction in recent years against the dehumanization of life and work in industrial society can therefore be viewed as a healthy response. It represents a victory of quality over quantity or, if you like, of mind over matter. It is an expression of man's revolt against the dominance of economic and material constraints.

121

13. Disclosure of information—all the way?

There is a James Bond touch about the phrase 'disclosure of information'—fast cars, beautiful girls, microfilms, sudden death, and top secret files bulging with sealed documents the guarding of which is essential for business success. All this may be fantasy but the fact is that European management faces an explosion of proposed legislation on corporate information disclosure. International bodies like the ILO, UN, OECD, and EEC, indeed governments everywhere, are scrambling onto the disclosure bandwagon as fast as the legislative procedures will allow.

A recent research survey by the Battelle Institute in Germany, in conjunction with the London–based Matrix, and Tidevo in Copenhagen, found that simply to detail all proposed laws on disclosure in 10 countries covered 32 closely typed pages—enough to give some managers apoplexy. To avoid being buried in a costly 'data' mountain, management should be looking at what is being prepared by the legislators, the trade unions, the business associations, and the various pressure groups. Mere protest on the grounds of being unprepared is futile. Companies should get involved in the policy–making process, try to understand the objectives behind the proposals, and inject their own ideas.

The practice of disclosing information is on the increase, for reasons linked with the development of the idea of democratic behaviour and participation by workers in management decision–taking. Everyone seems to want it, though in different ways and for a variety of reasons. Powerful arguments can be advanced in support of the virtues and likely advantages of workers being well–informed. Even during the last war army briefing officers 'kept the chaps in the picture' and joint production committees and advisory bodies made information available on production matters.

But this was in wartime, when there was a united will to get things done. Peacetime collective bargaining is a different situation, especially in Britain where industrial relations have a strong adversary flavour. Nevertheless, it still seems logical that, where collective bargaining is concerned, negotiations should be about facts rather than emotions. It must surely be right that workers are more likely to give of their best when they understand more clearly their role and function in the production process. This view has made disclosure of information a persistent theme over the past ten years in British industrial relations and induced both Conservative and Labour

Governments to include disclosure provisions in their industrial relations legislation, the former in the 1971 Industrial Relations Act and its attendant Code of Practice, and the latter in the abortive 1970 Industrial Relations Bill and the current Employment Protection Act.

There seems to be general agreement that the disclosure of information by companies is desirable, but there are differences of opinion as to what this implies. Employers, for example, tend to believe that it will lead to rational and objective bargaining. They feel it will moderate trade union demands, prevent rumours, and encourage productivity agreements, as well as giving workers cost–consciousness and a greater sense of involvement and identification with the firm. Trade unions, however, tend to support the disclosure concept for different reasons. They believe it will correct the power imbalance and help them to bargain as equal partners.

Moreover, unions feel that company information will help them to decide when an employer can least afford a strike, provide ideological reinforcement for claims, and force management to justify its decisions. Outside observers of both left and right have also mixed reasons for supporting disclosure. Some believe it can help to promote a more ready, albeit reluctant, acceptance of redundancy and the need for cooperation and change to avoid it; but others think it might give advance warning to a union to steel its sinews for factory occupation and other forms of resistance.

Leftist organizations like the CGT in France and the Institute of Workers' Control in England predictably see disclosure as one way of exposing the antisocial nature of capitalism and extending the traditional frontiers of collective bargaining and workers' control to include issues like investment and other company matters. These views are balanced by those who feel that disclosure will help companies to overcome the mystique surrounding profits and convince workers of the usefulness of their company's contribution to society. Information can be disclosed to all workers or to trade unions. In the former case the aim is usually to promote understanding of the company's affairs, while information to unions tends to be seen and used in a collective bargaining context.

Two types of information are generally provided—labour information (wages, manpower, training, etc.) and financial information, in the form of company accounts. Both these categories of information may contribute to a more advanced form of disclosure on the forward prospects for the company (order books, redundancies, expansion, closures, mergers, etc.) The problem with disclosure proposals throughout Europe is that they are being developed without much input from companies and without detailed assessment as to what is really needed and how the information can be interpreted and used.

The Battelle survey looked at what kind of information workers,

123

managers, company directors, trade unions, customers, governments, press- ure groups, business organizations, creditors, the media, and shareholders really want. The results showed that while the expectations of the most important groups are increasing they are reasonably modest. Less infor- mation appears to be required than the advocates of more disclosure would have us believe. The main thrust comes from managers and trade unionists, their thirst for information being rooted in a desire to do a better job—of management in the case of managers and of collective bargaining in the case of trade unions. All this emphasizes the great danger that the major inter- national push for greater disclosure will lead to an international infor- mation jungle, in which multinational companies in particular may incur huge costs while only providing minimal benefits to themselves or to those who receive the information.

While these pressures build up, however, European companies are doing well in publishing social reports. Within Europe, German companies are in the lead, 25 companies having published such information during the last two years. Moreover, 300 German reports are in various stages of prep- aration, the point being that this major effort has influenced the content and timing of German legislation. These reports, which are published separately from annual reports, are long and immensely detailed, covering health and safety analyses, pollutant emissions, and even supplier depen- dency, as well as wage and salary structures. The assessments within the reports stress the company's commitments to the needs and welfare of the various groups, and the way the company's activities affect the different groups is shown through indicators.

The tendency in Britain is to make economic performance more intel- ligible, both to workers and shareholders. A large number of companies have published short, simple reports to explain where the money comes from and how profits are used. These two approaches reflect the different industrial relations systems of the two countries. British business is under- standably trying to encourage a fuller understanding of the traditional accounts and profits, while German business is concentrating on clarifying the way it meets shareholders' needs while simultaneously contributing to social and economic welfare.

The French Employers' Association launched a sizeable research pro- gramme two years ago which had some influence on French legislation on company information. Dutch employers are urging companies to produce social reports, and Dutch companies are at present responding better than the non–Dutch multinationals in the Netherlands. Spanish and Portuguese employers are beginning to move in the same direction, no doubt spurred partially by the knowledge that when they eventually join the European Community considerable levelling–up will be necessary on their part in the field of industrial relations. Many companies are discovering that the mere effort of embarking on an information exercise has major internal value, in the sense that the information generated and the procedures devised for analysing it are creating a keener management awareness, an improved mutual understanding, and better planning and decision making.

Still on the question of attitudes resulting from imparting information, some British employers contend that most workers who show curiosity in the firm's activities are interested not merely in the actual answers to the questions they ask, but in whether the company is prepared and willing to give the answers. It is argued that to give it openly, honestly, and fully is as important as the information itself. Linked with this opinion is the view that some information should be available to workers but not necessarily imparted, while other information should be specifically provided. The information policies in each European country are mainly determined by the industrial relations system and the institutions (works councils, collective bargaining, or a mixture of the two) operating in a particular country.

Montesquieu once wrote on the subject of politics: 'It is not the means which need to be brilliant, it is the end result.' It could not be claimed that the disclosure situation in Belgium, France, Germany, and the Netherlands is perfect, but the information given to works councils in these countries is positive and concerns existing social and economic activities as well as the future prospects of the company. The Belgian Royal Decree of 27 November 1973 refers to the precise economic and financial information to be given to the works council and is a clear example of this trend.

Belgium

The situation on disclosure of information in Belgium is as follows. The works council has the right to information on personnel matters, and sometimes on the competition position of the company and its plans for future development and investment. The Belgian Royal Decree lays down a procedure for providing information and defines which financial and economic material should be disclosed to works council members. Each enterprise in which 150 people are employed is required to have a works council. Its members, both on the management and the workers' side, must receive all relevant documents 15 days in advance of a special meeting of the council, which is called to discuss information. Worker members of the council may call an expert for advice, and disagreements and complaints can be referred to the Minister of Economic Affairs for arbitration. The Royal Decree stresses that the objective of providing detailed information on production costs and intended future investments is to help works council members to

125

understand the relationship between the prevailing economic and financial conditions in the enterprise and their effect on work and workers.

France

There is also a good deal of activity on the subject of disclosure in France. All firms employing at least 50 workers are required to have a works council. Each council comprises management and workers' representatives. An Ordinance of 1945 lays down that works council members have the right to be informed on economic and financial matters and should have access to the company's annual report. Quarterly communications are also given to the Council on the progress of production and employment. In limited liability companies the Council has the right to see the balance sheet. The French Parliament is considering enacting new legislation compelling firms with over 750 workers to compile a 'social balance sheet' each year for submission to the works council. This social balance sheet will certainly contain information on employment, pay and related costs, conditions relating to health and safety, training, and industrial relations. This information will relate to the year in question and will also give comparisons of the company's policy over the past two years.

The Bill will also involve Ministerial Decrees for each sector of industry, specifying the type of information which each 'social balance sheet' in these sectors should contain. Furthermore, in multinational firms each establishment must have a separate social balance sheet, provided it has more than 750 workers. Each works council member must receive the social balance sheet 15 days before the next formal meeting of the works council.

West Germany

As one would expect, the German disclosure provisions are precise and extensive. The Works Constitution Act of 1972 gives works councils far–reaching rights of information, consultation, and participation regarding social, staff, and economic matters. The rights of German works councils under the terms of the 1972 Act are as follows:

1. The right to be informed and consulted on manpower planning, vacancies, training, termination of employment, construction, alterations or extensions of works and other premises belonging to the establishment.
2. The right to be informed about any proposed alteration which may affect the employees, or new work methods and production processes; where necessary they may try to reach an agreement concerning social compensation.
3. Where specific matters are not subject to regulation or collective agreement, works councils have the right to co-determination in many social

126

matters; these include hours of work, holidays, the introduction and use of technical devices to check on workers, safety and health regulations, and internal wage fixing.

4. The right to veto employers' decisions regarding dismissals.

Holland

In Holland too, disclosure of information is very much 'on-scene'. Works council members have the right to ask for information relating to the progress of the enterprise and to discuss important decisions before they are taken. Dutch laws also specify that trade unions be consulted in advance about any measures concerning the transfer of control of the enterprise.

In all four countries mentioned it will be seen that the right to information also includes the right of works council members to question and if necessary to challenge the employer in the courts if the necessary information is not given. The influence of legislation concerning information in Belgium, France, Germany, and Holland, can be seen in the proposals for a European Works Council, which have been prepared by the European Commission. The proposed statute for a European company requires the management board of a European company to give the following information to a European Works Council.

First, the management board must meet regularly with the European Works Council and in any case not less than four times a year. At least once a quarter, a report must be submitted on the general position of the company and its future development. The report must contain full and up–to–date information on general developments in the sectors of the economy in which the company and its subsidiaries operate; on the economic and financial position of the company and associated enterprises; on the development of the company's business; on the state of its production and marketing; on the employment situation of employees of the company and its subsidiaries, and its future development; on the production and investment programme; on working methods, especially the introduction of new working methods; and on any other fact or project which may have an appreciable effect on the interests of the employees of the company.

In Britain disclosure of information has been developed in the nationalized industries, particularly in discussions about the future of the coal industry and rail transport. Disclosure has also been officially supported by the TUC since 1952 and political parties have supported the concept as a means of improving communications in industry. This probably explains why the disclosure provisions in the current Employment Protection Act are

127

similar to those of the Conservative Industrial Relations Act in 1971. The main emphasis is on disclosure for purposes of collective bargaining; though companies are not compelled to produce a document against their wishes or to provide information when the cost or the amount of time involved in compiling or assembling it is out of reasonable proportion to its value in collective bargaining.

The problems of disclosure fall under three main headings. First, there is the behavioural difficulty—the assumption that 'facts' can bridge the gap between the goals and values of unions and management, two independent organizations with separate and sometimes incompatible goals. Secondly, there is the difficulty of presenting information which firms are willing to disclose. Unions tend to ask for economic and financial information and they often insist that it is presented in simple, comprehensible terms. The preparation of information in this way, especially in large firms, needs time and can be very costly. On the other hand the timing of disclosure is critical. To give information to workers when a decision has already been finalized is likely to be an exercise in futility. In matters involving changes affecting the majority of the workforce, provision of information in the formative stage of decision making can be helpful to the employees and their representatives. In the early stages, attitudes and opinions on both sides can be accommodating and proposals can be easily altered. Decisions arrived at in this way can be applied more easily. Timing in the release of information is important to management too. In some cases first line supervisors and other junior management people receive information about their company not from senior management officials, but through the grapevine, from members of the works council who have access to vital information much sooner than others. Obviously, this creates serious morale problems for management.

The third problem is confidentiality. In some countries works council members have to keep information confidential until senior management is able to release it to all parties simultaneously. In practice this creates problems and in Belgium, Holland, and West Germany, for example, there are legal provisions authorizing employers to withhold certain information. The drawing of the confidentiality line is done by management, but has to be justified. The definition of confidentiality varies; it usually includes details of projected company mergers and takeovers and other information to which stock markets might react sensitively. Marketing information which might affect the competitive position of the company is also considered confidential in most cases.

But while management decides what is confidential, the criterion on which such a decision is based is usually negotiated with the unions. The

128

obligation to keep information secret creates a dilemma for the unions. They often feel they cannot participate in a meaningful way in the affairs of the company if the information given to a minority of their representatives must be kept secret. Disclosing confidential information brings headaches for management too, as it can be used by unions to enhance their influence and power or even to further political ends. The French CGT, for instance, makes no secret of its view that works committees constitute a weapon in the class struggle and should not be considered as an instrument for cooperation between workers and management.

The use of confidential information by unions could also undermine the position of management in collective bargaining sessions. Not surprisingly, the level and quality of disclosure of confidential information bears some relationship to the state of industrial relations in the country and the industry in question. In the absence of legislation governing this type of disclosure both sides tend to interpret disclosure obligations to suit themselves. In general, employers tend to interpret disclosure obligations rather restrictively and workers' representatives interpret them broadly. The key consideration for management and unions, however, is that disclosure of information will be of little real value unless workers representatives are able to understand, evaluate, and use it.

The implications for training and education of all those involved in participative schemes are profound. The principle of disclosing information may be traumatic to management, but trade unions face immensely difficult problems of adjustment too. The focus of education and training for workers varies in different countries, due to their legislative and institutional arrangements. In West Germany and Holland, trade union representation at plant and enterprise level is indirect, so the main educational effort is aimed at the works councillors. But in Britain, where trade unions are directly involved in representing workers at various levels of the enterprise, the educational effort is concentrated almost entirely on shop stewards.

West German trade unions contend that the main purpose of their educational programme is to familiarize workers' representatives with their duties and to teach them how to translate political demands into social realities. The DGB runs schools for works councillors which analyse the functions of works councils, the priorities in trade union educational objectives, and basic information on economics, law, and science. In Holland, the unions have concentrated on three main areas of education:
1. Information on the legal framework within which the works councils operate.

129

2. Information on the Dutch socio–economic system and its functioning.
3. Information on the internal relationships within the firm—industrial management, economics, industrial sociology, etc.

In Britain and Italy, the subject–matter of collective bargaining has gradually been extended from the traditional areas of wages and working conditions to the role of workers and their representatives in the factory and to other areas. British unions in particular, during the past few years, have found themselves opposing plant closures and asking management not only for financial information but also for a 'social cost benefit analysis' in the handling of such a situation. With this trend British unions have realized the great need for a multidisciplinary educational system to enable workers to cope with such complex situations. All this indicates that the explosion of information disclosure has not yet found an acceptable Euro–form. As in so many other areas of industrial relations we are being swept along by events instead of controlling them.

Social and democratic pressures linked with fast technological change make the disclosure bandwagon roll faster by the hour; but management and unions have to wedge themselves firmly in the driving seat if the bandwagon is not to become a destructive juggernaut. Both trade unions and management require training in the meaning, consequences and presentation of information. In other words, those who disclose facts need to understand and communicate to others as well as to present information. Company accountants may have to be given industrial relations training. We may need a new skill of 'disclosure accountancy'. Those who ask for and receive information will have to be shown what it really means and how one group of facts relates to another. Trade unions will have to consider employing specialists. Paradoxically, while the social and democratic arguments for disclosure of information are well–rooted, there is no firm evidence that disclosure will, in itself, improve industrial relations. Indeed, information disclosed on profit ratios, directors' salaries, job changes, or planned redundancies may well stimulate conflict rather than reduce it.

Information given may not always be accurate, objective, and absolute; and there are various ways of presenting financial information. In any case, negotiations are not so much about facts as interpretations. Mark Twain once wrote: 'It is difference of opinion that makes horse races' and the same is certainly true of industrial relations. Trade union aims and policies and the bargaining strength of the parties can be as important as factual information, and neither side will be constrained by information or facts unless it wishes to be. Information can initiate as well as inform. In order to justify a sectional redundancy an employer may disclose information about comparative performances of one section with another. This might convince the unions to accept the redundancies, but might also reveal that some workers are more productive and more profitable than others. A wages claim born of disclosure and endorsed by employers' statistics might be the result. Information disclosed about company difficulties when refusing a wage claim may lead to an overtime ban to prevent feared redundancies. Creditors may hear of the problem, and in this way the original disclosure, based on the best of motives, could snowball into disaster.

Despite all these problems and difficulties, the pressures for disclosure of information will increase rather than diminish, fed by the uncertainties linked with high unemployment, technological change, and the thrust towards industrial democracy. The educational systems during the postwar years have also produced workers less willing to be deferential. In the long run some harmonization of disclosure practices will be achieved within the European Community, and the Commission is currently considering the possibility of proposals designed to achieve this aim, but because the nine are a patchwork of individual histories and different national institutional structures, the momentum will be in national legislation, and this will be governed largely by management and trade union relationships.

Employers and trade unions have reservations about the advantages of disclosure. Some employers regard requests for information as incompatible with obligations to shareholders and an interference with managerial rights. Others believe it will damage competitiveness and break confidentiality, and that unions will distort and misuse the information they receive. Some trade unions fear disclosure will curb their ability to manoeuvre, seduce them into acceptance of management philosophy and, by giving information directly to workers, bypass the trade unions. In fact social and political pressures are forcing both parties to consider a new style of collective bargaining, based more on facts than opinions. They are both singularly ill–equipped for the challenge. On the employers' side 'disclosure accounting' is in its infancy, and trade unions are finding it difficult to handle the information they are already receiving.

14. Industrial democracy—is it really democratic?

Is the concept of worker participation in management decision–taking an enlightened step towards humanizing the conditions of working life; or is it just another front on which the age–old conflict between capital and labour can be worked out? The name of the game is certainly power—more power for workpeople. The argument is how and to what extent this power should be balanced by responsibility.

'Beautiful theories are often killed by brutal facts', said Huxley. In Britain the Bullock Report on industrial democracy was certainly a bold plan to put workers on the boards of large companies, but it was destined for an early pigeonhole. It produced a lively, often trenchant, public debate with the CBI opposing it as implacably as the TUC opposed the Industrial Relations Bill some years ago. The plain fact is that an effective system of worker participation cannot be legislated into existence, nor can it occur overnight. A house must be built from the foundation upwards, not downwards from the chimney stack.

The undiluted application of the Bullock Report would have created bitterness and serious industrial unrest in Britain. The Report, however, had a negative value in showing what could not be done in the field of participation. Instant participation, pushed by politicians either from motives of sincerity or expediency, is a non–starter. It must start from small beginnings with attainable objectives within the competence of those who are participating. It is an organic growth that must be nurtured carefully by management and workpeople, not a pre–packaged transplant delivered to industry by eager politicians with electoral fish to fry.

European experience clearly shows that board–level worker representation has never been introduced as an isolated revolutionary change at the top. It has invariably been the final stage of an evolutionary process designed to develop and encourage worker participation at every level of the enterprise. Seven countries (Austria, Denmark, Sweden, Germany, Norway, Holland, and Luxembourg) have laws providing for workers' representatives on boards. These laws, however, followed decades of effort to expand worker participation gradually throughout all levels of the enterprises involved. Until the Bullock Report no country had even contemplated the introduction of board–level participation by workers, without lengthy experience of operating works councils designed to introduce industrial democracy at

132

the immediate place of work.

Moreover, in no country with legally–imposed directors from the shop–floor, is the system of industrial relations remotely comparable to that of Britain. The principle of industrial unionism, for instance, is firmly established in Austria, Germany, and Luxembourg. It is being pressed hard in Denmark, Norway, and Sweden, where an historical combination of craft and industrial unions exist. In all these countries it would be unusual if more than three unions were represented in the workforce of one company. In all six countries collective agreements are legally binding.

In short there is no other country in Europe where worker directors have been introduced into a British type of situation, where agreements are not legally binding and multi–unionism within plants abounds. Nevertheless, the industrial democracy debate in Britain continues, albeit controversially.

From the angle of efficiency and competitiveness, it does not really matter who runs the company provided they see their task as helping the company to make and sell its goods and services, and they are good at their job. This was the fundamental weakness of the Bullock Report. It assumed that the main function was the cutting up and sharing of the 'cake' which automatically and assuredly appeared on the board–room table. The Report does refer to releasing the energies and skills of the working population to their full potential, so raising the level of productivity and efficiency, but does not describe how this would happen.

As the Institute of Personnel Management pertinently observed in its evidence to the Bullock Commission: the history of the Industrial Relations Act revealed the danger of adapting a foreign concept which is not adapted to the particular culture of Britain: it would be equally disastrous to adopt some parts of a foreign system without accommodating the fundamental principles on which it is based. In the European Community the search continues for the consensus formula for the Fifth Directive (introduced by the Commission in 1972) which would enable the Council of Ministers to approve a Euro–law prescribing minimum standards of worker participation. The problem is both political and psychological—how to find an acceptable legal framework to yield effective and agreed participative management styles.

'A rose by any other name would smell as sweet', said Shakespeare; but worker participation and industrial democracy, with which it is linked, are high–sounding words which can mean all things to all men. Different groups of zealots with vested interests such as managers, politicians, trade union leaders, or social 'do–gooders', see in worker participation what they wish to see. It can be used to define anything from near revolution to a gentle tinkering with the existing system. At one end of the ragbag of ideas there are the socialist aspirations for workers' control, and at the other end of the

133

spectrum a limited reform which offers consultation whilst preserving the management's right to take a final decision.

Worker participation is not a panacea, a sort of social liniment to rub on society to ease industrial arthritis. Nor is it meant to banish all shop stewards or give a soft option to those managers who feel that the industrial headaches of those they manage can be cured by a few verbal bromides. It is already happening on a wide scale in the European Community. On the basis of existing systems a widely acceptable definition of worker participation might be 'a more effective involvement of people at work and in the success of their companies'. But still the basic questions arise, either from genuine doubts or confirmed cynicism.

Worker participation for what—and by whom? The answer is clear. It means participating in management decision–taking, first at the lower levels and then in the upper reaches of management. It is a way of using fully the resources of an organization. As to who should participate, the aim should be to allow participation at all levels in a company—office workers, staff managers, supervisors, and professional workers as well as manual workers. The topics will generally be those on which the participants have knowledge and experience; for example, overtime policy, manning rates, job evaluation, promotion, recruitment, and training are clearly issues on which much knowledge and information in a company goes unused.

Before looking at more specific aspects of worker participation in the European Community, it is worth remembering that the idea of worker directors is completely at variance with the private enterprise philosophy of many industrialized countries—Japan, Australia, Canada, and the USA, for instance. In other countries where there are powerful trade union organizations with a Marxist philosophy, the concept of worker directors has received little support, as such a move is seen as being incompatible with the outright rejection of capitalism which these trade unions favour. France, Italy, and to a lesser degree Belgium, fall into this category, though the mood is gradually changing.

Where trade unions are well–established and closely linked to Social Democratic political parties, as they are in countries like Norway, Sweden, Germany, Denmark, and the Netherlands, then worker directors are either well–established or being introduced. The British and Irish cases are interesting because they do not fall neatly into any of these categories. Until quite recently they could have been grouped with Australia, Canada, Japan, and the USA as opposing worker directors, but membership of the European Community and exposure to the different participative systems and the complex discussions on European Company Law have forced British and Irish politicians, managers, and trade unionists to reconsider their position.

There are different structures for industrial decision–taking in the nine member states of the Community, due to different legal traditions and social conditions. These differences create obvious problems when searching for a consensus formula for worker participation. On the other hand, the differences pinpoint the need for a common approach. For example, the stated aim of the Community is to improve and harmonize living and working conditions in the member states. It will be hard to do this in a situation where, in some countries of the nine, wage–earners enjoy extensive rights and legal status within their firms, while in others workers' rights remain embryonic. As part of the Community objective of creating a common market with a single industrial base, one of the tasks of the European Commission is to work towards the harmonization of national company law legislation.

The typical form adopted by most of the important industrial and commercial enterprises in the Community, is that of a corporation with limited liability and a share capital. These enterprises are the main producers of wealth and as employers they have an immediate impact on the lives of large numbers of Community workers. They are institutions of strategic importance in relation to the economic and social systems of the Community. At present these companies are incorporated under the separate laws of the nine member states. These national laws vary widely, especially in relation to the internal structure of companies, the powers of directors, and the rights of shareholders and of the employees. This situation creates a real barrier to cross–frontier activities, both for the company and those with whom it deals, as there are no common legal standards.

A company trading in a foreign state through a branch company, often does not offer those doing business with the company the same assurances and guarantees as a company incorporated in the state in question. But if a company tries to overcome these problems by setting up a subsidiary incorporated in another member state, the subsidiary will have a different structure from the parent. For an enterprise which wishes to trade in all member states, the result is a complex, expensive and inefficient organization. It is true that some enterprises are able to operate internationally, even with these difficulties, provided they have the right resources; but only at a cost which is much higher than it need be.

It is precisely because every company is incorporated under a particular national system that serious barriers prevent the rational restructuring of enterprises to exploit Community–wide, rather than national, markets. Even if a company tries to transfer from one country to another, it has to undergo the trauma of dissolution and reconstruction. In short, with the present system of nationally based company laws, each company is virtually imprisoned within its national system, and cannot expand or combine with another company beyond its national frontiers in the same way and with the

135

same freedom as it can inside the member state in which it is incorporated. With the creation of a wholly new community company law, commercial activity will be free to develop across the boundaries of member states and the Community will assume a more robust and mature attitude to industry.

In drawing up its company law proposals with these points in mind the Commission has looked at the role played within firms by those who represent shareholders and workers. Reform of these roles has seemed to be urgent, as over the years there has been a tendency in public companies towards concentration of real power in the hands of a few top men, while shareholders and sometimes directors are no longer in a position to exercise supervision. The European Community has adopted a number of measures of a limited kind during the past few years which move elements of decision–making in the direction of the workers. As part of its social action programme, for instance, the Community drew up a draft directive on collective dismissals which was adopted by the Council of Ministers in 1975. This means that employers who plan such dismissals must now first consult with workers' representatives about the possibility of avoiding or reducing the redundancies and of mitigating the consequences of those which seem unavoidable.

Redundancy plans must also be notified in advance to the competent public authority. They may then not usually take effect until a period of 30 days has elapsed, during which the authority is empowered to seek solutions to the situation. In the same field, the Commission's acquired rights directive, adopted by the Council in 1977, means that before a merger takes place, workers' representatives must be told about the reasons for it, its likely impact on wage–earners and the measures to be taken on their behalf. In the case of a transfer of ownership, the acquiring firm normally inherits the liability for the rights and advantages accumulated by the workers in the firm being transferred. If an argument arises and no agreement can be reached, an arbitrating body rules on the arrangements to be made for the workers. A European card–index of collective agreements is being developed, covering a number of industries, and joint committees are already operating in several sectors. These committees are discussing common problems in a Euro–setting, and engaging in a dialogue with the Commission on the social problems which concern them.

But the real crunch of the Commission's work on worker participation and company structure comes in two major proposals. The first, originally made in 1970, is the proposal for a Statute for European Companies. It involves a complete company law which companies operating in more than one member state will be able to use, if they wish, instead of relying on a combination of the laws of the member states. The structure of the Statute is sophisticated and complicated. European companies would need to have a dual board system, consisting of a supervisory board and a separate management board. The supervisory board would have the power to appoint, supervise and, if necessary, dismiss the management board and would tend to look at longer–term strategic matters of major importance to the company, such as programmes of expansion or contraction, organizational changes, and links with other enterprises. The management board would have the legal responsibility for managing the company's affairs and would deal with day–to–day activities. Provision has also been made in the Statute for workers to influence decision–making in a number of ways.

First, conditions of employment applying to the workers of the European company may be regulated by European collective bargaining, and agreements made by the company and the trade unions represented in its establishment. Second, a European works council is to be set up in every European company having establishments in more than one member state. This Council will have specific rights to information and consultation and the right to give or withhold its consent on important affairs such as social plans to deal with the consequences of redundancies. Third, workers will have the right to participate in the appointment of members of the company's supervisory body. As the proposal currently stands, the shareholders would elect one–third of the members, the workers one–third, and the two groups together would coopt the remaining members, who would represent the general interest and be independent of both workers and shareholders.

This amended proposal for a European Companies Statute is currently being considered by the Council, which is not likely to reach a final decision on it for some time; or at least until after the Commission has submitted an amended version of its second major proposal, namely the proposal for a Fifth Directive relating to the decision–making structure of public companies.

The draft Fifth Directive was first submitted to the Council in 1972. It would require all public companies formed in the member states to have a dual board structure and, if they employ more than 500 persons, worker participation in the appointment and dismissal of supervisory board members. Two options would be available to member states, based on the two systems of participation in force when the proposal was made. Either, provision should be made for at least one–third of the supervisory board members to be elected by the workers of the company or their representatives, or the supervisory board should be allowed to perpetuate itself by cooption, with shareholders and workers having an equal right to veto any proposed appointment. Of the two proposals, the Fifth Directive has tended to be more controversial than the European Companies Statute. The Fifth Directive would be mandatory, and through national laws would require the

137

observance of specified company structures, while the Statute would be optional.

In this whole area the arguments have been, and still are, fierce, as the proposals raise issues verging on the traumatic for trade unions and employers in some member states. This is especially so in Britain where, for historical reasons, the conflictual form of participation through bargaining mechanisms is already well developed. Do British workers really want more worker involvement in decision–taking, or are they content with the traditional battle with the boss? And if unions opt for involvement, have they men and women trained to take on the exacting responsibilities which eventual Board membership might entail? Are British managers who are sceptical or opposed to enhanced worker participation aware of the growing industrial alienation which larger firms and fast technological change are generating? And can they and the community logically deny workers the same democratic rights in industry which they enjoy in their political citizenship?

The post–Bullock White Paper on industrial democracy was inevitably a compromise and indicates that there are many unresolved points to be discussed before legislation can be introduced. Three of the large unions in the TUC, the municipal workers, the engineers, and the electricians, appear unenthusiastic about worker directors and hold varying views about lower–level participation. The British dilemma is agonizingly clear—company boards are seen by the trade unions as the citadels of industrial power. If unions are to have a direct influence on them, it means their members or officers sitting on such boards. But with this extra power must go additional responsibilities for trade unionists. You cannot sit on a company board and be part of management and still retain the unbridled luxury of criticizing it. If unions accept these extra responsibilities then they must change or modify substantially their adversary–style of operation. Their whole rationale is called into question. They must become instruments of positive change, not weapons of defence. One suspects that this is why the Bullock Report aimed for instant industrial democracy through legislation, with the trade union members of the boards being responsible to their sponsoring trade unions.

In one sense the argument about industrial democracy in Britain has taken most organizations by surprise, especially the trade unions. Because industry and democracy are good, it is assumed that the need for industrial democracy is self–evident. Paradoxically, the pressures which have created the need for industrial democracy have been largely generated by trade union activity: better living standards, improved educational facilities, and better welfare cover, for example. These trends have produced a workforce which is more easily bored by routine work, less deferential and more willing to challenge authority, and with expectations of permanently high lifestyles. But all good things have to be paid for sooner or later. The price of more democracy in industry and workers on boards is a more constructive, cooperative approach to industrial relations and the willing acceptance of wider responsibilities. The key consideration for any worker participation scheme is that it should avoid the confrontation of opposing interests that would be damaging to the company as a whole. Any participation structure should be designed to encourage all parties to work together in the common interest. The rapid evolution of industrial democracy concepts in the West has hoist British trade unions with their own philosophical petard.

There is time, however, for Britain and other member states to introduce experiments in the field of worker participation. The Fifth Directive has still to be approved in a plenary session of the European Parliament, before it can be revised by the Commission and submitted for decision by the Council of Ministers. It is generally felt that the Directive will not reach the Council before 1980–81; and if it is accepted there will be a 'phasing-in' period for member states to adjust their laws or pass new legislation to bring their participative systems to the level which the Fifth Directive will prescribe. This 'phasing-in' period is usually two years, but there is already talk of a longer period for the Fifth Directive in the light of its controversial concepts. So we are speaking of the mid–'eighties as a deadline for participative legislation in the European Community—not a time–scale to induce the pressing of panic buttons, but a clear warning to member states without participative systems to take firm action in consultation with all the interested parties. The Draft Statute for European Companies will follow a similar timepath. Its approval by the Council is unlikely, at least until after the Commission has submitted an amended version of the Fifth Directive to the Council.

In some EEC member states it is laid down that the decision–making bodies of companies must include members appointed by the workers, or whose appointment has been approved by them. In others, participation in the decision–making bodies of private companies is neither statutory nor generally practised, except in the public sector where throughout the Community companies have to allow worker representatives or unions to participate in their decision–making bodies. A few words about the trends in member states in the field of worker participation will probably help the reader.

Five member states will need to change their systems quite substantially in order to conform to the plans put forward by the Commission. These are Belgium, France, Ireland, Italy, and Britain. In four of these five member states things are happening which suggest gradual progress towards the Commission's ideas. In Belgium, the major trade unions have been looking at worker participation, both separately and together. The possibility of introducing supervisory boards in large companies is also being considered, following an agreement on economic and social policy in 1977 with the Coalition Government. In Ireland, a recent law introduces a system giving workers in five large state enterprises the right to appoint up to one–third of the board members of the enterprises. Since the majority of board members will have no executive functions, the resulting structure will be dualist in reality, if not in name.

In Italy, despite traditional opposition to the idea of worker participation by the trade unions, they are considering suggestions made by some leading politicians for some form of worker participation in certain state enterprises. France has worker participation in theory, but in practice there is much to be done. The subject is mentioned in the preamble to the French constitution, and French law lays down provisions for participation by workers in public companies. The Sudreau Committee recommended a new form of participation to be known as co–supervision. The present relative weakness of collective bargaining and the mutual suspicion and hostility of employers and most trade unions makes any radical extension of participation a difficult task. The British position has already been discussed and the established systems of participation in Germany, Holland, Denmark, and Luxembourg are well known.

The Commission's Green Paper on the subject of participation, published in 1975, analysed the participative trends in member states and made suggestions of a general kind to stimulate debate between all the interested parties, bearing in mind that the discussion on the Fifth Directive has dragged on since 1972, when it was first introduced. The Green Paper stressed the Commission's firm conviction that the basic principles of the Directive were still valid. These are, first, the introduction of a dualist board system, thus drawing a clear institutional distinction between those with legal responsibility for the management of public companies and those with the responsibility for supervising management. Second, the chance for workers in large public companies to participate in appointing those who supervise management. Of course, legislative action at Community level must always take account of different national situations that have resulted from different historical development. On the other hand it is vital to adopt, with the least possible delay, flexible minimum Community standards of participation. One reason for this relates to the difficult industrial and economic problems which many companies are facing. It is often necessary in these circumstances to make radical changes fairly quickly. This can be done more effectively and with less disruption to industrial relations by involving those immediately concerned in the task of finding solutions which they can understand and accept.

During the transitional period suggested by the Commission, four possibilities might emerge: the dualist board system with workers on the supervisory board; the dualist system with a workers' representative institution at company level; the single board system with workers on it; and the single board system with a workers' representative institution. These, then, are the main themes of the arguments surrounding worker participation—diverse industrial relations systems, political pressures and the need to reform and widen company law on a Euro–basis to facilitate cross–frontier activities, and the full development of the Community's resources. The key legislation will probably not be approved by the Council for some time yet, perhaps until 1980–81, and the transitional period is still being discussed. The Fifth Directive will probably take the form of a framework, giving a range of options and a phasing–in period for a specific participative system. The commission feels that this should be the dualist board structure with workers on the supervisory board, but the nine member states will decide, through the Council of Ministers.

Finally, it should be remembered that those countries which already have workers on boards, all have long experience of works council systems designed to increase industrial efficiency as well as industrial democracy. In other words, worker participation is a psychological threshold to be crossed gently and firmly with one's eyes wide open, not a precipice to be rushed over wildly and blindly. It is ethically right, democratically desirable, and likely to be economically beneficial. It is designed to change the adversary–style of industrial relations for something more cooperative and productive. This is why the Bullock Report, bold and imaginative though it was, missed the whole point. Advocating worker directors on unitary boards without the supporting framework of works councils, and with responsibilities only to the unions who select or elect them, is a sure way of making the boardroom a battlefield, strewn with vetoes and venom.

Sidney and Beatrice Webb are reputed to have said that 'a worker on a board is as useless as a financier at a forge'. It is not clear, however, whether the Webbs were being critical of workers or financiers. But one thing is certain: worker directors are coming, not because of arid, academic formulae emanating from Brussels, but by the sheer pressure of social forces on Western industrial society. Financiers, like everyone else in industry and politics, will have to help to forge a system which will give workers more responsibility and the democratic rights in industry which they already enjoy in politics. At first sight, trade unions seem to gain most from these trends, but there is always a price to pay for something valuable. British unions in particular need to mount their biggest ever training exercise to prepare their members for the new responsibilities which are coming their way.

141

15. Incomes policy—has it a European context?

Whether we panic, yawn, or reach for the tranquillizers after seeing or hearing the words 'incomes policy', the fact remains that many European countries have been using incomes policies in various forms for the past 30 years. The frequent changes which have been rung on this theme illustrate the continuing need and the relative failure of the prescriptions which have been tried. Some regard the concept as essential for economic progress; others see it as an irrelevancy, like a blush on a dead man's cheek! It was indeed the possible death of democracy which many people saw in Britain when they looked into the economic abyss in 1975. They were profoundly relieved to have pulled back in time.

European experience shows the value of a permanent modification of collective bargaining in the area of pay negotiations. The spectrum is wide and ranges from the indexation systems in Finland, Holland, Denmark, and Italy, to the concerted action plans of Germany and Sweden. 'Freezes', 'statements of intent', 'norms', 'guidelines', 'legal limits', and 'social contracts', are a few of the phrases in the emotive, controversial vocabulary of incomes policy. Moreover, the distinction between incomes policy, fiscal policy, and monetary policy is not clear–cut. In Britain, Holland, and Sweden, for example, there have been attempts to influence the size of wage increases by trading tax reductions against lower wage demands. Incomes policies do have a Euro–context, in the sense that persistently high unemployment and recurring inflation are forcing wage and price disciplines on many countries.

Britain, Denmark, France, Germany, Holland, and Sweden are examples of countries where different incomes policy techniques have been tried. Exhortation, centrally–agreed criteria, and legal controls have all been used. But the striking and paradoxical thing about an incomes policy is that most new governments when they come to power abjure the idea, but resort to it after a year or two in office, either just before or after a crisis. Inevitably, therefore, incomes policies have restrictive connotations in the public mind. When an incomes policy, however justified it might be in terms of a particular economic crisis, is screwed down on top of a national wage structure bristling with anomalies and inequities—as in Britain—the resentment felt by certain groups is obvious and understandable. It is often forgotten that wage injustices are also frozen in a 'wages freeze'.

All this leaves disgruntled workers vulnerable to seduction by the political left or right, whose motives may be genuine, sinister, or just naïve. The trouble is that few people are prepared to speak the truth and say that in principle a country, like a family, must live within its income or take the consequences. Even the voluntary wage restraint embodied in the social contract in Britain recently was sold to trade unionists as a way of keeping Labour in office, and not as something intrinsically desirable and the only feasible alternative to a statutory wages policy. The problem is that every industrial and professional group sincerely believes its wage and salary claims are justified at a level more optimistic than is economically possible when all the claims are added together. Multiunion structures in many industries perpetuate this competitive thrust and make it impossible for free collective bargaining to work for very long, or to be conducted responsibly, even though its advocates may be sincere in wishing this to happen.

No one who looks seriously at what a democratic society means can come to any other conclusion than that there must be a continuing public presence in the collective bargaining situation. That presence is probably best provided by trade unions themselves acting collectively. 'The only liberty I mean,' Burke once said, 'is a liberty connected with order.' To think that any country can manage without planning its wages sectors is surely as naïve as to suppose that turning off all the traffic lights in London or Paris during the rush hour would not be disastrous. Of course, in theory civilized people should be capable of self–discipline at all times, but we are a long way from that blue–sky Utopia. Our laws and police force remind us that freedom in a democratic society is a very relative thing. Absolute freedom is anarchy. That is why talk of free collective bargaining is meaningless, whatever euphemisms are used to cloak its implications.

Moreover some of those on the political left who are rabid in their advocacy of a wages free–for–all, probably support political systems which would not give any bargaining freedom to trade unions. Paradoxically, too, the countless injustices in British wage structures, for example, are a powerful indictment of the 'free' system. The jungle is indeed a fine place for the lions, but what about the rest of the inhabitants? Some people wish to hang on to free collective bargaining because it is an area in which they can create the greatest industrial disturbance. But here is the crowning irony: incomes policy, which is the price society pays for its profligacy, has as its most bitter opponents the advocates of the free system whose failure has made incomes policy necessary in the first place. In theory it should be possible to combine free collective bargaining with financial and political responsibility. But people are human and fallible. They are sometimes envious of those with higher incomes and often genuinely aggrieved at wage differentials which are unfair and inexplicable.

Nor is it easy for a trade union leader to argue for an incomes policy, even

143

of limited duration. The enormity of asking workers to give up or modify, even temporarily, their right to bargain with their only saleable asset, their labour, must be understood. Furthermore, workers will not opt for training or retraining for skilled work unless the rewards are reasonable and employers are free to obey the rules of the market and pay realistic wages. These arguments, however, do not diminish the stubborn fact against which Britain and other European countries have bumped their noses frequently during the past 30 years. A complete free–for–all in wages, particularly in a society with a large public sector, leads inevitably to inflation. Clearly, incomes policies are not a panacea designed to bring higher living standards automatically. A genuine increase in productivity and efficiency is needed before an increase in real wages can be sustained. But a sensible national system to settle basic wages is certainly not inimical to higher productivity. Indeed, without a central policy incentive schemes and justifiable differentials tend to get lost in the avalanche.

Since the last war the governments in Britain, Denmark, and Holland have at various times intervened directly in the outcome of collective bargaining. In Sweden, on the other hand, there has been no state machinery dealing with incomes policy since 1938, and the trade union and employers' central federations have been responsible for the implementation and formulation of such policies. In France, incomes policies are seen as a necessary part of economic planning exclusive of collective bargaining. In other words, incomes policy is enforced via the employer rather than the trade union. This approach has been used since 1966 in a whole series of agreements between government, employers and trade unions, designed to achieve effective price controls. As part of these agreements, firms who introduce excessive price increases forfeit certain financial incentives which are otherwise available to them. This controversial system implicitly controls wages, since a firm conceding wage increases above the national norm is unable to pass these on in price rises. It must seek to offset them by productivity improvements.

In Britain the responsibility for observing pay limits was also shifted to the employer in the incomes policies introduced in 1975, 1976, and 1977. In the private sector the policy was policed by not allowing firms which granted excessive wage settlements to pass these on in higher prices to the consumer. In addition to this indirect control of prices, the Government would not give financial assistance under the 1975 Industry Act to firms who were considered to have broken the pay limit—nor were Government contracts awarded to firms who so behaved. In the nationalized sectors during the social contract period, the government would not finance breaches of the policy by providing subsidies, or extra borrowing, or higher prices to the consumer. Local authorities were similarly restricted by relating the govern-

144

ment rate support grant only to pay settlements within the specified limits. Between 1966 and 1970, and 1972 and 1974, statutory incomes policies existed in Britain and unions were held responsible for ensuring the observance of the pay limits laid down. It was a criminal offence under the Prices and Incomes Act for a trade union to take industrial action to force an employer to pay a wage increase which the Government had vetoed after an adverse report from the Prices and Incomes Board. It is fair to say, however that the social contract was not only more effective as a form of voluntary wage restraint, but highly beneficial to the British economy, reducing the rate of inflation from a staggering 26 per cent to below 8 per cent.

Sweden offers the best example of an incomes policy conducted solely by the central organizations of employers and trade unions. In the early 'fifties, after a wage freeze lasting two years, the Swedish Employers' Confederation and the Confederation of Swedish Trade Unions developed the practice of negotiating future wage increases for Swedish manual workers annually. The system has two important features. First, it tries to arrange simultaneously settlements for the greater part of the Swedish economy and second, it sets out to narrow the spread of pay differentials. This is an effective way of eliminating low wages, though the narrowing of differentials raises other problems. The second or 'solidarity' aspect of the system is dependent on the first or 'centralized' aspect. It requires central organizations of employers and unions possessing considerable power and influence over their constituent members. The loose confederations of employers and unions in Britain, for example, are not equipped to operate in this way. The Swedish Government only directly affects collective bargaining via the annual budget, and the unions and employers operate the incomes policy. The collective bargaining partners have also established their own expert agency with the task of analysing the economic role of wages.

In Holland, incomes policy was introduced immediately after the war when the country's economy was in a critical condition due to wartime devastation. A Foundation of Labour was established by the unions and employers with the aim of promoting 'better understanding between the two sides of industry'. For some years the system worked well and all wage increases had to be absorbed by an increase in labour productivity, though exceptionally high increases were given to correct certain cases of hardship—especially in the agricultural field. This system seemed to work well, mainly because of the strong spirit of cooperation between the unions and employers which were rooted in the experiences of the Second World War. A Social Economic Council was set up in 1950 with more flexible ideas, one of which was to recommend that increases in the average wage rates should be given in proportion to increases in the real national income.

145

Since then several Government interventions in wage bargaining have been necessary, a minimum wage law was introduced in 1965, and wage indexation had been extended to many industries by 1971. After a breakdown in the collective bargaining arrangements, a statutory incomes policy was introduced in 1976, followed by a resumption of automatic wage indexation.

In Denmark, index–linked wages have operated continuously since 1945, and collective agreements have on average lasted two years. When Danish Governments tried to end indexation in 1970 and 1973, they met stiff opposition from the trade unions, the only concession being given in 1973 when the government was allowed to substitute a tax–free allowance for the first three cost–of–living rises in 1974. In March of the following year, the government gave statutory support to its incomes policy, the effect of which was to give legal backing to the flat–rate cost–of–living increases in wages. The Government also agreed about this time to give financial assistance to industry if indexation led to more than two increases in 1976. Some years previously the Government had actually agreed to reimburse industry when large cost–of–living adjustments were made with a view to preserving industrial competitiveness. An incomes policy was introduced in 1976 limiting wage increases to six per cent and a further short–term incomes policy of a statutory kind was introduced in March 1977.

Incomes policies do have a European context, in the sense that they are being consistently tried in many European countries, all with different styles of collective bargaining reflecting their particular values and cultural characteristics. The Austrian system, for example, rests on a spirit of national consensus and social partnership, but other countries have felt the need to maintain the purity of the adversary process. In Switzerland, government intervention is reduced to an absolute minimum and collective bargaining remains an essentially private system; while in other countries governments have come to play an active, significant, and even indispensable role. Moreover other stages of the bargaining process reveal differences of an important kind. Union recognition is a critical issue in the UK, but not vital in Belgium, Denmark, and West Germany. Recourse to conciliation services is compulsory in Finland, but entirely voluntary in other countries.

European experience suggests that we need to be more rational and less emotional about incomes and collective bargaining. We do not need permanent, formal incomes policies—they involve economic and political costs out of all proportion to any possible benefits. What is needed is an attitude towards incomes and bargaining based on common sense and expressed in words which ordinary people understand. When it comes to the crunch most workpeople realize that 'free' collective bargaining is a form of anarchy which can never produce a civilized and fair wage structure. The much–vaunted free system has produced the tangle of wage injustices which bedevil our industrial relations system. The criteria for success are not the skill, effort, or responsibility of workpeople, but the strength or weakness of the union concerned and whether the industry involved is old and declining or new and expanding. Free collective bargaining is neither fair nor efficient and stands condemned by the wage structures it has created—and yet it still has passionate advocates. These fall into two categories. One group naïvely, though sincerely, believes that the working of market forces will produce a fair and efficient result on their pay claim, especially if they are in a prosperous industry. This narrow though understandable view overlooks the position of other workers in the declining private sectors, or in the public services where there are often no profits but still the desire to keep up with the wages leaders.

The second group of 'free bargaining' advocates are more concerned with exploiting the understandable frustrations of low-paid workers or inequities in the wages structure, especially if the groups involved are doing hazardous, responsible, or vital work. In Britain in particular, the advantages of the normal market processes of pay–setting are often put by learned professors and economists, who are concerned with market adjustments but not the injustices and human problems the system creates. Many trade union leaders and politicians, aware that a planned system of collective bargaining would deprive trade unions of much of their *raison d'être,* take the easy way out and call for free collective bargaining, so pandering to individual selfishness instead of contributing to new thinking. Ironically, the same leaders usually call for planning and greater fairness in society generally.

Other trade union leaders have genuinely tried to tiptoe on the edge of credibility by referring to an 'orderly return to free collective bargaining'— surely a contradiction in terms spelling economic suicide. And suicide must be bad, whether you queue for it or drift into it slowly. There were many red faces among trade unions during the turbulent early months of 1979. The weakness of the free–for–all solution is its social crudity and the strains it puts on democratic institutions—assuming, of course, that all its advocates wish to see those institutions preserved. Economic realism must be reached by a saner route, involving less hardship and disruption. To aim for it without a plan is asking for responsibility without leadership. Those who believe that by some magic a free bargaining situation would induce responsible behaviour are naïve, foolish, or forgetful.

A planned approach to incomes is needed for three reasons: as a shield against economic catastrophe, as a bridge to a new bargaining system, and as a platform from which to launch an inquiry into wage relativities. In Britain, incomes policies have been mainly responses to crises and the second and third aspects have never been taken seriously. In Germany and Sweden,

147

however, and to a lesser extent in Denmark and Holland, all three aspects are being used with a fair amount of success. There is no blueprint for a European incomes policy. Each country must devise its own approach to fit its own collective bargaining system. The aim should be to have an orderly growth of incomes, linked to economic resources, and to preserve free bargaining arrangements within that framework, and the love of the ritual which go with those arrangements.

There is a strong case, too, for examining wage relativities, perhaps, in Britain, through a revived Prices and Incomes Board or Differentials Commission which would have the necessary time and detachment for such a sensitive task. It would be desirable if this body had permanence, through all–party support. Politicians, however, would have to decide on the role of nationalized industries. Should they be regarded as a public service or should they pay their way in strictly business terms? If the former, should there be a limit to subsidies given, and do not subsidies presuppose extra responsibilities on union bargainers who can operate without the check of the financial stringency? But if the balancing of the books has to be the rule, who ensures that workers in the nationalized sector get fair rewards and keep up with the private sector? Any such system would produce endless arguments, especially in Britain, due to the myriad institutions and intricate patterns of relativities; but at least they would be within a framework of economic reality.

It was Samuel Butler who said that 'all progress is based upon a universal innate desire on the part of every organism to live beyond its income'; but this is a luxury we cannot afford in today's crisis–ridden society. Learning to live within one's income is good national housekeeping as well as sound domestic strategy. It is a concept which even the critics of the idea at national level apply to their own affairs. But the most compelling argument for the injection of more realism into collective bargaining is to ensure the preservation of our democratic system and the supremacy of our freely–elected government. During the 'sixties and 'seventies British governments fought out single-handed a series of duels with trade unions on incomes policy and industrial relations policy, and lost on both issues. The merits of the particular arguments are not relevant. What is important is that a country cannot be run in this way. The fact that trade unions kept on talking and are still talking through bodies like the NEDC shows that they understand that such conduct ultimately harms everyone.

This points the way that the debate on the future of incomes policy in Britain should go. It is a question of incorporating the realities of policy and rulemaking in our society into the machinery of government, in such a way as to recognize the legitimate interests of the various parties and to put the government above the battle as the representative of the broader national

148

interest. There are two sources of guidance, one from British past history, when governments have had to struggle to survive against the pressures of power blocs, and the other from attempts by other European nations to solve the same problem. On the first point, mediaeval parliaments in Britain were based on the sensible assumption that if there were powerful barons in the country whose understanding and agreement had to be obtained before any common policy could be enforced (and taxes raised), then it was far easier if these groups could be gathered together, the common problems examined, and a certain unity obtained. The barons could not then escape responsibility for the rules and their enforcement.

It is this gentle therapy which is being tentatively tried in discussions about annual talks in Britain between the Government, the TUC and the CBI on the state of the economy, and collective bargaining possibilities. The price of having one's say at this level (which is difficult to refuse) is to match words with deeds. The object is to get greater mutual understanding, to have an open record of views expressed and to give greater legitimacy to any rules or policies which have been endorsed by such a body. Thus the extra power given to pressure groups by giving them a say in the determination of national economic policies is balanced by more involvement and more obligations.

This brings us to the second point, which is that various European countries have set up a range of bodies varying from advisory planning organizations of the British NEDC type to virtual third chambers like the French Economic and Social Council, whose powers are set out in the Constitution. In Belgium, a Central Economic Council was created in 1948 and a National Council of Labour in 1952. The second body deals with social objectives and has been kept as a separate body to overcome Labour's fear that, if only an economic council existed, economic efficiency would take priority over all other considerations.

In the Netherlands, a Social and Economic Council was set up in 1950 and has proved extremely useful. In fact, it was because three of the original members of the European Community had bodies of this kind that the Treaty of Rome established an Economic and Social Committee, appointed by the Council of Ministers as 'representative of the various categories of economic and social life'. In certain cases the Council of Ministers has to seek the advice of this body, while in others consultation is optional. The advice does not have to be taken but some important interests are represented and their views are given due weight.

If this European experience is to be heeded—and it would be wise for Britain to do so—it seems there are two broad possibilities for developing the national dialogue which might create the right mood for collective bargaining. NEDC could be expanded and made more accountable. Edward

149

Heath was pressing for this in the election campaign of October 1974. He wanted NEDC work to be extended, formalized, and conducted before the media so that those taking part could be held to what they had said and undertaken at the Council. The second option would be to expand the House of Lords to take representatives from the various pressure groups. If this was linked to a select committee system, the case of the pressure groups could be put and members prepared for broader debates in the House, during which the country's industrial options could be clearly stated.

It is time for radical new thinking on incomes policy. The sterile repetition of free collective bargaining slogans help no one to understand our real economic problems, or that in a democratic society freedom is always relative. There are only two ways of getting people to work together—one is force, the other is the observance of laws based on consent. We must learn to live within our income as a nation. All other incomes–policy problems are secondary to this. The TUC, CBI and the Government must work together to define the economic parameters within which the nation can live without worry or fear. Unless sensible wage–restraint can be achieved by consent, as a prelude to the gradual removal of the countless anomalies in our wage structures, then pressure groups will begin to defy democratically–elected governments. It is surely better to try the institutional alternatives which are already working on the Continent than to allow force and civil disorder to become the preferred solution for influential sections of the community.

Part 4
Future developments

_____

16. The European Parliament—its impact

Churchill's comment that 'democracy was the worst form of government, except all those other forms which have been tried from time to time', has a special relevance for the newly–elected European Parliament. This is the first time *real* democracy has been tried in the European Community and it is likely to prove painful in the early stages. No one expects sudden or even slow miracles from the new Parliament, which has still very few real powers, despite its grandiose title; but its representative character does mark the first step in bringing democratic accountability to the Community's institutions. At a time of slack water in the tide of European affairs, the challenge is whether these Euro–Parliamentarians can speed up the tortuously slow evolution of its representative role and use the Parliament as a catalyst to introduce fresh thinking, new policies and the political will to make progress with Europe's industrial problems— especially unemployment, on which the solution of many other problems hinges.

The 410 new members of the Parliament are an impressive array of political figures, many of them eminent and some still members of their national parliaments. It seems unlikely that they will be satisfied with the mainly consultative role of the old Parliament. On the other hand, constitutional changes to the powers of Parliament are a sensitive topic and raise emotional arguments among the federalists and functionalists. They force people to think about the future of the Community. In the democratic tradition all elected parliaments are divided into political groups, the largest group having the right to form a government and rule, though remaining responsible to the people through the parliament. Unless the European Parliament is to remain a toothless tiger, the logic of this democratic evolution seems inescapable, though the time–scale will be long. The fact that direct elections to the Parliament have started this democratic train moving has prompted everyone to try the signals and inspect the track! But the Community must move forward, even if it muddles along; the alternative is for it to disintegrate or slowly wither away. The democratic legitimacy and potential political authority of the European Parliament make it an ideal lever for change, though the price of boldness will be to raise the ideological arguments about the future of the Community.

This controversial strategy is on balance justified for another reason. The tendency of the Council of Ministers in recent years has been to search for a consensus on most issues and this, allied to the wide economic divergences between member states, has limited its capacity for innovative political leadership. After the successful early completion of the Customs Union, the Commission's mandate from the Treaty of Rome has often seemed uncertain—a matter of deducing consequences from it rather than obeying directions in it, and its capacity for innovation has accordingly been diminished. Power has been shifted to the Council of Ministers and this change has been symbolized by regular meetings of heads of governments. Prestigious though these are, they have not guaranteed any acceleration or simplification in the decision–making process. This has depended on the political will among the member governments. The statesmen who manage European affairs in the coming years will need to exercise imagination and courage, as the penalties for failure will become increasingly severe.

The European Parliament is now the largest political forum in Europe. It is the only Community institution in which both the representatives of government and opposition parties in all member states sit together—and the only body that meets and reaches its decisions in public sessions. Members take their seats in the House according to political conviction rather than nationally. They have formed six European political groups which usually speak and vote together. These groups, which disregard national divisions, give the Parliament its special character, its political drive and its sense of purpose. They are the Socialists, the Christian Democrats, the Liberal and Democratic Group, the European Progressive Democrats, the European Conservatives and the Communists and allies. Members of the European Parliament are not, of course, obliged to join a group and a few members remain unattached. The European Parliament has three main tasks:

1. To tell the Council of Ministers what it thinks of the Commission's legislative proposals.
2. With the Council, to hammer out the Community Budget.
3. To exert some political control over the Council and Commission.

Law–making in the Community is a triangular process. The Commission proposes and, after consulting Parliament, the Council decides. On a great many topics the Parliament must be consulted on the Commission's proposals before the Council can come to a decision on them. In practice, the Parliament is consulted on all important matters, even when this is not expressly stipulated in the treaties.

Parliament's opinions, given in the form of resolutions prepared by specialist committees and voted on in full sitting, influence the final legislative texts. Apart from the detailed and expert scrutiny which they reflect, they carry political weight with the Council of Ministers when decisions are made. National governments know that the same political forces they face at home are represented in the European Parliament. There are twelve specialist committees in the Parliament, broadly matching the various areas of Commission activity. They are as follows:

1. Political affairs
2. Legal affairs
3. Economic and monetary affairs
4. Budgets
5. Social affairs, employment, and education
6. Agriculture
7. Regional Policy, Regional Planning, and Transport
8. Environmental, Public Health and Consumer Protection
9. Energy and Research
10. External Economic Relations
11. Development and Cooperation
12. Rules of Procedure and Petitions

The year begins for the European parliament on the second Tuesday in March, with the appointment of President and Vice–President and the members of the Parliamentary Committees. During the year the Parliament meets once a month on average and sits for a week at a time. Most of the Parliament's meetings are held in Strasbourg at the Palais de l'Europe. Other sittings are held at the European Centre in Luxembourg, where the Parliament's secretariat works. No decision has been taken yet about a permanent meeting–place. Although the sittings of Parliament are open to the public, the Committee meetings are not, unless otherwise stated. The preparatory work for the Parliament's sittings is done in the committees, who appoint 'rapporteurs' to draw up reports on specific questions. A report comprises a motion, together with an explanatory statement which gives the result of the committee's vote. The reports of the various committees are laid before the House which then votes on the motions for a resolution.

History shows that all Parliaments gain influence through their money power and their inquisitorial functions. The European Parliament has some powers in both these fields which it may well extend, now it is genuinely representative. Parliament can, by a censure motion carried by a two–thirds majority of the votes cast and representing a majority of its members, force the Commission to resign as a body. It is possible that the special committees of the Parliament might wish to hold public hearings on various subjects at which officials would be required to testify. Such hearings would have the advantage of satisfying public opinion that mistaken policies can be investigated and those responsible held accountable. The Commission has already to submit an annual report on the activities of the three Communities to

Parliament and Commissioners take part in the meetings of the parliamentary committees, where they discuss their plans and programmes of action. The European Commission is also accountable to Parliament for the standpoint it adopts at meetings of the Council. Members of the European Parliament may address written questions to the Commission. These and the answers given are published in the official journal of the European Community. Subject to certain preliminaries, members may put oral questions too, without debate.

So the Parliament has already achieved a fair measure of effective supervision, mainly in respect of the Commission's own decisions, which are usually of an executive nature. More important, however, are the decisions taken by the Council on proposals from the Commission. Since the latter is accountable to the Parliament, a permanent dialogue has been developed between the two bodies and this enables Parliament to exert influence up to the final stage, which is the Council's decision. To this dialogue with the Commission has now been added a dialogue between Parliament and the Council, via the consultation procedure within the legislative process and the consideration of the budget. Deciding on the budget itself is a matter for both Parliament and the Council. Originally, the European Parliament had only advisory responsibilities in this field, but the introduction of the Community's 'own resources' scheme (based on import duties and levies and, in principle, part of VAT revenue) made it necessary for Parliament to have certain real budgetary powers. Parliament and Council now share responsibility for the Community budget, which covers the income and expenditure of all the Community institutions. The draft budget is drawn up by the Commission and considered in two stages by the Council and Parliament alternately, who each finalize one category of expenditure.

There are two categories of expenditure defined by the Treaty—'obligatory' and 'non–obligatory'. The Council controls the former as it concerns expenditure arising from acts adopted in accordance with the Treaty. On all other expenditure, Parliament has, within certain limits, the last word. The European Parliament may, if there are overwhelming reasons for doing so, reject the budget in its entirety. Such a rejection makes it impossible for the European Commission to implement the budget, so that fresh proposals then become necessary. This naturally strengthens the hand of Parliament in its discussions with the Council. The budget procedure is as follows. The Commission submits a preliminary draft to the Council—and, for information, to the Parliament. The Council draws up the draft budget and presents this to Parliament, which can propose changes to both 'obligatory' and 'non–obligatory' expenditure. During the next stage, the Council can take the final decision on all items of 'obligatory' expenditure and can re–amend 'non–obligatory' items. At the final stage, the European

Parliament can take the final decision on 'non–obligatory' items—and either adopts the budget as a whole or rejects it as a whole.

From the point of view of Parliament, Community laws are enacted in the following way:

1. The Commission prepares a proposal which is forwarded to the Council and sent for information to the European Parliament.
2. The Council decides to consult Parliament and officially forwards the Commission proposal to the Parliament, with a request for an opinion.
3. Parliament gives its opinion, which may call for amendments to the proposal—and this is sent to the Council and the Commission.
4. The Commission may amend the proposal in accordance with Parliament's opinion (or for other reasons). The Council discusses the Commission proposal and takes the final decision.

This very brief outline of the work of the European Parliament brings out the two sanctions it can employ, if it so wishes—the rejection of the whole budget and the dismissal of the Commission. Parliament has flexed its muscles on both issues in recent years, particularly on budget questions, as the 1975 revisions to the Treaty of Rome gave Parliament more control over the Community budget. It has the right to revise, within certain financial limits, those parts of the budget which are not 'obligatory': for example, the regional and social funds, but not the allocations for the Common Agricultural Policy, which are 'obligatory' because they are laid down in the Treaty of Rome.

In December 1978, Parliament felt so strongly about the budget that the 'conciliation procedure' had to be invoked. This involves discussions between parliamentarians and members of the Council and Commission on issues with major financial implications. In this specific case, Parliament attributed the priority of priorities to regional policy and its budgetary expression, bearing in mind the acute industrial problems affecting regions in member countries.

Now direct elections have been held, Parliament is being taken much more seriously. There is much work to be done in the field of public relations. It is not surprising that many people confuse it with the Assembly of the Council of Europe. Others are not sure where it sits—nor is the Parliament, one might add. At present it holds half its monthly meetings in Luxembourg and half in Strasbourg, while the members of the 12 committees spend a great deal of their time in Brussels, quizzing Commission officials. It has been estimated that a huge monthly convoy of removal vans shifts the files and office equipment back and forth between Luxembourg and Strasbourg at a cost of £1 million per year. But Parliament is in the public eye, which is good. Some see it from an aura of hopeful green, others of idyllic rose and yet others of hellfire red.

157

It would not only be premature, but rash, to expect too much too soon, but a number of major consequences are expected from the direct elections. The European Parliament will acquire greater moral authority—its members will be representing 'somebody' and 'somewhere', instead of 'nobody' and 'nowhere'. Secondly, a Parliament doubled in size with full-time members, will be able to conduct its affairs more efficiently, including a more vigorous questioning of the work of the Commission. Thirdly, ordinary people will be involved in Community affairs for the first time, through the elections, and fourthly, national parties will have to become more involved in European affairs with other European parties. Fifthly, industrial affairs will figure much more prominently in the Parliament's work—top trade union leaders now sit in the Parliament. Moreover, the fact that many of the newly–elected Parliamentarians represent industrial con-stituencies means that a great number of day–to–day industrial relations problems will be raised and discussed. The questioning of Commission officials too, will have a hard practical dimension, especially on industrial subjects. From the Commission's viewpoint, the steady trickle of parliamen-tary questions received before direct elections is already becoming a fast-flowing stream and could engulf the Commission, unless remedial action is taken.

The asking of questions symbolizes the democratic accountability of the Commission to parliament and few would complain about that, certainly not the officials of the Commission. But if this accountability is to be squared with the need to maintain a competent civil service function, in terms of producing draft legislation, preparing meetings, and so on, then the resources of the Commission will have to be adjusted to match these dual pressures. There will also be pressures on members of the European Parlia-ment. The average electorate per member is some five or six hundred thousand persons. On this basis, by the way, Luxembourg would be entitled to half a member. It has, in fact, six members. The smaller countries, Benelux, Denmark, and Ireland, are keenly interested in the European Parliament; but they face the problem of the separate or dual mandate, not because of political balance, but because of the sheer limit of available talent.

On the other hand, representatives of small countries can wield more power in the European Parliament than in their own country. An Irish deputy in the European Parliament, for example, represents the equivalent of several national constituencies and has considerable influence on the formulation of the EEC budget, which gives him more influence on national affairs than a junior minister in Dublin. This is especially so in Ireland, which has the largest percentage of agricultural workers in the whole Com-munity, some 28 per cent of the population. At present the Agricultural

Budget absorbs 73 per cent of the whole of the Community's expenditure. On the industrial side there could be equally wide–ranging effects. The applicant countries, Greece, Portugal, and Spain, together with Italy, provide the bulk of the estimated six million migrant workers in the Community. If each citizen of the Community has a right to vote for his European deputy at his place of residence, then the political complexion of many areas will change in relation to national representation. The European Parliament, then, raises a great dilemma. The introduction of democratic accountability was necessary, both as a desirable objective and as a means of blasting the Community clear of its retarding nationalistic forces. But it opens up the issue of the Community's future as surely as prising open an oyster. Whether the pearl inside is federation or a loose–knit jumble of European states remains to be seen. Robert Schuman spoke wisely when he said in 1950: 'Europe will not be built in a day; nor as part of some overall design. It will be built through practical achievements that first create a sense of common purpose'.

17. Enlarging the Community—what effects?

'Where there's a will, there's a way; but where there are several wills, there may be no way', warned Shakespeare. Securing the 'political will' to do something in the European Community has meant getting nine apricots in a row on the Community fruit machine—a favourable political conjuncture only present for short periods of the Community's existence. After enlargement, an even more elusive line of twelve apricots will be a necessary prelude to serious political progress. Just as the search for consensus will be made more difficult politically, the complications of enlargement will initially dilute progress towards coordinating industrial relations' policies, especially in the field of labour legislation. Both Greece and Portugal have 9 million inhabitants and Spain has a population of 35 million. Accession by these three countries will increase the economic and social diversity within the Community and widen the gap in living standards between richer and poorer member states.

Their absorption into the Community will provide a real challenge at a time when the full consequences of the 1973 enlargement are still being felt. Apart from the effects on the agricultural policy, a drastic overhaul of regional and social policies will have to be carried out to ensure that they are effective in an enlarged Community. For Greece, Portugal, and Spain, membership of the Community has advantages which are both political and economic. As members of the Community, they will participate effectively in all important political decisions affecting the Community. They will also benefit from common economic policies, particularly the Common Agricultural Policy and the abolition of trade barriers within the Community. This aspect is important to them as all three countries have a high degree of trade dependence on the Community. They will, of course, also participate in trade arrangements made by the Community with third countries. All three countries compete with Community producers in the production of a number of agricultural products. This could lead to friction between the producers in the Community and the applicant countries who are seeking to sell their products on the same market (wine, olive oil, citrus fruits, and vegetables).

The total vineyard area in Spain, for example, is greater than in France and Spanish wine is sold more cheaply than French. Spain and the other two applicants, however, will buy more cereals, butter, and wheat from their

160

northern neighbours thereby reducing current surpluses or near–surpluses in these products. In the current Community of the nine, 42 per cent of those employed work in the industrial sector, but the figures are considerably lower in the applicant countries. In Spain, industry accounts for 38 per cent of those employed, in Portugal 33 per cent, and in Greece 28 per cent. The main difficulties likely to complicate industrial relations activities are the economic disparities between the applicant countries and the Community. Despite varying standards of living and economic development, the three applicant countries are each poorer than any of the nine Community nations. The disparities within the present Community are already troubling. But while the differences in terms of gross domestic product per inhabitant is 1 to 5 between Calabria (Italy) and Hamburg (Germany), it will be 1 to 15 between Braganza (Portugal) and Hamburg. Nevertheless, it is a happy coincidence that Greece, Spain, and Portugal have simultaneously managed the transition from totalitarianism to parliamentary democracy. Their applications for Community membership constitute an offer which the nine member states cannot refuse. But this implies a willingness to pay the price.

Politically it is imperative for the Community to consolidate the over-throw of the Mediterranean dictatorships and sustain the new democracies. A regression to authoritarian regimes of the right or left, would be tragic for social democracy. The surest way to support the new regimes is to give the countries concerned the economic benefits of Community Membership, such as they are, as in the last resort political stability rests on economic strength. It is also important to show that the Community is not exclusively a rich man's club of northern nations. But institutionally, however, the nine member states are already a good deal more cumbersome than the original six. The Council of Ministers sometimes resembles a mass meeting rather than an embryo European government. With the addition of new ministers, new members of Parliament and new languages, progress towards majority voting in the Council, and the emergence of European political parties in the European Parliament, is bound to be more complicated. With the accession of Britain, Denmark, and Ireland in 1973, Community institutions remained essentially the same as those which had operated for the original Community of six. But three further members will double the original number of nations for which the institutions were designed and criticism has already been voiced about the creaking institutional machinery.

The European Commission's 'fresco' or overview of the enlargement process emphasizes the necessity of gradually resolving all these problems. Britain, Ireland, and Denmark had a transitional period of more than four years before fully integrating their economies into the European Community. With Greece, Spain, and Portugal the Commission has proposed a minimum of five years and a maximum of ten. It is expected to take place in two stages. During the first five years, the new members will implement Community policy to the fullest possible extent in the free circulation of goods, competition rules, agriculture, free movement of workers, Community budget contributions, and external relations. After five years the Commission and Council will review each new member's progress and determine whether a continued transition period of up to five years is necessary. The Commission 'fresco' also stresses that while the Community is bound to be realistic about the negative aspects of enlargement, the positive elements of political commitment, additional markets, and the growth dynamism of the applicant countries should also be taken into account. Enlargement will challenge the already sluggish picture in the nine member countries. The economists theorize that the annual growth rate for the nine member states will need to be at least four per cent and for the applicant countries six per cent to make a resolution of all these difficulties possible.

It is also felt that if Community growth should decline to less than 2 per cent, the applicant countries could soon be dragged down to near–stagnation. The internal regional imbalances in the three new countries are best exemplified by Spain, where only seven of the 50 provinces have *per capita* incomes above the national average. There is likely to be intense competition for the Community's Regional and Social Funds. From the participants' viewpoint it will be as controversial as spreading the same amount of jam over 12 slices of bread instead of 9. So enlargement is a step that cannot be taken lightly, nor without adequate preparation. Politically, enlargement is important for the Community and the applicants. For Greece, Spain, and Portugal, the Community represents a buttress for their fledgling democracies. For the Community, enlargement is a chance for it to extend and consolidate its position in a wider European dimension. There are qualitative differences on the economic side, however, as the 1973 enlargement brought into the Community three countries whose economies were broadly similar to those of the six and therefore more easily assimilated. The gap between the present applicants and the nine is much more pronounced. The GNP *per capita* of Spain and Greece is only half the Community average and a third that of its richest member states. Portugal's position is even weaker.

These points raise not only the questions of how easily the Community can absorb these three economies without damaging its own, but also to what extent the applicant countries can survive economically within a competitive common market. The other institutional difficulties are obvious: the size of the Commission, the number of working languages, and the principle of proportionality in the appointments to higher positions. The introduction of three new languages would be stultifying, though it might be

162

feasible just to add Spanish as a working language. Equally, a Commission of sixteen would be difficult to manage as a working unit, though an extension of the management committee procedure, which is permitted by the Treaty, might help to simplify the taking of smaller decisions. But the social aspects of enlargement pose the real problems. The three candidate countries still lack an effective industrial relations structure, especially as far as trade union organization is concerned. For example, the Greek Government has already informed the Commission that it will be unable to apply the directive on collective dismissals in the near future, due to the absence of effective worker representation at shop–floor level without which it would be difficult to implement and police such Euro–laws.

Obviously, a realistic phasing–in period is the answer, though this will have to be devised carefully to avoid the suspicion that preferential treatment is being given to the applicant countries on industrial relations topics. The overall industrial relations picture does not give unlimited room for manoeuvre. Too much dilution of the Commission's proposed labour legislation in order to accommodate the candidate countries, could reduce the labour standards to little more than the level of ILO Conventions—or the European Social Charter, which would be of little interest to advanced industrial countries. In nautical terms, the convoy needs to travel at the speed of the slowest ship, so to speak, but one needs to have a minimum of movement to ensure reaching the appointed destination!

Further sensitivities in the industrial relations field stem from the fact that none of the Portuguese trade union organizations are members of the ETUC. The main central trade union organization (Intersyndicate) is intent on maintaining a unitary system of representation, rather than the system of multiple federations desired by the Socialist party. Outside the Intersyndicate, about thirty other organizations, mainly in the service sector, are grouped in the 'Carta Oberta'. The agricultural workers are organized in the Confederation of Portuguese farmers (CAP), while the small farmers are in another organization called MARV.

Doubts still persist about the representativeness and authenticity of Portuguese employers' associations, which were closely associated in the past with the state machinery. The Greek General Workers Federation is a member of the ETUC, and few problems should therefore be experienced in involving its members at an early date in the various consultative bodies linked with the Commission. Spain, as the most industrially advanced of the three applicant countries, provides an example of the complications which enlargement will bring to the industrial relations scene. The UGT (*Union General Trabajadores*) is affiliated to the Spanish Socialist Workers' Party, but the CCOO (*Comisiones Obreros*) is affiliated to the Spanish Communist Party. The UGT and STV (*Sindicate Trabajadores Vasco*) are affiliated to

163

the ETUC. A problem of representativeness seems likely to arise in this area. The primary employers' organization CEOE (*Conferaciones Empresares Organizacion Espanol*) is the federation which speaks officially for business to government. The second employers' group is the *Cirulo Empresarios,* covering the 100 largest employers in the public and private sectors.

Spanish industrial relations are emerging from an era of control and domination by a vertical syndicate system. Direct involvement by the Franco government in industrial relations took various forms. It included control of worker representatives, control of the data system used as a basis for adjusting compensation, and control of the entire system for resolving disputes. The problems are basically those of transition. The prolonged illegality of the trade union movement has not prepared it for a free industrial relations situation. Independent trade unions, collective bargaining and the right to strike now exist, but they have not emerged through a gradual evolutionary process. So the participants in the industrial relations scene are forced to play difficult and sometimes impossible roles. They have not been rehearsed for their parts, so to speak. Furthermore, they believe that the legal structure, the information they work with and the Government are not to be trusted. There are practical problems too—below national level there are virtually no statistics and neither management nor labour have much confidence in the limited statistics now available. There is a dearth of reliable information on wages, labour costs, and productivity. While strikes are now constitutional, debate is going on about wage and price guidelines and the possibility of limiting strikes to economic as opposed to political issues. Procedures are also being examined for resolving industrial disputes.

These sensitive and explosive industrial relations topics are not new and most of them are presenting problems in Community countries at the present time. The difficulty for Spain, Greece, and Portugal is a cumulative one: a combination of controversial industrial relations issues, a new political system, high unemployment, unacceptable levels of inflation, a fragile balance of payments picture and an uncertain economic climate. Key industries in Spain, too, are precisely those which are currently in crisis in the Community (shipbuilding, steel, textiles, and footwear). Various forms of assistance are being used to help construct the new Spanish industrial relations system. Foreign management experts are helping employers with sessions on industrial relations problems, with particular reference to legal strategies to improve the management position. On the trade union side, considerable technical and financial assistance has been given by the IMF (International Metalworkers' Federation) to the UGT. Separate foreign trade union support has gone to the STV and the CCOO. The AFL–CIO has also assisted with training programmes. There is no neatly packaged solution to the transitional industrial relations problems of Greece, Spain, and Portugal.

It is a question of setting out the various options available and encouraging a constructive and democratic dialogue between employers and trade unions. It is interesting to note that the main organizations of employers and trade unions in Spain believe that the close examination of industrial relations practices in Belgium, France, Italy, Germany, Sweden, the UK, and the USA, will be of the most value in their own policy developments. Average productivity in Spain amounts to 55 per cent of average Community productivity, that in Greece to 51 per cent, and that in Portugal to only 33 per cent. The industrial structure consists in the main, particularly in Greece and Portugal, of small firms which account for a large part of the working population and these are protected from external competition by tariff and non–tariff barriers which the Commission itself says are far from negligible, though it is hard to establish the exact level. Internationally competitive companies do exist, but they are often wholly or partly controlled by foreign interests and their development strategies are fixed by the parent company—in other words by the multinationals. In Spain in particular the multinationals frequently operate through a system of concessions. This means that the eventual application of Community competition rules might affect their continued production in certain cases.

The opening of frontiers and lowering of tariff and non–tariff barriers for the three countries and the need to increase productivity in order to withstand Community and international competition, will clearly mean large scale re–structuring of industries in the candidate countries. It will obviously be hard to prevent unemployment figures from rising. Prospects for women in employment is another sensitive area. In 1975, the number of women at work amounted to 19 per cent of the total female population in Spain, 11 per cent in Greece (in 1971), and 18 per cent in Portugal, whereas the Community average was 28 per cent. In addition, many women in the three countries perform seasonal or casual jobs, or work in family concerns. In Greece, the difference between minimum wages for men and women has been reduced to 9 per cent which indicates that discrimination exists, though progress is being made. The Community is faced with the problem, therefore, in applying in Greece, Spain, and Portugal, the directives on equal treatment in respect of pay, recruitment, and working conditions. Greek and Portuguese labour law already contain certain minimum provisions, but there is a long way to go. The directives on collective redundancies and the protection of employees' rights in the event of mergers need also to be introduced. Deadlines, however liberally conceived, need to be established as quickly as possible.

Migrant workers are another important issue in the enlargement 'fresco'.

165

For the three new countries, migration not only represents an outlet relieving the pressures on the domestic labour markets, but also produces a substantial inflow of valuable currency remitted by migrant workers. Figures for 1976 indicate an approximate total of $1\frac{1}{4}$ million workers from the candidate countries in the Community, of which 448 000 are Spanish nationals, 239 000 Greek, and 569 000 Portuguese. Apart from the effects of enlargement on the flow of these migrant workers, the Commission intends to remove existing discrimination in respect of recruitment and working conditions for those migrant workers from the applicant countries who are already working in the Community. The deadline dates are the dates of accession.

The enlargement of the European Community, then, meets specific political needs namely, to consolidate the democratic regimes recently restored in the three countries after long and sombre periods of dictatorship; to tackle the problem of the slower development of southern Europe with a view to removing economic and social divergencies; and to strengthen the idea of European unity, whose centre of gravity has hitherto been in the centre or north of Europe. 'We boil at different degrees', said Ralph Waldo Emerson. Therein lies the argument for a carefully–phased approach to enlargement and its related industrial relations problems.

18. Industrial relations legislation— protective or punitive?

'Every convert to the cause of socialism', said Bernard Shaw, 'has in the first five minutes of his novitiate the dazzling idea of bringing capitalism to its knees at one stroke by a general strike.' At the time, the older hands replied to this comment by saying: 'Why not commit suicide?' But apart from this practical objection to the political use of the strike weapon, trade unions in Britain have generally accepted the parliamentary road to political change; though the fall of the Conservative Government in 1974 and the severe industrial troubles experienced by the Labour Government early in 1979 made it clear that this constitutional principle could not be taken for granted. The worker as a citizen is expected to use the ballot box, the right of petition, and peaceful demonstration in order to secure changes in the system of government.

This theory is simple enough, but modern governments increasingly intervene in the economic sphere, sometimes provoking reactions which pose dangers. Lawyers still argue, for instance, about whether the 1926 General Strike in Britain was aimed at the government's withdrawal of the coal subsidy, or was basically an industrial dispute between miners and owners. The problem remains topical. Is a dispute with an employer (especially a public corporation) political if it is caused by that employer succumbing to a compulsory or even voluntary incomes policy? Or is a strike in support of nationalization, or for worker participation on the boards of companies, politically motivated? These questions are of vital and increasing importance throughout Western Europe, particularly as unions press for government intervention against the growing economic power of multinational companies.

In addition to this pressure for balancing legislation, there are at least two other reasons for the growing network of Europe's labour laws. Legal remedies for grievances have tended to be used more on the Continent than in Britain and industrial relations have retained this legal tone over the years. Many European countries had laws regulating collective agreements long before Britain had laws dealing with trade union organization. Works councils, too, have evolved into powerful bodies with legal rights, and do much to compensate for the fragmented nature of Continental trade unionism since they represent the work force of whole plants, irrespective of individual union affiliations. The other influence on legislative activity is of a *quid pro quo* nature—in other words legislation favourable to trade unions is sometimes offered by governments as a reward for wage restraint. The 'social contract' in Britain is a classic example of this influence, which was a key factor in drastically reducing the British rate of inflation between 1975 and 1977.

A cynic once remarked that if all Europe's labour laws were laid end to end there would be no end. This nightmare vision must occasionally haunt the British personnel manager as he staggers under the avalanche of legislation by British governments which has been rumbling over him since 1965, especially in the field of employment rights; and, since 1973, from the European Community's institutions in Brussels. Chapter 9 on multinational companies lists over thirty measures which are currently being developed in Brussels, all of which directly or indirectly concern industrial relations practitioners.

This string of labour laws may seem like suffocating red tape to employers, but to British trade unionists it ties up with red ribbon a massive package of protective legislation. Since 1965 a transformation in the employment laws has taken place in Britain. There has been a Redundancy Payments Act; two sets of amendments to the Contracts of Employment Act; action on unfair dismissal under the Industrial Relations Act strengthened by virtue of the Trade Union and Labour Relations Act and supplemented again by the Employment Protection Act; the Equal Pay, Sex Discrimination, Race Relations and Rehabilitation of Offenders Acts; and the Employment Protection Act itself, with its range of individual rights all giving rights of action before Industrial Tribunals. The surge of legislation in the 'seventies, mainly rooted in the 'social contract' has completed the quiet revolution in British labour law.

British trade unions have traditionally been opposed to laws in the industrial relations field, preferring to rely on tough collective bargaining based on strong membership. Trade unions felt—and may still feel—that anything which hinders trade union growth should be opposed. Legal remedies for grievances at work mean that the employee gets satisfaction through the workings of the law rather than through the efforts of trade unions and there is accordingly less incentive to become or remain a union member. That was the rationale, and it still accounts for the TUC's opposition to a statutory national minimum wage and the reluctant acquiescence of trade unions to wage–restraint policies, which are seen in this sense as the thin end of a statutory wedge.

But change is being forced on British unions by events. Since the advent of unfair dismissal legislation in 1972 and the repeal in 1974 of parts of the Industrial Relations Act to which unions objected, representation by trade unions of their members before Industrial Tribunals has become a key function in most unions. This has led to the expansion of union legal departments and many full–time officers have acquired much expertise in unfair-dismissal cases before Tribunals. In other words, unions have developed new and more sophisticated skills by this form of representation. Legislation, therefore, has not proved a disincentive to recruitment as unions feared. On the contrary, this new role has balanced the diminishing influence of full–time officers on wage questions, due to successive phases of incomes policy and the steady devolution of union power to shop stewards and lay officials.

All this means that British trade unions have a credibility problem, at home and abroad. It is one thing to argue that there is no place for law in British industrial relations—for reasons which are understandable, though of doubtful validity—and then to proceed to accept labour laws which are favourable to trade unions, while continuing to oppose those suggested which would place restraints or new responsibilities upon unions. Moreover recent industrial relations legislation in Britain has favoured unions and is not now matched by voluntary wage restraint as it was during the social contract—but the new laws remain. It is now the employers who regard labour laws as punitive, whereas this was previously the view of the unions. Some argue that the answer lies not in producing laws in the controversial areas of secret balloting, unofficial strikes, and picketing, but in working out acceptable codes of practice.

Picketing is a particularly difficult problem in Europe, due to the close interdependence of industry and the consequent havoc which can be wrought by its aggressive and indiscriminate application. The noticeable feature of any comparison of picketing laws is the tolerance shown to peaceful picketing. In Italy, mere propaganda (without intimidation) seeking to induce potential strike–breakers not to work, is protected by the 'right to strike' guaranteed by the constitution. In France, the criminal code provides for the offence of fettering the exercise of a person's freedom to work. The aim of this is to prevent strikers exerting certain forms of pressure on those who wish to continue working.

In interpreting these provisions the French courts have drawn a distinction between peaceful and aggressive pickets. If pickets refrain from acts of violence, duress, threats and fraudulent conduct, they do not commit the crime of interfering with the freedom to work. Moreover, it has to be shown that the intention of the pickets was to coerce the strikers into stopping work. If their intention is to threaten the firm's plant or property they commit a different crime. There is little doubt that the mass picketing which occurred at the Saltley Gasworks in Britain during the miners' strike in 1972 was unlawful, since it was a public nuisance. There is, therefore, no need for legislation to control mass picketing. The real issue is the way in

169

which the police exercise their very wide discretion to control the number and conduct of pickets. Effective mass picketing can and does occur only when the police decide there is no serious danger of violence despite the obstruction which large numbers of pickets are bound to cause. As the law stands at present there is no statutory right to picket, but there is nothing to prohibit it either. The Trade Union and Labour Relations Act of 1974 says that 'it shall be lawful for one or more persons in contemplation or further-ance of a trade dispute to attend at or near a place where another person works or carries on business, or any other place where another person happens to be, not being a place where he resides'.

It looks a straightforward statement but it does not cover issues like the arrival of mass transport on the picketing scene, or the way in which employers can now drive large lorries or hired buses full of strike–breakers through picket lines with police support. Nor has the law cleared up the position on secondary picketing, which caused enormous problems during the strike of road haulage workers in Britain in 1979 by involving innocent companies in disputes in which they had no part, and laying–off thousands of workers. The blunt fact is that the vagueness of the law on picketing at a time of serious industrial unrest can quickly lead to the view that picketing by any means is justified. This is not only bad for society generally but bad for trade unions in the longer term. Irresponsible picketing is bound to discredit the whole concept of picketing as a method of securing common trade union action.

It was this fear which prompted the Irish Congress of Trade Unions in 1970 to make a clear distinction between a picket which is placed with the object of securing a stoppage of work by all trade unionists employed by a particular firm, and a picket which is placed with a view to informing the public that a dispute is in progress and informing other workers so that they will not undertake the work of those on strike. It was decided that only Congress should be entitled to issue picket notices of the former kind for an all–out strike.

Industrial relations legislation is likely to continue unfolding at a steady rate. Whether it is seen as protective or punitive will depend on the courage and judgement of governments. No doubt at different times employers and unions will feel like a drowning man being thrown both ends of a rope! But laws providing individual employment rights will keep coming from Brussels and reflect the influence of Western Europe in this field. There are three pressures. The first is the persistently high unemployment levels, which pose a growing need for protective labour laws in most European countries. Secondly, the obvious inadequacies of the British industrial relations system, and the failure to transplant the American system of legally enforceable agreements via the Industrial Relations Act, are inducing a close

British scrutiny of labour law systems in West Germany, Holland, Denmark, and Sweden. British interest in worker participation falls into this category, though it is generally seen as a device for promoting greater cooperation rather than a means of giving unions more power—hence the robust criticism of the Bullock Report and subsequent proposed legislation.

The third European influence on British labour law has been in developing the concept of the job property right, which gives the intellectual justification for the structure of individual employment rights. Traditionally, the legal basis of the employment relationship in Britain has assumed that the employer and employee were free and equal parties to the contract of employment. On this basis, the contract of employment could be terminated by either side at will. In Holland, France, and Germany, postwar legislation has been based on an entirely different premise: the notion that an employee, through his work, invests his 'asset' in a particular job and that when he is deprived of this 'asset' through no fault of his own he should be compensated. He should not lose his 'asset' arbitrarily. This is how Continental countries define the concept of an employee's property right in his job. The 1965 Redundancy Payments Act in Britain was the first law to be based firmly on the property right concept, with severance pay depending on age, service and pay (the employee's investment in his job and the effect of his losing his 'asset'). The other aspect of the property right principle concerns the circumstances in which an employee can be dismissed. Protection against unfair dismissal is also embodied in a number of Acts and loss of employment on the grounds of sex, married status, pregnancy, trade union membership, colour, race, nationality, or ethnic or national origin is now unlawful in Britain due to a number of statutes passed during the 1974–76 period, while the social contract was running.

Other concepts from the labour codes of other European countries have found their way on to the UK Statute book in recent years—such as the legal right to a written reason for dismissal, an obligation to consult trade unions in advance where redundancies threaten, and a right to time–off to look for work in a redundancy situation. ILO Recommendation 119 is itself an amalgam of Western European good practice in these areas and was the reference point for the Department of Employment when the unfair dismissals sections of the Industrial Relations Act were drafted. So industrial relations legislation rolls on, irritating some and pleasing others, setting new parameters of social responsibility.

Despite the surge of labour laws in Britain in recent years there is much leeway to make up yet. One British labour law, however, has unique status in the Community. It is the 1976 Trade Union and Labour Relations Amendment Act, which among its provisions specifies that a person dismissed for refusing to join a union has no legal rights under the unfair

171

dismissals procedure. In the same way an employer has no right of redress against a union which brings industrial action to bear against him in pursuance of the closed shop. So, unlike other countries in Europe, the closed shop in Britain is not only lawful, but encouraged by the law. In Belgium, Denmark, Holland, Norway, and Luxembourg, unions have fought for and obtained laws establishing the right of workers to join a union. The right not to join a union is obviously implicit in these laws. This 'freedom of association', as it is called, reflects the later industrial development on the Continent and the attitude of trade unions, who regarded the law as a protective and helpful device for winning freedoms. In West Germany the closed shop concept would breach the 1949 Federal Constitution and is therefore unlawful; but the issue has always been a controversial aspect of British trade unionism, shrouded in emotional hysteria.

The general idea of a closed shop can be defended on the simple moral grounds that it is wrong for a man to take the benefits which come from the collective efforts of his fellows acting through a trade union. If compulsory trade unionism means a loss of personal liberty, so does living together in a modern community. Rules have to be made for the regulation of traffic, for the protection of public health, and a vast number of other social purposes. It is argued that a non–unionist's behaviour is antisocial in the sense that it makes his fellows unwilling to work with him. Can personal freedom be carried to this point? So run the arguments of the trade unionist. On the other hand we have to guard against the use of compulsion to bully people, or to be politically vindictive. The purpose of the closed shop is surely to attain maximum trade union strength with a view to securing the best possible wages and working conditions for those whom the union represents. Curiously, the closed shop in Britain is not justified on either of these two counts. Trade union membership in Britain is around 50 per cent of the whole labour force, while in Belgium it is 66 per cent, in Norway and Denmark around 70 per cent, and over 80 per cent in Sweden—all of these countries being without the closed shop. Moreover, it need hardly be said that the wages, and in particular the fringe benefits, of British workers compare in general most unfavourably with their Continental counterparts.

The closed shop in Britain, then, does not seem to fulfil its basic tasks, though it remains an area of intense political argument. If the advocates of the closed shop are absolutely honest, they must admit that it is better to recruit *trade unionists* than trade union members—those who are genuinely prepared to work for the union because they believe in it. The closed shop then is a quirk of British history, which has become a political shrine rather than a means of increasing overall membership density and improving wages and conditions. It would be suicide for any British Government to try to abolish it. The right course is to press for adequate safeguards in the form of 'conscience' clauses. Trade unionists in Britain should remember, too, that they exist to fight injustice and oppression. In many ways, Continental trade unions are doing this job better without the closed shop than their British counterparts are doing with it.

19. British industrial relations/Euro–style

'A map of the world that does not include Utopia is not worth looking at', said Oscar Wilde. It is indeed utopian to imagine British industrial relations functioning on the European pattern. On the other hand Britain is not so rich in industrial relations wisdom that good ideas which are working well abroad can be dismissed out of hand. The key Continental practices which could transform the industrial scene in Britain are: higher productivity, legally–binding agreements, better fringe benefits, works councils, industrial unionism, good–conduct bonuses, worker participation, concerted action programmes, better trade union education facilities, no closed shops, national minimum wages, and no strike clauses in public service agreements. This list is not comprehensive, though it shows in a devastating way the need for fresh thinking in British industry.

Of course, a straight transplant of all these activities would be neither possible nor desirable, as they reflect different social attitudes and historical developments. But many British trade unionists, including some senior officials, dismiss these different though successful concepts on the grounds that they are too simplistic, too legal, and anyway quite foreign. Yet the 12 items mentioned are the framework of industrial success and the secret of the less volatile industrial relations systems in many European countries. Before considering the feasibility of introducing some of these continental ideas into our industrial relations, it is necessary to look at some wider economic and political trends. The problem is that Britain is trapped by an outdated industrial relations system. Crises come and go, but, like Tennyson's brook, the system meanders on, seemingly forever. When each industrial crisis subsides, people feel the glorious sense of relief of a man who has stopped banging his head against a wall. The negative pleasure rarely lasts longer than a year or two, then the whole masochistic business starts again.

The frightening aspect is that few people are prepared to criticize our industrial relations constructively, let alone speculate about possible future changes. To do so risks incurring the charge of union–bashing or knocking one's country. Politicians and trade union leaders are inhibited, too, by a mixture of electoral apprehension and cowardice, or muzzled by conference decisions all too often taken without a firm lead from the so–called leaders. This is the shameful side of the power game. But unless the industrial relations system is changed soon, and drastically, Britain seems doomed to relative economic backwardness. The basic problem is that British workers want to emulate Continental lifestyles without the productivity and the industrial attitudes which have created the wealth on which these higher living standards are based.

Between 1949 and 1963, Britain's annual growth was at the rate of 2·6 per cent. This compares with 4·6 per cent in France, 7·8 per cent in Germany, and 5·8 per cent in Italy. Over the past 20 years it has averaged about 2·8 per cent, less than half the average growth rate of the French, the Italians, and the Spaniards, and two-thirds of that of the Dutch. In fact, since 1955, the British GNP has grown by more than 4 per cent on only four occasions: 1959, 1963, 1964, and 1973. This is why superior pensions, higher family allowances, better fringe benefits, and more generous living standards are prevalent on the Continent. The unions consciously aim to create more wealth, with a view to securing the best possible distribution of it. In Britain the arguments seem to centre on distributing the economic cake, which is assumed to bake itself. It is sometimes argued that Britain has reached a stage of maturity which implies low growth, and in that sense international comparisons on productivity are irrelevant. This ostrich–like approach conveniently ignores Britain's trading commitments and the need to be competitive.

In theory more competition is supposed to invigorate an economy, but intense competition during the past 20 years has significantly eroded Britain's position in the international economy. This is surely one major cause of the decline of British economic strength. Although in absolute terms wages have remained low in Britain in recent years, higher wage costs and lower productivity increases have brought about a damaging change in unit labour costs. Since, then, we could be more efficient and are not, is it that we prefer an easier life in the factories than more leisure and more goods in the home? This seems unlikely, as workers demand higher real wages and strike, sometimes ruthlessly, as we have seen in 1979, to get them. Managers too are not exactly silent on the need for higher salaries and improved differentials. But while many admit that British industrial relations are a shambles, few are prepared to do anything about it. There is no mystery about industrial efficiency. The blunt truth is that British workers and management use basically the same equipment less effectively than their foreign counterparts, though we can all point to the things that are wrong: low productivity, lack of enterprise, low investment, poor industrial relations, and too many unions—the list is endless.

To ignore or rationalize the economic retardation of the country on the grounds that industrialism is morally and aesthetically objectionable is naïve in the extreme. Those who object to industry and growth on these grounds must say clearly how people are to be fed and clothed without it.

175

Britain is not a self–supporting country and its standard of living is in relative decline. Even if Britons were prepared to accept a radically changed system (and there are no signs that they might, despite the occasional talk of protectionism and a siege economy by some politicians), Britain would still find itself with the problem of how to supply the country with the necessities of life. It must trade successfully simply to have enough food. During the war everyone understood with utter simplicity and urgency that the country was on the verge of catastrophe and that practical things had to be done. War simplifies everything—but economic decline merely muddles and confuses everyone. Without decisive, responsible leadership, confusion reigns, militancy in trade unions is seen to pay, and ordinary decent people have no option but to revert to naked individualism.

The lesson of history is that acute and prolonged economic and social crises lead to political instability and even at times to the collapse of the system. It was Aneurin Bevan who said: 'The safety of free political institutions depends upon reducing social tensions before these become intolerable.' The question for the 'eighties for Europe generally, and Britain in particular, is how the stability of our democratic systems can be maintained, when rising aspirations are matched by increasing economic difficulties. The traditional combination of national interest, civic pride, respect for property, industry, thrift, and Christian morality, is now largely shattered. Fewer and fewer people accept a residual moral commitment to the social and national interest, though most are still anxious that the world should be a decent place in which to live. In theory politicians should give birth to the new national spirit needed to turn the slack industrial tide in Britain; but the central contradiction of political life in modern society is that the role of the government in securing the best long–term interests of the country conflicts with its desire to make a plausible showing of short–run achievement at the next election. Any party enacting the unpopular measures which the economic situation demands would strain the loyalty of the average voter beyond breaking point.

It seems that the solution to economic and social problems is in motivating man, rather than in analysing statistics or using technological expertise. It is the opinion of ordinary people about the society in which they live which in the end will prove decisive. Political stability hangs on economic success and a pre–condition for this is a good industrial relations atmosphere. To make British industrial relations more realistic and more responsive to people's needs is surely the first step to the fairer, more prosperous society we all seek. The TUC/Government agreement on industrial relations reached in February 1979 would have been sensible and helpful in the longer term, but it dodged the immediate crunch issues. If you are drowning, a manual on swimming is not of immediate use—you need a lifebelt, as the main thing is to survive. There are three flashpoints in the British industrial relations system: low pay, narrowed differentials, and unofficial industrial action. They all interact, sometimes in a devastating way. Arguments about low pay explode periodically, but the increases won give rise to 'leapfrogging' claims, as skilled workers and those with industrial muscle attempt to maintain their differentials, knowing that the establishment of fair relativities will take a long time to solve. Both issues provide fertile ground for unofficial strikes. By selecting a few European ideas already working well in other countries, a six–point short–term plan could be devised, which would tackle the three immediate problems intelligently and constructively and at the same time point the way to more sophisticated, fundamental longer–term reforms.

1. The foundation would be a national minimum wage, automatically indexed to retail prices. The actual level could be set by NEDO on a fair and realistic basis. Systems of this kind already operate in five Community countries, Belgium, France, Holland, Luxembourg, and Denmark. In Belgium there is a three way indexation: first, to prices; then to occupational categories of which there are five, each with its own national minimum wage; and to the age of the workers, the minimum wage rising as the worker gets older. Thus there is not one minimum wage, but several, all indexed by criteria jointly agreed by employers and trade unions. The triggering mechanism is an increase of two points in the price index which then puts 2 per cent on the minimum wage levels the month after is it recorded. The five occupational categories are set by the National Labour Council, on which sit trade unionists and employers.

2. These arrangements are legally binding and it would be a good idea to link this concept with a national minimum wage in Britain, as large sums of public money would be needed to devise realistic wage levels in the public sector. To introduce the legally binding agreement selectively in this way, as a *quid pro quo* for a guaranteed minimum wage with automatic indexation, would avoid generating the mass hysteria likely to arise from a more comprehensive package of legal reforms. Despite the electrifying effect of this idea on trade union activists, it would only affect the small minority of trade unionists who persistently misbehave.

3. Good conduct bonuses for those workers who do not strike during the duration of their agreements should also be introduced in Britain. In several Community countries this concept has proved useful and the bonuses vary from 1 per cent to 2 per cent of gross earnings. Cynics describe the arrangement as buying loyalty, but in Britain we do the opposite thing. We penalize people who behave responsibly in industry by not recognizing that fact, and by making little or no attempt to deter or punish those who behave irresponsibly. The Government could set an example by introducing these

arrangements in the public sector.

4. A Differentials Commission should be established, preferably with all–party support. It would look generally at wage and salary levels and would examine as an urgent priority the comparisons between public sector grades and their linked grades in the private sector. Such a body would help to prevent the national minimum wage structure becoming a launching pad for 'leapfrogging wage' claims. The Clegg Comparability Commission, set up by the last Labour Government is a step in the right direction, though its future seems doubtful. To function usefully in the short and long term such a commission should have the security which stems from all-party support. It also needs a staff reflecting this general acceptability and the widest possible terms of reference. It will need to prescribe a healthier and fairer pay structure as well as performing emergency operations on pay disputes. Unless society feels that dukes and dustmen, porters and Prime Ministers, should all be paid the same, some workers will always be paid less than others. The push for complete equality may well suit heaven or the cemetery, but it has little relevance to human nature. It discourages the acquisition of skills and the assumption of responsibility. It limits the scope of firms to recruit the people they need and the mobility of those they already employ. The aim should be to set the rates for the lower–paid workers at a realistic level, bearing in mind the cost impact on the public and private sector and the consequential upward adjustment of differentials which are genuinely based on skill, responsibility, training, and effort. Moreover, the system is more than just a numbers game. It must enable goods and services to be produced at competitive prices. This clearly means a searching examination of manning levels, productivity, and restrictive practices, particularly in the public services. To say less than this would be dishonest. Such a structure will not be achieved by thrashing around wildly and destructively in the jungle of free collective bargaining.

5. The arguments for secret ballots are well known. Secret ballots should be strongly encouraged and Government funds provided where necessary to assist their organization. This would not avoid strikes; it might, however, produce fewer, bigger, and longer disputes. Secret ballots would certainly deter many frivolous strikes, and those which result from the clever manipulation of meeting procedures by unscrupulous individuals. The wide use of secret ballots would at least ensure that a reasonable proportion of people vote on all important industrial issues. The commonsense of ordinary people, formally released in this way, would provide a crushing answer to the strike–happy militants—which is why they usually oppose the idea. They know their limitations. In Germany a 75 per cent vote for strike action is required, the initial call coming from the executive committee of the union concerned.

6. The British picketing laws need to be clarified, and if necessary changed, to prohibit 'secondary' picketing (picketing of outside firms or factories not involved in a particular dispute). A combination of weak legislation and controversial court rulings, has made picketing law a legal minefield. In today's turbulent industrial relations climate secondary picketing is a licence to intimidate and a short–cut to anarchy. In other Community countries, picketing in any form is relatively rare and secondary picketing almost unknown. In Belgium, Denmark, France, Germany, Italy, and the Netherlands, there is no basic legal right to picket. In practice, however, it is tolerated, provided it is peaceful and concerns those directly involved in the dispute. In any case, French and Italian unions are too poor to afford the lengthy stoppages of work which secondary picketing might produce. German unions are rich and well–disciplined and do not need secondary picketing as a standard weapon. Their union codes strictly control picket behaviour.

The foregoing six points would be a first–phase action programme. They would tackle the three flashpoints mentioned, encourage loyalty, and discourage irresponsibility in industry. They would also introduce the law into collective bargaining in a more specific though selective way and bring in some well–tried European concepts, thus paving the way for further changes later. Without this modest foundation of discipline and encouragement of responsible behaviour it is difficult to see how the longer–term, more complex changes can be introduced with any hope of success.

The items for the second phase of reform have all been well publicized and need only to be briefly listed: concerted action by the Government, TUC and CBI, to plan a fairer wages structure within an overall framework of economic reality; the synchronization of settlement dates of the centrally–bargained wage claims within a defined period of time each year; an easing of the closed shop provisions; a gradual introduction of worker participation in management decision–taking; and, most important of all, a 'social' wage rather than an 'effort' wage for vital groups of public service workers, in short, no–strike clauses in these sectors in return for agreed guaranteed wage differentials.

There would probably be wide public support for a careful review of the use of the strike weapon in key industrial sectors. This would not be a form of union bashing, but a recognition of changing industrial circumstances. Free collective bargaining was conceived in a society which was loosely integrated, compared with our own. The morality of strikes may be dismissed as irrelevant in the context of sacrosanct collective bargaining, but the truth is that modern society is almost completely dependent on certain groups of workers. A dispute in the power industry, for example, means more than lighting a candle or missing a favourite television programme. It

179

can mean shivering old age pensioners, people trapped in high–rise flats because the lifts do not work, or even the lives of people on kidney machines. Strikes in 1979 disrupted hospitals, causing delay and distress to the sick and the old, and in some cases there were no emergency services for those dangerously ill. Airport strikes affecting Britain's long–suffering holiday families further illustrate that the use of the strike weapon in key sectors has a devastating effect on the public and is socially quite indiscriminate. There must be a more civilized way—even of being difficult—than bashing a suffering and innocent public.

There is something fundamentally wrong with a society which tolerates abysmally low rates of pay in certain vital public services. It is monstrous, however, when fundamentally decent people are driven to seek a solution to these problems by taking ruthless and inhuman actions, often against the weakest members of society. We must be bold enough to consider other ways of doing this. The TUC, for instance, might consider compulsory and binding arbitration for these key sectors, and give those who waive the right to strike a reward by putting them in a higher range of wage earners with a self–adjusting differential well above an agreed base. Responsible behaviour must be balanced with a meeting of material needs, so that the best–behaved do not always have to be equated with the lowest paid. Moderates have always tended to be penalized for their reasonableness, in British trade unions. Over the years the TUC has forced the pace of change and made a firm and largely beneficial impact on governments and society; but primarily as a weapon of defence, not as a positive instrument of change. Britain's industrial problems are now so urgent and complex that unions must accept change themselves in order to be more effective in changing society.

The central dilemma of British industrial relations is that a system of collective bargaining which is essentially voluntary can only work if it is linked to a firm, responsible leadership and accepted procedures at all levels of trade unions and employers' associations. And yet the competitive thrust of multiunionism prevents free collective bargaining from being pursued in an orderly and responsible way, even if its participants wish that to happen. There is no way of being gentlemanly in the wages jungle if you want to stay alive. It is painfully evident that social justice can only come from order and not from anarchy. It is a sad though obvious fact that some trade union leaders are content to drift with the militant tide they have helped to generate in their own unions; others who might wish to speak out are prevented from doing so because power and authority in their organizations has been moved to the shop–floor. They respond to pressures from below, therefore, instead of launching initiatives from the top.

But other influences have helped to destroy the credibility of the voluntary bargaining system. First, the simmering industrial unrest, which emerged during the late 'sixties in France, Italy, and to a lesser extent, in the UK, sparked off moves to 'democratize' many unions. Some British trade union leaders, who have recently retired, rode to power during the 'sixties on the theme of 'shop–floor democracy'. This was probably the right strategy, but they moved too fast and without adequate preparation—if events are any guide. Shop–floor power has not generally been balanced by responsibility and the authority of the new leaders has been seriously undermined. The forum for real discussion is no longer the branch, but the multiunion meetings at the workplace which still remain largely outside the union rulebooks. The vast majority of shop stewards have unquestioned integrity, but the informality of the system leaves it highly vulnerable to the actions of the ruthless and reckless few.

The second influence is the complex interlocking structure of British industry, which means that an unofficial strike by a few key workers in a vital sector can prevent several thousand other people from working. The third factor hitting the voluntary bargaining system was the energy crisis in 1973, which saw Britain—indeed the whole of Europe—moving from the golden age of growth into an age of anxiety, bringing unemployment on a scale not known since the 'thirties, with its related social pressures and conflicts.

The higher level of material wellbeing and education experienced in the postwar years has strengthened the resolve of ordinary people to maintain and improve their living standards, despite persistently high unemployment. Against this acquisitive background it was not surprising, in one sense that the TUC in 1978, officially adopted a policy of 'free collective bargaining'—although it highlights the weak and divided leadership. Events since then have demonstrated the futility of the free–for–all approach, though its social crudity has been apparent for years; indeed, low pay is one of its products. The wages scramble during the 1974–75 crisis pushed inflation up to frightening levels and resulted in the three years of wage restraint embodied in the social contract. The frustrations and injustices generated by this restraint probably contributed to the ruthless and ferocious attitudes which emerged during the industrial disputes in early 1979.

The time for reconstructing British industrial relations is now. 'Muddling through' is fine if the only aim is to survive with our battered system intact. But if British workers want the best European living standards (and they are right to do so) then they must be prepared to accept the discipline and the application which makes those higher standards possible. It would be fatuous and arrogant to dismiss Continental industrial relations as unworkable in Britain because they have a strong legal flavour. It is simply a question of Britain being humble enough to try a few of the concepts which are working well in other European countries.

In any case British unions can no longer say the law has no place in industrial relations. Paradoxically, the Labour Government's pro–union legislative package has seen to that. The real danger to British trade unionism is not from a rampaging Conservative Government, but from within its own ranks—from those members who are willing to let it remain a prisoner of its history in order to avoid the trauma of change. In other words, innate conservatism rather than militancy is by far the more serious problem for trade unions in Britain. The country's national recovery hinges on a swift and substantial improvement in its industrial relations system. We need an absolutely unfaltering determination to allow neither sentiment nor political prejudices to stand in the way of the changes needed. The ideas and suggestions in this chapter are a modest attempt to start the dialogue.

Appendix Comparisons of European industrial relations practices

The nine diagrams and charts which follow, embellish points made in the book on different aspects of industrial relations in Europe. They also give an impression of the social and economic climate in the different countries.

1. How the European Community works

This is a reminder of the basic procedures at Community level—as industrial relations problems have often to be worked out within this framework (Appendix Figure 1).

2. A survey of current picketing practice in eight Community countries

The right to communicate information to workers, to persuade them not to work in support of an industrial dispute, is widely practised in Community countries by activities generally classed as 'picketing', but appears to have little specific legal backing. Provided the picketing is peaceful and concerns those directly involved in the dispute, it is usually permitted. There is not the same pressure from trade unions in the other Community countries for more positive legal rights in this field as there is in the UK (Appendix Figure 2).

3. A survey of various aspects of working life

The diagram reveals interesting trends in the use of flexible working hours. On-the-job accidents are worrying, but traffic accidents per thousand drivers would hardly look better. Expenditure on training is surprisingly low, given the structural changes rolling over the European economies (Appendix Figure 3).

4. Government anti-unemployment measures

This list is self-explanatory and shows the wide range of measures being used by governments, not always with success, to combat unemployment (Appendix Figure 4).

5. Statistics on unemployment and wage and price changes

These interesting tables outline the problems and the opportunities. It will be noted that Belgium, Denmark, France, and Italy have a higher rate of unemployment than the UK. The problem of matching people with jobs is also revealed in the high number of job vacancies in West Germany and the UK (Appendix Figure 5).

6. The night-work league

Some 15 per cent of the Community labour force (about 25 million people) do occasional or regular night work (Appendix Figure 6).

7. The different uses of leisure

This table has a serious and light-hearted aspect. The Dutch, Swedes, Belgians, and Danes top the non-working days league—and the columns on swimming pools and bicycles are interesting (Appendix Figure 7).

8. The list of organizations affiliated to the ETUC

A total of 31 national trade union centres are shown, in 18 countries, giving a total affiliated membership of 40 millions (Appendix Figure 8).

9. International and European trade union structure

This diagram shows the complex network of international trade unionism. An individual trade union may have three links—to the national trade union centre, to the international trade secretariat, or to the European industry committee. A national trade union centre like the TUC can and does affiliate to the ETUC and ICFTU (Appendix Figure 9).

Community rules affect our everyday lives. Some we like, such as stricter safety laws for electrical goods. Some we don't, such as the agricultural policy. How are these decisions made, and how can we stop rules being made we don't like?

Here is a simplified diagram of the rule-making machinery

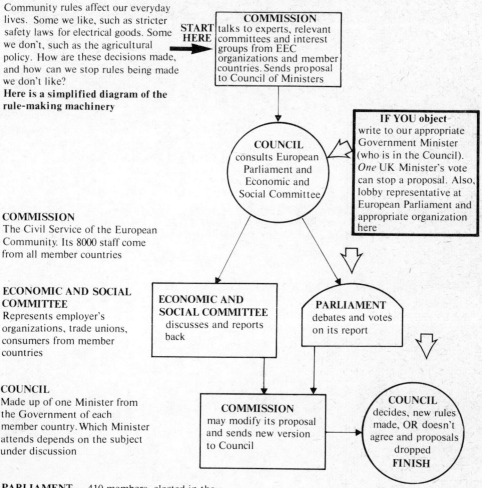

COMMISSION
The Civil Service of the European Community. Its 8000 staff come from all member countries

ECONOMIC AND SOCIAL COMMITTEE
Represents employer's organizations, trade unions, consumers from member countries

COUNCIL
Made up of one Minister from the Government of each member country. Which Minister attends depends on the subject under discussion

PARLIAMENT – 410 members, elected in the nine member states – 81 for UK chosen by us

Appendix Figure 1 How the European Community works. (Source: *Woman's Own*)

Appendix Figure 2 A survey of current picketing practices in eight Community countries. (Source: *European Industrial Relations Review*, 1978)

	Belgium	Denmark	France	Germany
1. Is there a right to picket?	No basic legal right to picket. In practice, however, any form of peaceful picketing is permitted	No basic legal right to picket. In practice, however, picketing in support of lawful disputes is permitted	No specific basic legal right to picket. In practice, however, peaceful picketing has not been held to constitute a 'grave misdemeanour' by the Courts	No basic legal right to picket. In practice, however, most non-violent forms of protest or demonstration are permitted
2. What activities are lawful?	All forms of peaceful persuasion, including obstruction of the highway for short periods of time, are allowed. Where actual violence is involved, however, pickets may be liable for criminal offences	Activities such as obstruction of the highway and breach of the peace are technically unlawful. In general, however, the police are reluctant to intervene in industrial disputes unless serious dislocation (of supplies, etc.) involved	In general, picketing only becomes unlawful where violence or a hindrance of the freedom to work of those not in dispute is involved. If the strike picket is 'sufficiently intimidating' to constitute a threat, the offence of hindering others' freedom to work will be committed	All forms of peaceful demonstration, including obstruction of the highway at the discretion of the local police, are allowed. Demonstrations are not, however, permitted on private property–i.e., within the plant. Where actual violence or serious breach of the peace is involved, pickets may be liable for criminal offences

3. Who can engage in such activities?	Any individual can engage in peaceful picketing—not simply trade union members or their representatives *Note:* Belgian trade unions have consistently resisted attempts to give them a legal 'persona', on the grounds that this would involve them in unnecessary litigation	In line with the provisions of most collective agreements—which contain a 'peace' clause during the term of the agreement—those to whom such agreements apply may take strike action or support action, such as picketing, when established procedures for settlement have been exhausted	Any individual may exercise the implied right to engage in such activities as would constitute peaceful picketing	Any individual can engage in peaceful demonstrations –no special distinction is made as between those involved in industrial protests and those concerning other (e.g. political) issues

Appendix Figure 2 (continued)

	Ireland	Italy	Netherlands	United Kingdom
1. Is there a right to picket?	In accordance with the Trade Disputes Act 1906, 'peaceful picketing' is permitted where it is 'in contemplation or furtherance of a trade dispute'	No basic legal right to picket. In practice, however, picketing in support of industrial disputes is regarded as a normal labour practice	No basic legal right to picket. In practice, however, most non-violent forms of protest or demonstration are permitted	In accordance with the Trade Union and Labour Relations Act 1974, 'peaceful picketing' is permitted where it is in contemplation or furtherance of a trade dispute'
2. What activities are lawful?	In general, the immunity conferred by the Trade Disputes Act extends to attendance at but not serious obstruction of the highway, for the purpose of peacefully communicating information or persuading others not to work. Violent actions are not protected. Since, however, the Supreme Court has ruled that certain provisions in the Constitution can override this Act, the extent of the protection it affords remains unclear	In general, picketing only becomes unlawful where serious violence or breach of the peace occurs. The Courts have shown a tendency to diminish the penalties for such offences where the actions taken can be shown to relate to an industrial dispute	Most forms of peaceful demonstration are permitted, subject to prior authorization by the municipal authority. Where serious obstruction of the highway, violence, or breach of the peace is involved, pickets may be liable for criminal offences	The immunity conferred by the Trade Union and Labour Relations Act, and amplified in the proposed Employment Protection Bill (EIRR 16), appears to extend only to attendance at the workplace, falling short of obstruction of the highway, for the purpose of peacefully communicating information or persuading others not to work. There is no specific right to stop vehicles. Where violence is involved, the criminal law applies

| 3. *Who can engage in such activities?* | The right to engage in such activities as constitute peaceful picketing is restricted, by the terms of the 1906 Act, to workers employed by persons engaged in trade or industry. This has been narrowly construed by the Courts to cover only those in commercial or profit-making undertakings. The situation is further complicated by the fact that the Act applies only to unions holding negotiation licences issued by the Labour Ministry | Although the right to engage in trade union activities is specifically provided in the 'Workers Statute' 1970, the implied right to picket is exercisable by any individual or group of persons | Any individual can engage in peaceful demonstrations –no special distinction is made between those involved in industrial protests and those concerning other issues | The right to engage in such activities as constitute peaceful picketing is granted, by the terms of the 1974 Act, to any person undertaking such action in furtherance of a trade dispute. (Previous case law under the old Industrial Relations Act had ruled that union officials were not protected where such actions involved inducing breaches of commercial contracts) |

Appendix Figure 3 A survey of various aspects of working life. *Notes:* □ Not available ■ Impossible to estimate. (a) Estimate or extrapolation; (b) government expenditure only; (c) only private sector expenditure; (d) 80 per cent of basic wage plus cost of living allowance; (e) up to a maximum of 3900 F per month; (f) only after age of 30, and ceiling varies according to occupation; (g) including company pensions; (k) women lose their job on marriage. (Source: *Vision*, July/August 1978)

	Unemployment rate at end 1977 (%)	Number of unemployed per job vacancy end 1977	Percentage of employees working flexible hours	Expenditure on training per head of working population in 1977 ($s)	Number of accidents at work per worker in 1977	Unemployment benefit in the sixth month as percentage of last	Minimum retiring age men/women	Worker's pension as percentage of final salary
Belgium	8.2	29	10 (a)	14 (b)	97	60	60/55	70
Denmark	6.9	8	10 (a)	31 (c)	9	90	67/63	75 (g)
W. Germany	4.3	7	15 (a)	20 (b)	79	68	63/63	66
Spain	6.7	8	10 (a)	15 (a)	88	85	65/65	85
France	4.6	14	10 (a)	58	67	90	60/60	50 (h)
Italy	7.6	20 (a)	5 (a)	■	55	80 (d)	60/60	80
Netherlands	4.4	5	10	17 (a)	■	80	65/65	70
Norway	1.0	1	20 (a)	7 (b)	9	50 (a)	67/67	60
Austria	2.7	2	8 (a)	■	74	50	60/55	70
Portugal	9.1	■	■	■	■	60	65/60	65
Switzerland	0.1	2	8 (a)	■	43	75 (e)	65/62	75 (g)
Finland	7.0	12 (a)	15 (a)	■	91	70	65/65	40
Sweden	1.8	2	20 (a)	■	36	85	65/65	70
United Kingdom	5.4	10 (a)	5 (a)	4	12	30 (a)	65/60	60 (g)
Japan	2.0	■	□	■	22 (a)	60 (f)	55/□ (k)	60 (g)
USA	6.5	■	3 (a)	■	23	50 (i)	62/62	50

Appendix Figure 4 What European governments are vainly trying to do to combat unemployment. (Source: *European Industrial Review*, 1978)

	Belgium	Denmark	Germany	France
Job creation	Six month exemption from social security payments for firms which hire people who have been jobless for more than six months	£1.16 per hour subsidy for six months for new workers aged from 15 to 24	Subsidy of 60 per cent of salary for a year for unemployed workers hired	Exemptions from social security payments for firms who hire young unemployed workers
Preferential hiring	Until December 1978 firms with more than 50 employeees were obliged to hire one jobless worker under 30 for every 50 employees	State aid to hire young long term unemployed workers	Subsidies for firms which hire the long time unemployed and the handicapped	Exemptions from social security payments for a year for firms which hire those under 26
Deferred sackings	No special state aid to help firms put off or avoid sackings because of temporary economic problems	No special state aid to help firms put off or avoid sackings because of temporary economic problems	Subsidies to maintain wages at 90 per cent during four weeks if working hours reduced for economic reasons	State aid to firms to avoid sackings if working hours are reduced

Appendix cont.

	Belgium	Denmark	Germany	France
Temporary job creation	Unpaid temporary work for public bodies under special state plan for those on the dole	State financed 'useful work' for local authorities and ministries lasting six months	State programme of subsidized, temporary social work for local councils	No public works programme
Early retirement	Special pension for those who retire five years early, at 60 for men and at 55 for women	Opportunity to retire at 53 not 60 with a guaranteed substantial income	Retirement at 63 for men who have worked at least 35 years and at 60 for those who have been jobless for 12 of the previous 18 months	Guaranteed 70 per cent of weekly pay based on last pay packet for those sacked or who chose to retire after 60
More time at school	No move to raise school leaving age from 14	No move to raise school leaving age from 14	School leaving age has been raised from 15 to 16 in several Länder	No move to raise school leaving age from 16
Labour mobility	Right to claim social security and unemployment pay on the basis of previous salary	Special aid to encourage mobility such as moving and travelling expenses	State loans and aid for unemployed workers to encourage mobility	A wide range of special aid to encourage mobility such as travelling expenses
Controls on overtime and moonlighting	Firms must notify all overtime plans. Crackdown on moonlighting	No special control of second jobs	Reinforcement of current rules governing second jobs	No special control of second jobs

	Ireland	Italy	Luxembourg	Netherlands	United Kingdom
Job creation	Subsidies for firms which hire new workers amounting to £20 for adults, £14 for school leavers	Reduced social security payments to create new jobs in Mezzogiorno and other high unemployment regions	No aid to encourage job creation	State aid for firms which organize production which will create jobs	A subsidy of £20 a week for six months for firms with less than 50 employees which hire a new employee
Preferential hiring	State aid for job creation	Subsidies from 12 to 19 per cent of the salary of a new employee aged between 15 and 29 for the first year	State measures to encourage firms to hire young unemployed	Subsidies up to 30 per cent of the salary of a new employee over 45 for the first six months	A subsidy of £30 a week for firms which hire handicapped workers who have been jobless for more than six months
Deferred sackings	Wages at 80 per cent guaranteed by state and employer fund in case of temporary work stoppage	Wages at 80 per cent guaranteed by state and employer fund in case of temporary work stoppage	Wages at 80 per cent guaranteed by state in case of temporary work stoppage	Subsidies to ship builders and machine tool companies to avoid mass redundancies	A subsidy of £20 a week for a year for each employee kept on who would otherwise have been sacked
Temporary job creation	Temporary public work for those looking for their first job for six months	State financed temporary work for four to eight months within government and regional bodies for those under 30	No public works programme	State pays wages of those who do temporary work for public bodies for up to a year	Temporary work for young unemployed and special training programmes

	Ireland	Italy	Luxembourg	Netherlands	United Kingdom
Early retirement	No early retirement plan	Early retirement for men at 60 and women at 55 for those who have made pension payments for 35 years	Retirement at 57 not 60 for steel workers with a state pension equivalent to 85 per cent average salary in last three years	No retirement before 65	Retirement a year early for those who are replaced by a younger unemployed worker
More time at school	No move to raise school leaving age from 16	No move to raise school leaving age from 15	No move to raise school leaving age from 15	No move to raise school leaving age from 16 but part time training from 16 to 18	No move to raise school leaving age from 16
Labour mobility	Removal aid, including up to £150 towards the legal costs for buying and selling a house	Aid from a mobility fund to cover some travelling costs and moving costs	State aid to help recycle workers after industrial changes	State makes up pay of unemployed who take a job at a lower rate	State aid to encourage job creation in regions where unemployment is high
Controls on overtime and moonlighting	No special control of second jobs	No special control of overtime but weekly and monthly limits in some sectors	Special control of overtime and extra laws on second jobs	Firms must notify all overtime plans	No special control

Appendix Figure 5(a) Unemployment and job vacancies in the countries of the EEC (February 1979). *Notes:* Unemployment refers to registered wholly unemployed. Job vacancies are those unfilled at the end of the month. The unemployment figure for Denmark is provisional. (Source: European Commission and national offices)

Country	Unemployment		Change on same month of previous year		Job Vacancies	Change on same month of previous year	
	Number	% of working population	Number	%	Number	Number	%
Belgium	341 200	8.6	+ 16 500	+ 5.1	5300	+ 2 100	+ 65.6
Denmark	173 100	6.8	+ 9 000	+ 4.7	1900	+ 600	+ 46.2
W. Germany	1 134 100	4.4	− 90 000	− 7.4	266 900	+43 200	+ 19.3
France	1 341 900	6.1	+233 700	+21.1	72 200	−10 700	− 12.9
Luxembourg	1 236	0.8	− 92	− 6.9	200	N/C	N/C
Holland	225 800	4.7	+ 6 800	+ 3.1	57 300	+ 7000	+ 13.9
Ireland	N/A	—	—	—		N/A	N/A
Italy	1 660 300	7.8	+ 88 900	+ 5.7		N/A	N/A
United Kingdom	1 452 000	5.6	− 56 700	− 3.8	216 000	+43 900	+ 25.6

Appendix Figure 5(b) Wage and price change. *Notes:* Numerical notes refer to wage index only; letters to prices. 1. November; 2. 3rd quarter; 3. October; 4. 2nd quarter; 5. 1st quarter; 6. January 1978–79; 7. quarter; 8. earnings; 9. males. (a) Excluding indirect taxes; (b) November; (c) excluding rent; (d) excluding items which show marked seasonal fluctuations. (Source: OECD)

Country	Indices of wage rates in industry			Consumer price indices all goods services		
	December 1977	December 1978	% Increase over past 12 months	January 1978	January 1979	% Increase over past 12 months
Austria	121.7	130.2	7.0	115.5	119.6	3.5
Belgium	126.0	133.0	5.6	120.3	125.1	4.0
Denmark [1] [8] (a)	128.7	141.0	9.6	123.2	130.0	5.5
Finland [2] [8]	127.0	135.0	6.3	134.0	143.0	6.7
France [1]	133.2	150.1	12.7	124.5	137.2	10.2
W. Germany [3]	114.9	120.7	5.0	110.2	113.4	2.9
Greece [4] [8]	154.0	189.0	22.7	136.6	157.0	14.9
Ireland [5] [8] (b)	127.0	144.0	13.4	137.8	148.7	7.9
Italy	166.3	191.1	14.9	148.2	167.4	13.0
Luxembourg	—	—	—	119.0	123.4	3.7
Holland [6] [8]	122.0	126.0	3.3	117.5	122.2	4.0
Norway [7] [9]	133.0	142.0	6.8	125.0	132.0	5.6
Portugal (c)	—	—	—	155.5	193.3	24.3
Spain [3] [8]	174.3	216.9	24.4	160.5	187.0	16.5
Sweden [8]	132.5	140.7	6.2	126.1	138.4	9.8
Switzerland [8]	103.0	107.3	4.2	103.6	104.8	1.2
UK (d)	127.3	157.8	24.0	140.8	153.1	8.8

Appendix Figure 6 The night work league. (Source: *Industrial Relations Europe, February 1979*)

Belgium, Denmark, Ireland, Holland top
Market's regular night work league

Some 15 per cent of the total Common Market labour force—or roughly 25 million people—do occasional or regular night work, according to statistics compiled by the European Commission, whose proposals for Market-wide rules on the subject have just been shelved in the face of opposition from both employers and unions.

However, the figures, published last year, need to be viewed with caution. The fieldwork on which they are based was carried out in 1975, and the percentages include not only employees, but the self-employed—and employers.

The Commission says that the countries with the highest proportion of regular and occasional night workers are Luxembourg (22.6 per cent of the labour force), Ireland (21 per cent) and Denmark (19.3 per cent).

But when only regular night workers are counted, Holland, Ireland, Denmark and Belgium all come out about the same—at 8 per cent or slightly more.

Among male night workers, the proportions are more or less equally divided between industry (43.6 per cent) and services (46 per cent), with most of the rest in agriculture.

Of 2.3 million women night workers, around 75 per cent are in services and only 10 per cent in industry.

The Commission study examines other aspects of what it calls 'the seamy side of work'. Among its findings:

Sunday working Almost 30 per cent of people with one main job regularly work on Sundays and holidays.

Noise More than half the industrial workers in the five countries surveyed on this topic (Germany, Belgium, Holland, Ireland and the UK) complained that noise is a problem in their working environment. The same complaint was voiced by about 30 per cent of people in selected services—transport, commerce, restaurants and repairs.

Hygiene In the five countries surveyed, between 10 and 20 per cent reported unhygienic or dirty working conditions. In some industrial sectors, more than 40 per cent complained of lack of hygiene.

Appendix Figure 7 The different uses of leisure. *Notes:* ■ Impossible to estimate. (1) Weekends, holidays, and public holidays; (2) in the evening, but not necessarily for dinner; (a) Estimate; (b) some people work on Saturdays; (c) more in some states; (d) dollar figures not comparable; (e) not including school and company swimming pools, even if open to the public. (Source: *Vision*, July/August 1978)

	Number of non-working days in 1977 (1)	Percentage of population that took a holiday away from home in 1977	Expenditure per head on food and drink away from home in 1977 ($s)	Number of occasions per month visitors are invited to the home (2)	Percentage of population that belongs to a sports club	Number of inhabitants per swimming pool (thousands)	Number of bicycles purchased in 1977 (thousands)	Number of cameras purchased in 1977 (thousands)	Number of pleasure boats (sail and motor) (thousands)
Belgium	140	90	170	1—2	■	20	480 (a)	252	4.7
Denmark	140	50	■	1—2	40	25	300 (a)	185 (a)	50.0 (a)
W. Germany	136	54	270 (d)	7	24	15	3 850	3 600	173.0 (a)
Spain	125	70	■ (d)	2—3	5	21	55 (a)	70 (a)	5.0
France	133	54	120	4	15	18	2 050	2 400	420.0
Italy	120	45	95 (a)	2	5	112	1 100 (a)	2 000 (a)	400.0
Netherlands	145	54	120	4	■	15	1 200	■	250.8
Norway	132	74	220	1—2	27	10	170 (a)	170 (a)	300.0
Austria	137	38	175	3	1	6	315	500 (a)	■
Portugal	131	22	■ (d)	4—6	■	■	■	92	10.0
Switzerland	130	76	475 (a)	3	37	8	100 (a)	■	■
Finland	130	73	210	4—6	38	35	250	140	215.0
Sweden	144	86	130	1—3	30	46	400 (a)	400 (a)	320.0
UK	127	80	120 (a)	4	18 (a)	70	1 000 (a)	1 500 (a)	■
Japan	111 (b)	75	90 (a)	0	9	43	2 900 (a)	2 000 (a)	10.8
USA	116 (c)	50	290	1—2	25 (a)	1	7 500	16 500	8 020.0

Appendix Figure 8 List of organization's affiliated to the ETUC

Name		Country	Membership*
Fédération Générale du Travail de Belgique	FGTB	Belgium	900
Confédération des Syndicats Chrétiens	CSC	Belgium	1 100
Landsorganisationen i Danmark	LOD	Denmark	990
Fællesrådet for Danske Tjenestemands-og Funktionarorganisationer	FDTF	Denmark	210
Deutscher Gewerkschaftsbund	DGB	Germany/Federal Republic	7 200
Union General de Trabajadores de España	UGT	Spain	—
Solidaridad de Trabajadores Vascos	STV	Spain	—
Confédération Générale du Travail—Force ouvrière	CGT–FO	France	1 000
Confédération Française Démocratique du Travail	CFDT	France	860
Trade Union Congress	TUC	Great Britain	11 500
Irish Congress of Trade Unions	ICTU	Ireland	547
Althydusamband Islands	AI	Iceland	42
Confederazione Italiana Sindacati Lavoratori	CISL	Italy	2 100
Confederazione Generale Italiana del Lavoro	CGIL	Italy	4 300
Unione Italiana del Lavoro	UIL	Italy	800
Confédération Générale du Travail de Luxembourg	CGTL	Luxembourg	30
Letzbuerger Chrëstleche Gewerkschaftsbond	LCGB	Luxembourg	15
General Workers Union	GWU	Malta	26
Nederlands Verbond van Vakverenigingen	NVV	Netherlands	700
Nederlands Katholiek Vakverbond	NKV	Netherlands	340
Christelijk Nationaal Vakverbond	CNV	Netherlands	210
Landsorganisasjonen I Norge	LON	Norway	200
Österreichischer Gewerkschaftsbund	OGB	Austria	1 600
Schweizerischer Gewerkschaftsbund	SGB	Switzerland	471
Christlichnationaler Gewerkschaftsbund der Schweiz	CNGS	Switzerland	106
Schweizerischer Verband Evangelischer Arbeitsnehmer	SVEA	Switzerland	14
Toimihenkilö ja Virkamicsjäjestöjen Keskusliitto	TVK	Finland	240
Suomen Anmattiliittojen Keskusjärjesto	SAK	Finland	920
Landsorganisationen I Sverige	LOS	Sweden	1 750
Tjänstemännens Centralorganisation	TCO	Sweden	922
Confédération Génerale du Travail de Grèce	CGT	Greece	300

*In thousands members.

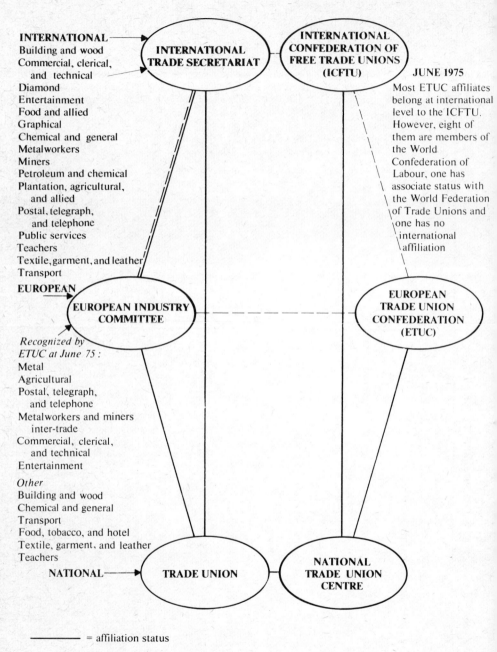

Appendix Figure 9 International and European trade union structure (June 1975). (Source: Trade Union Division of the European Communities)

INTERNATIONAL
Building and wood
Commercial, clerical,
    and technical
Diamond
Entertainment
Food and allied
Graphical
Chemical and general
Metalworkers
Miners
Petroleum and chemical
Plantation, agricultural,
    and allied
Postal, telegraph,
    and telephone
Public services
Teachers
Textile, garment, and leather
Transport

**INTERNATIONAL
TRADE SECRETARIAT**

**INTERNATIONAL
CONFEDERATION OF
FREE TRADE UNIONS
(ICFTU)**

JUNE 1975
Most ETUC affiliates
belong at international
level to the ICFTU.
However, eight of
them are members of
the World
Confederation of
Labour, one has
associate status with
the World Federation
of Trade Unions and
one has no
international
affiliation

EUROPEAN

**EUROPEAN INDUSTRY
COMMITTEE**

**EUROPEAN
TRADE UNION
CONFEDERATION
(ETUC)**

Recognized by
ETUC at June 75 :
Metal
Agricultural
Postal, telegraph,
    and telephone
Metalworkers and miners
    inter-trade
Commercial, clerical,
    and technical
Entertainment

Other
Building and wood
Chemical and general
Transport
Food, tobacco, and hotel
Textile, garment, and leather
Teachers

NATIONAL

TRADE UNION

**NATIONAL
TRADE UNION
CENTRE**

———————— = affiliation status

– – – – – = other type of close relationship

Abbreviations

ACP	African, Caribbean, and Pacific Countries
AFL/CIO	American Federation of Labour and Congress of Industrial Organizations
AFRO	African Regional Organization
AI	Althydusambard Islands (Iceland)
ARO	Asian Regional Organization
BDA	Federal Association of German Employers
CAP	Common Agricultural Policy
CAP	Confederation of Portuguese Farmers
CBI	Confederation of British Industry
CCOO	Comisianes Obreros (Spain)
CEA	European Assurance Committee
CEEP	European Public Enterprises Committee
CEOE	Conferaciones Empresares Organizacion Espanol (Spain)
CFDT	French Democratic Federation of Labour
CFTC	French Confederation of Christian Workers
CGB	Christian Trade Union Federation (W. Germany)
CGC	General Confederation of Supervisory Staffs (France)
CGIL	General Confederation of Labour (Italy)
CGPME	General Confederation of Small and Medium Sized Employers (France)
CGSLB	General Centre of Belgian Liberal Unions
CGT	General Confederation of Workers (France)
CGTFO	General Confederation of Labour Worker's Force
CGTL	General Confederation of Luxembourg Workers
CIO	Liberian Trade Union Congress
CISL	Confederation of Workers Union (Italy)
CJD	Centre of Young Managers (France)
CLC	Canadian Labour Congress
CNPF	National Council of French Employers
CNT	National Council of Labour (Belgium)
CNV	Protestant National Trade Union Federation (Netherlands)
COCCEE	Committee of Trade Organizations of EEC Countries
COPA	Agricultural and Professional Organizations Committee
CSC	Confederation of Christian Unions (Belgium)
CTM	Mexican Trade Union Congress
DAG	German Salaried Employees' Union
DB	German Civil Servants' Union
DGB	German Trade Union Federation
E and P	Enterprise and Progress (France)
ECFTU	European Confederation of Free Trade Unions
ECOSOC	Economic and Social Committee
ECSC	European Coal and Steel Community
EEC	European Economic Community
EFTA	European Free Trade Association
EIB	European Investment Bank
EMF	European Metalworkers' Federation
ETUC	European Trade Union Confederation
FAO	Food and Agriculture Organization
FCWV	Federation of Catholic and Protestant Employers (Netherlands)
FEB	Federation of Belgian Enterprises

FEN	Federation of National Education (France)
FEP	Federation of Private Sector Employers (Luxembourg)
FGTB	Belgian General Federation of Labour
FIET	International Federation of Commercial, Clerical and Technical Employees
FO	Force Ouvrière
FUE	Federated Union of Employers
GATT	General Agreement on Tariffs and Trade
GDP	Gross Domestic Product
GDP	Union of Police (West Germany)
GNP	Gross National Product
IAEA	International Atomic Energy Agency
ICF	International Federation of Chemical and General Workers
ICFTU	International Confederation of Free Trade Unions
ICTU	Irish Congress of Trade Unions
IFBWW	International Federation of Building and Wood Workers
IFCTU	International Federation of Christian Trade Unions
IFFTU	International Federation of Free Teachers' Unions
IFPAAW	International Federation of Plantation, Agricultural, and Allied Workers
IFPCW	International Federation of Petroleum and Chemical Workers
IFTU	International Federation of Trade Unions
IGF	International Graphical Federation
ILO	International Labour Organization
IMCO	Intergovernmental Maritime Consultative Organization
IMF	International Metalworkers' Federation
ISETU	International Secretariat of Entertainment Trade Unions
ITF	International Transport Workers' Federation
ITGLWF	International Textile, Garment, and Leatherworkers' Federation
ITS	International Trade Secretariat
IUF	International Union of Food and Allied Workers
LCGB	Luxembourg Christian Workers' Federation
LO	Danish Federation of Trade Unions
LO	Swedish Federation of Trade Unions
LO	Norwegian Federation of Trade Unions
MARV	Organization of Portuguese Small Farmers
MIF	Miners' International Federation
MNCs	Multinational Companies
MTN	Multilateral trade negotiations
NATO	North Atlantic Treaty Organization
NEDC	National Economic Development Council (UK)
NEDO	National Economic Development Office (UK)
NKV	Netherlands Catholic Trade Union Federation
NVV	Netherlands Federation of Trade Unions
OECC	Organization for European Economic Cooperation
OECD	Organization for Economic Cooperation and Development
OGB	Austrian Trade Union Federation
ORIT	Inter-regional Organization of Workers
PIACT	International Programme for the Improvement of Working Conditions and the Environment
PSI	Public Services International
PTTI	Postal, Telegraph, and Telephone International
RTUI	Red Trade Union International
SAK	Organization of Salaried Employees (Finland)
SEC	Social and Economic Council (Holland)
SGB	Swiss Trade Union Federation

SIEA	Steel Industry Employers' Association (Luxembourg)
STV	Sindicate Trabajadores Vasco (Spain)
TCO	Organization of Salaried Employees (Sweden)
TOC	Finnish Trade Union Organization
TUC	Trades Union Congress (UK)
UACEE	EEC Craftsmen's Union
UADW	Universal Alliance of Diamond Workers
UGT	Union General Trabajadores (Spain)
UIL	Italian Union of Labour
UK	United Kingdom
UNCTAD	United Nations Conference on Trade and Development
UNESCO	United Nations Education, Scientific, and Cultural Organization
UNICE	Union of Industries in the European Community
UN	United Nations
US, USA	United States of America
VAT	Value Added Tax
VNO	Association of Netherlands Enterprises
WCL	World Confederation of Labour
WFTU	World Federation of Trade Unions
WIPO	World Intellectual Property Organization

Index

compiled by K.G.B. Bakewell

Organizations are entered under their full name as given in the text, and there are no cross-references from initials for organizations which are included in the list of abbreviations on pages 201–203. The index is arranged 'word by word' or 'nothing before something', so that 'Industrial relations' precedes 'Industrialization'. Initials and acronyms are filed as words, so that 'BSN' follows 'British'.